Jesus and Ubuntu

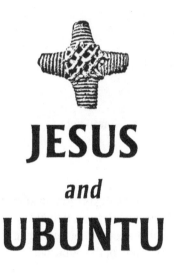

JESUS
and
UBUNTU

Exploring the Social Impact of Christianity in Africa

Edited by
Mwenda Ntarangwi

AFRICA WORLD PRESS
TRENTON | LONDON | CAPE TOWN | NAIROBI | ADDIS ABABA | ASMARA | IBADAN | NEW DELHI

AFRICA WORLD PRESS
541 West Ingham Avenue | Suite B
Trenton, New Jersey 08638

Copyright © 2011 Mwenda Ntarangwi
First Printing 2011

Book and cover design: Saverance Publishing Services

Library of Congress Cataloging-in-Publication Data

Jesus and Ubuntu : exploring the social impact of Christianity in Africa / edited by Mwenda Ntarangwi.
    p. cm.
"Essays in this volume come out of a conference on the social impact of Christianity in Africa held at the campus of Calvin College in the summer of 2009"--Introd.
Includes bibliographical references and index.
    ISBN 978-1-59221-842-4 (hardcover) -- ISBN 978-1-59221-843-1 (pbk.)   1.   Christian sociology--Africa, Sub-Saharan--Congresses. 2. Africa, Sub-Saharan--Church history--Congresses. I. Ntarangwi, Mwenda.
    BR1430.J47 2011
    276.7'083--dc23
                              2011020289

Contents

Acknowledgments   vii

1. Introduction: African Christianity, Politics, and
Socioeconomic Realities   1
Mwenda Ntarangwi

2. Faith and Freedom in Post-Colonial African Politics   25
David Hoekema

3. Culture, Missions, and Africa's Lessons for Western
Christianity   47
Caitlin McGill

4. Charismatic Renewal in the Catholic Church in Ghana   67
Ross Acheson

5. Charismatic Renewal: Lessons in Missions from the
Kenyan Church   81
Joshua S. Kuipers

6. The Gospel for Ethiopia by Ethiopians: Mapping the
Contested Terrains between Pentecostals and Marxist
Radicals   101
Tibebe Eshete

7. From the Fringes to the Centre: Pentecostal Christianity in
the Public Sphere in Kenya (1970-2009)   123
Damaris S. Parsitau

8. The Catholic Church and Civic Education in the Slums of
Nairobi   147
Christine M. Bodewes

9. Reflecting on Church-State Relationship in Kenya   175
    Njonjo Mue

10. Literacy teaching and learning in Sierra Leone   191
    Johanna Kuyvenhoven

Notes   217

References   237

Contributors   249

Index   253

Acknowledgment

The workshop for which chapters in this volume were developed was generously funded by Deur funds from the Department of Sociology and Social Work and from The Nagel Institute for World Christianity, both at Calvin College, Grand Rapids, Michigan. A book reading group that germinated the idea of this book was generously funded by the Calvin Center for Christian Scholarship to whom I am also very grateful.

Introduction

AFRICAN CHRISTIANITY, POLITICS, AND SOCIOECONOMIC REALITIES

Mwenda Ntarangwi

It is January 1st 2008 and Kenya is tittering on the brink of a full-scale civil war following a disputed presidential election. Njonjo Mue, a Human Rights lawyer, is seated at Nairobi's Ufungamano House amidst a hundred top church leaders from all denominations desperate to try and deliberate on a Christian response to the violence. Instead of the usual prophetic voice that has come to represent Kenya's mainline Christian leaders when pitted against oppressive political regimes, Njonjo notices that the church leaders cannot even agree on the wording of a simple press statement without degenerating to finger pointing in the now-emerging camps formed along ethnic lines. Njonjo is taken aback. He had agreed to join this group of clergy because he knew of the role the church had played in such crucial national moments. This time around, however, something was amiss. What happened? Where is the prophetic voice that Kenyans were expecting of clergy in times such as these? Has the Kenyan church lost its critical role in challenging the status quo? This collection of essays applies a broad brush to respond to some of these questions as a frame to explore the social impact that Christianity has had in Africa today. While the scenario above is very much tied to a specific country, the context and even emerging issues are observable in many parts of Africa that are going through political and socioeconomic challenges.

Recent studies of Christianity in Africa variably engage issues of ethnic identity, democracy, development, and the public role played by Christians.[1] These studies have probed and analyzed various manifestations of Christianity in Africa in the recent decades. Essays in this volume come out of a conference on the social impact of Christianity in Africa held at the campus of Calvin College in the summer of 2009 to explore similar issues but with a specific focus on the role Christianity plays in African social life. The conference itself was a follow up from a faculty book reading group that I organized in the 2008-09 academic year, in which fourteen faculty members and two graduate students read eight books focusing on Christianity in Africa.[2] I organized the conference for two key reasons: first, I was attracted to the expanding literature focusing on the explosive growth of Christianity in Africa compared to Christianity's decline in the West. Specifically, I was curious to find out the specific social impact that this explosive growth in Christianity was having on individuals, communities, and nations in Africa. Further, I was curious to find out what effects this impact would have on a continent rife with stories of socioeconomic and political decline. As a Christian myself I was also curious to explore the false dichotomy depicted about Christianity in Africa by, on the one hand Paul Gifford's work that concludes that "African socio-political systems . . . certainly needed radical restructuring, and it is not self-evident that . . . churches will contribute much in that direction,"[3] and on the other Katherine Marshall's conclusion that faith is critical for Africa's development.[4]

Surprisingly none of the books we read provided convincing examples of Christianity's significant social impact in Africa, either negatively or positively. However, one cannot deny the positive role played by Christianity in dismantling apartheid in South Africa and in the second liberation of many African countries. That notwithstanding, shocking news of civil and political strife in many African countries where the majority are Christian (and not to mention the fact that development indicators are no better in Muslim and religiously plural countries) is enough reason to question the role of faith in people's lives. This apparent duality of African Christianity's identity led me to my second reason for the conference. I sought to bring together a diverse group of people—scholars, practitioners, and students—to offer examples of personal experiences, primary research among practitioners of Christianity (what often is considered the "grassroots"), and practical tips about African Christianity and its place in the continent's socioeconomic, political, and development spheres. I was convinced that people with vast and diverse experiences on the ground in Africa would provide a nuanced analysis of Christianity in the continent. I wanted them to share their observation and experiences of how Christianity was socially impacting the parts of the continent in which they had lived and worked. Did they have more positive stories than those told by the scholars whose books we had read?

Undoubtedly an analysis of African Christianity based on direct experience would present a unique perspective that is useful for understanding various manifestations of the daily workings of faith in what is now a growing field of academic endeavor. Much to my delight the two-day conference turned out to be an intimate, high energy, and intellectually stimulating interdisciplinary experience for the participants. My earlier perceptions of the kind of impact Christianity was having in Africa begun to expand as I learned about the diverse ways faith was mobilized by different people in different places. I heard about sacrifice and selfless service to others among people with very little; I heard of Churches providing alternative communities to those shunned by their own families because of disease (such as HIV and AIDS) or socioeconomic challenges; and I heard of ways in which African Christian's dedication and dependence on God influenced Western Christians themselves and made them self-reflexive about their own faith practices. At the end of the conference, I also found out that I was not alone in my enthusiasm for understanding African Christianity because in our final meeting for the conference, participants were quite passionate about making the gathering a regular occurrence. We agreed that an edited volume would be an important tool for creating a wider dialog with scholars, practitioners, and students interested in this important field of study. Participants also saw such a volume as a forum through which to invite a conversation on a topic we felt passionately about.

In retrospect I now can see that the outcome of the conference highlights the complexity and diversity of African Christianity itself, reflecting varied experiences and practices. Christianity is experienced through existing cultural frames that very much focus on the good of community even though political and economic structures, fashioned by years of interactions between external and internal practices, have tended to pull communities away from the collective orientation often present in many African societies. This collective orientation often geared towards the flourishing of others and commonly crystallized in the concept of Ubuntu is an important framework from which to analyze the social impact of Christianity in Africa. As a religious tradition predicated on "loving thy neighbor as thyself" Christianity is very much primed to be compatible with much of the African culture and philosophy entailed in Ubuntu. The essays in this volume provide numerous examples of this exciting but complex phenomenon, pointing at some areas where African political philosophies may have missed an opportunity to embrace Christianity, while also showing the ways in which Christianity has provided different frameworks to engage the world. In asking how Christianity has socially impacted Africa, these essays are keen to highlight African's cultural practices that emphasize community over the individual and in turn how Christianity, as a faith that itself reflects similar cultural practices of Ubuntu, manifests itself in Africa. Simply put, how does Jesus' ministry of loving one's neighbor as self (that often defines the cultural or horizontal religiosity of Christians) interact with the philosophy of Ubuntu that emphasizes the diminishing of self for the sake of others and community?

In this set of essays there is a shared thread of responses to this question that use various examples from different countries in Africa. The essays also have something else in common—their constant use of the terms Christian, Church, and Africa. While scholars show the underlying problematic of a term such as Africa, the use of the term here denotes the geographic space occupied by the continent, which lies south of the Sahara desert. By this focus, therefore, we exclude much of North Africa and only focus on East, West, and Southern Africa even though only a handful of countries provide case studies for the essays. Indeed I am drawn to the "idea of Africa" that Zairian scholar Valentine Y. Mudimbe espouses in his 1994 book. Mudimbe portends that Africa is both an invention and an affirmation of certain natural features, cultural characteristics, and values that contribute to Africa as a continent and its civilizations as constituting a set of differences from those that we may attribute to such areas and cultural groups as Asia and Europe (Mudimbe 1994). I am happy to retain this ambivalent definition of Africa. Wherever the term Christian is used in this volume it denotes a follower of Jesus Christ as expressed through multiple denominations spanning from African initiated churches to Catholic and protestant churches. The term church is used here in two ways, one to denote the corporate body of Christians (the community of Christ followers) irrespective of denomination and two as the physical structure where worship and other related practices carried out by Christians take place.

REVIEWING AFRICAN CHRISTIANITY'S ROLE IN SOCIETY

Africa's place in this rapidly globalizing world seems at most ambivalent with some even wondering where to place it in the global sphere.[5] There are questions to be asked of what role is being played by Christianity in Africa today and why churches play or do not play a positive role in the lives of individuals and societies in their respective locations in the continent. Two scenarios emerge as we contemplate answers to such questions. On the one hand recent trends and events across sub-Saharan Africa, including, the dramatic and tragic eruption of violent conflicts and massacres, increased HIV infections and AIDS deaths, constant reports of corruption and misuse of public resources, and irregularities in national and civic elections, drive this volume's questions of social change, democracy, political and economic change, and Africa's place in a globalizing world. On the other hand, however, the world has witnessed a relentless growth and expansion of Christianity in Africa with new converts increasing daily. How then do we relate these two scenarios?

Renowned religious studies professor Philip Jenkins, for instance, states that, "the center of gravity in the Christian world has shifted inexorably southward, to Africa, Asia, and Latin America."[6] What with the growth of Christianity in Africa shifting from about 10 million in 1900 to 370 million in 2000? However, as Robert Wuthnow warns, "we must pay less attention to demographic shifts and more to the complexities of global interdependencies."[7] Rather than see Christianity shifting from one location to another and reflecting a decrease in one location and an increase in another, Wuthnow suggests that the narrative of global Christianity be seen as the body of Christ. "A story that focuses on the withering of one appendage and the strengthening of another," he says, "makes no sense. A better story acknowledges each limb or organ's dependence on others."[8] While Wuthnow's argument is necessary here one cannot deny the fact that the numbers of Christian adherents in the West and North America have continued to decline while those in Africa, Asia, and Latin America have continued to grow. That notwithstanding, however, global processes have gone on for many years and Christianity is no exception. What is different this time around is the speed and expansion with which these global processes are taking place especially as a result in improvements in communications, travel, and exchange of ideas, goods, and other resources across social, geographic and economic boundaries. As Lamin Sanneh shows between 1970 and 1985 "there were over 16,500 [Christian] conversions a day [in Africa] . . . [while] some 4,300 people were leaving the church on a daily basis in Europe and North America."[9] Such growth is a direct result of population growth as Wuthnow notes but it is also a result of many leaving behind their erstwhile religious persuasions for Christianity.

This apparent shift in the numbers of Christians in the world leads Lamin Sanneh to ask, "Whose Religion is Christianity?" because as it stands now Christianity's identity cannot be exclusively linked to its European roots of the 19th century but rather has to incorporate the current religious character of the world. Indeed, this delinking of Christianity from its European ties is what makes Sanneh differentiate between world Christianity—"as the movement of Christianity . . . [that] takes form and shape in societies that were previously not Christian . . . [as] received and expressed through the cultures, customs, and traditions of the people affected . . . [and] global Christianity —- the faithful replication of Christian forms and patterns developed in Europe."[10] Other scholars offer similar interpretations of Christianity in Africa. Adrian Hastings observes that, "Black Africa today is totally inconceivable apart from the presence of Christianity"[11]; Jonathan Bonk reported in 2007 that, "Christian population growth in Africa is estimated to be 2.4 percent per year, the fastest of any continent."[12]

This growth is both internal (with notable expansion of congregations and Church planting in Africa by Africans themselves and in their own countries independent of any external influence) and external (as many African Church leaders continue to establish branches of their churches in different countries within and outside the continent including in Europe and North America). Moreover, African Christians see a clear connection between their faith and politics. A survey of Pentecostals in ten African countries carried out in 2007 shows that 83%, 75%, and 63% of Christians in Kenya, Nigeria, and South Africa, respectively, see a clear role for religion in politics and public life.[13] Given this overwhelming presence of Christianity in Africa how then do we explain the many socioeconomic and political challenges facing the continent? How can a continent that is seeing exponential growth in Christianity also have the highest level of economic and political decline? What relationship, if any, is there between Christianity and economic and political growth or lack thereof?

David Kasali, a Congolese scholar and former president of Nairobi Evangelical Graduate School of Theology (NEGST) responds to these questions by suggesting that African Christianity lacks theological and spiritual depth necessary for individual transformation that in turn leads to better economic and political practices. Kasali, who is now rector of a Christian university in eastern Congo (The Bilingual Christian University in Congo) argues that Africa's Christianity is "a mile wide and an inch wide," saying that this explains why in 1994, for instance, Rwanda was 84% Christian and yet witnessed the worst genocide in the continent.[14] Kasali's perspective seems to align with that of other scholars including Saskia Van Hoyweghen who argues that Christianity in Rwanda had minimal impact on Rwandan society specifically because many members of the Catholic Church (the dominant denomination) had been attracted to Christianity for social and economic reasons without significant influence from the Church's core beliefs.[15]

Providing an alternative perspective Paul Gifford, John Lonsdale, and David Gitari show that the church has had a prominent political role especially in what has come to be referred to as the "second political liberation" in such countries as Kenya, Madagascar, Malawi, and Zambia, whereby Church leaders challenged the political status quo of the day and created space for masses to criticize their political leaders.[16] Taking a political economy approach, however, Jeff Haynes argues that mainstream religious leaders in Africa actually collaborate with the state to achieve a hegemonic ideology that defuses or reduces any serious political challenges to the status quo.[17] Rather than being this alternative voice that is being presented of Christianity in Kenya, Madagascar, Malawi, and Zambia, Haynes sees these as exceptions rather than the norm. Indeed, Paul Gifford's analysis of the church in Liberia during the reign of Sergeant Samuel Doe shows that the church was often complacent and appropriated by Doe's government to serve its ulterior motives. The church focused more on the next world and not on life here on earth.[18]

Given this scholarly trajectory on Christianity in Africa one can conclude that the relationship between the state and the church is not always cordial and predictable neither is it altogether antagonistic. Christianity in Africa is complex and no easy explanations suffice. Sometimes the church reflects the same political-structural tendencies associated with state machinery, while in others the church is an alternative system to the state, offering the citizenry a platform to express discontent and disapproval of the political, economic, and cultural realities of the day. As Timothy Longman's study of the role of Rwandan Church in the 1994 genocide, for instance, concludes, "far from simply adapting to and reflecting Rwandan society, the churches actively shaped the ethnic and political realities that made genocide possible by acting to define and politicize ethnicity, legitimizing authoritarian regimes, and encouraging public obedience to political authorities."[19] Instead of sharing the message of love and unity the church in Rwanda socialized its members to become divisive, obedient, and attentive to power.[20] A similar scenario seems to have been repeated in Kenya in which the role of the Church in Kenya's political life was especially compromised following the post-election violence of early 2008, leading the National Council of Churches in Kenya (NCCK) to publicly apologize for "... sins of among others taking partisan positions on national issues [and] elevating our ethnic identities above our Christian identity..."[21] One cannot forget a gruesome scene of a church in Eldoret being burned with congregation members (from the "wrong" ethnic group) inside as members of another ethnic group kept watch to make sure none escaped the inferno. Such events point to the interrelated nature of Christianity, economics, and politics even though many African church leaders have been advised to stay away from politics.

These negative attributes that have befallen Christians only go to show how fallen humans are and also how much one's faith cannot be divorced from one's socio-cultural, economic, and political realities within which one is socialized and nurtured daily. Christians like other citizens have to respond to the same human demands and failings and as a result, Christianity takes on the culture of the place it is embodied as Christians become very much part of their own erstwhile culture. What is different for Christians, however, is that they do have templates and examples to act on and the demand to live differently as mandated by Scripture. Indeed, the church has been instrumental in opposing political tyranny and injustice in Africa, pointing to a different reality than the negative one exemplified above. In 2010 when Kenyans were working towards a referendum that would allow them to vote for or against a new constitution a number of church leaders went against their Church organs and supported the constitution, showing clearly that churches were not all united in matters affecting the country's political destiny. At last the new constitution was voted in and the opposing sides were left to seek newer ways of showing their moral legitimacy especially because the NCCK had again tried to spearhead the campaign against the new constitution. Such a defeat to the church organs can raise questions about the legitimacy of the church in Kenya to claim any moral leadership in matters political. What role does the church in this case play in influencing and shaping society?

One of the most celebrated examples of the role of the church in impacting the society of the day is the case of South Africa especially those churches operating under the auspices of the South African Council of Churches (SACC). Its key leaders—Desmond Tutu and Beyers Naude—will forever be remembered for their role in fighting apartheid through the actions and sacrifices of ordinary citizens who made the country ungovernable even as their counterparts in the Dutch Reformed Church defended and supported apartheid.[22] How then do we understand this mixed bag of Christianity's role in the political and economic life of many African societies? Essays in this volume take up this complex reality of Christianity in Africa to explore with numerous examples from different countries at different time periods, how the practice of Christianity sheds light, challenges, and also helps us understand these issues in new and different ways. We can see in Tibebe Eshete's chapter, for instance, that Christian students in Ethiopia successfully challenged their Marxist counterparts in ways that laid down important foundations for socioeconomic and political practices witnessed in the country today. As Andrea Freidus (2010) shows young Malawi pastors challenge notions of modernity that often tends to relegate faith to the fringes in development projects, and provides an interesting read on the place of Christianity in the emerging civil society in Africa. Indeed, we cannot understand the social impact of Christianity in Africa without exploring the relationship Christianity has had with notions of modernity and development especially in the latter part of the 20th century.

CHRISTIANITY, MODERNITY, AND DEVELOPMENT

African Christianity is growing at a time when there are mixed feelings about modernity (a post-traditional individualism anchored in capitalism, urbanization, industrialization, secularism, and the individual as the locus of change and growth) and development. Christianity's connection to modernity and development goes back to such missionaries as David Livingstone. It is well known that Livingstone's mission was to promote commerce, Christianity, and civilization. When Livingstone went to Mozambique as consul for the British government he was charged with the exploration that would lead to "the promotion of commerce and civilization with a view to the extinction of the slave trade."[23] Promoting commerce was part of the civilizing mission that was primarily based on a European notion of modernity. Part of this modernity involved the centrality of the state as the agent of change and in this case the state was fashioned after the colonial government to serve colonial ends. As a result Christian converts in many parts of Africa found gainful employment working for the colonial government where they learned the new cultural practices associated with this modernity. Missionaries provided mission schools that trained workers for the colonial government. In Zimbabwe, for instance, nine out of ten Zimbabweans were, in the period between 1950 and 1980, educated in mission schools. Many of them such as Robert Mugabe, who trained at Kutuma Mission School, used this opportunity to create networks with other Zimbabweans that they later used to mobilize politically against the colonial government. Writing in 1966, Raymond Hopkins argues that, "Christianity contributed to social change and the rise of nationalism... and the growth of indicators of development such as education, wage labor, electrical consumption and urbanization."[24]

Despite these attempts to "modernize" Africans, however, many of the beliefs and values that Africans needed to change remained, albeit below the veneer of modernity. Consequently even when Africans converted to Christianity and denounced their past beliefs they did not find an appropriate and fulfilling set of values and beliefs that they could mobilize in their everyday lives. Instead of seeing explanations for daily occurrences in the Western world of logic and reason, many Africans saw them within the realm of good and evil, of witchcraft and magic. Terrence Ranger's work in Zimbabwe is an appropriate example here. Ranger's research and writing on the Matopos Hills illuminates some spiritual negotiations between Zimbabweans and American Christian missionaries. Black farmers in Matopos Hills accepted the plough that was introduced by the missionaries because it increased food production. The farmers, however, thanked their traditional Mwali shrine for the productivity of their farms.[25] As a consequence Africans seem to have accepted the material merits of Christianity without giving Christ dominion over their spiritual and everyday lives. Does Christianity only have a role to play in availing instruments or artifacts of modernity such as a good Western education and new ways of farming and not in changing the spiritual life of the African people? What happens when these promises of modernity fail?

Since the 1970s many African nations have been experiencing the challenges of economic and political pressures brought by the failure of "modernity." The promises of Africa coming out of the economic challenges of the oil crunch of the 70s and structural adjustment programs of the 1980s were later transformed into a neoliberal economic model hinged on a stronger "free" market and a weaker state that gave up its monopoly on service delivery (however poor these services may have been) and economic control (in the form of tariffs and foreign exchange regulation). This new notion of development, framed in the discourse of modernity that would assure its recipients of technological advancements (modern transportation and communication), democracy, nuclear families, capitalism, urbanization, and a secular worldview shaped by enlightenment, collided with an African reality dominated by growing poverty, inequality, disease, and degradation. It is no coincidence that scholars working in much of Sub-Saharan Africa recorded increased incidents of activities associated with the occult especially sorcery, magic, and witchcraft[24] as well as the rise of new forms of Christianity especially Pentecostalism. These activities increase as the promises of modernity fail. When crops fail, bodies are struck with incurable disease, natural disasters befall a community, and when one wants to secure a political office against a tough opponent, all tend to lead the actors to the occult where they hope to find better solutions.

Clearly an interesting relationship emerges between socioeconomic challenges facing many Africans and the common Christian responses they apply. Modernity and Western Christianity share something in common—their unwavering focus on the individual as the ontological unit of redemption or empowerment. Success in many socioeconomic projects framed in the language of development often places emphasis on the individual as does Christianity, which emphasizes salvation and prosperity through the individual. Notions of Human Rights and even some development projects such as micro-credit and micro-finance activities are very much tied to the individual rather than the collective good. As some scholars have noted, the world is today often divided into the evangelized and the unevangelized, which in turn mirrors the division of the world into the developed and undeveloped. In the case of sub-Saharan Africa, "the world [is] divided into two realms: evange-lized/developed and unevangelized/undeveloped."[26] Individual success championed by a Protestant ethic of hard work and personal salvation shapes many people's regard and response to many socioeconomic challenges. As a result many public problems are often conceptualized as a failure of individuals rather than systemic failure and as a result many respond to them with private solutions. When there is increased insecurity, for instance, people build stronger gates and fences and hire guards instead of mobilizing to work together to seek large-scale security measures that are shared across the community or country; when potholes increase on the roads, they buy 4x4 vehicles, and when public schools deteriorate, people send their children to private schools. This individualization of faith and development reflects the growth and expansion of American global economic and social reach noted by Wuthnow. Amidst all this individualization of faith is increased prayer and church attendance. Many African churches try to pray for change and organize church gatherings to strategize how they can spiritually manage the situation while quite oblivious or ignorant of the structural basis for these challenges. As Ghanaian pastor of a Pentecostal Church, Mensa Otabil, states, "we can get everyone in Africa saved but that won't solve our problem. The poverty in Africa is not spiritual. Poverty is physical. Poverty is a social condition. You can bind, it won't be bound. If you are in a poor nation you will be poor. Your personal individual prosperity is tied up with the prosperity of the nation."[28] This relega-tion or elevation of structural issues to the realm of the spiritual is best exemplified by the response undertaken by many in the management of

Ghana Airways as it became clear that the national carrier was operating at a great economic loss. In a provocative essay titled "Christ is the Answer, What is the Question?" Ghanaian scholar Asamoah-Gyadu discusses how Ghana Airways staff held a prayer vigil to reverse the national carrier's misfortunes and wondered how prayers could be used in the place of following basic business practice that required charging those that had embezzled funds from the airline (2005b). What is the place for such "mystical causality" in a "modern" state seeking to use secular economic strategies to make an airline self-sustaining and profitable? Why would a company that is clearly set up to operate within specific business practices turn to spiritual practices to solve its economic challenges? Why did the airline bring in Lawrence Tetteh, a London-based Ghanaian evangelist, to lead what was termed a "healing and deliverance" service aimed at exorcizing evil spirits from the affairs of the airline and releasing it from its predicaments? Asamoah-Gyadu argues that it is because this worldview of mystical causality reflects the intertwined nature of Africa's public and spiritual lives, often separated and unimaginable in Western cultural contexts.

In the absence of a clear path towards being developed and modern, in the absence of defining clearly what ails a local airline that is supposed to bring about national prosperity, many Africans felt (and continue to feel) insecure and unable to control their immediate realities as well as their future and resort to a world in which they are often familiar—that of the supernatural. It has been argued that African worldviews of the spiritual and physical realms are interconnected, working within and for each other to structure daily lives.[29] In this perspective respecting the spiritual realm will bring health, prosperity, cohesion, and protection to the community while ignoring the spiritual realm leads to death, suffering, conflict, and marginalization. This worldview shapes the way many Africans, who have been frequently targeted as recipients of development projects by many Christian NGOs experience and interpret their daily lives. Moreover, because the principles of individual success encapsulated in the discourse of modernity brought by development to many African communities are closely tied to a protestant ethic of hard work and personal salvation, Christianity is an important player in this reality. Lying beneath these modern principles of development is the power of the African worldview, often a window shaped by a spiritual realm that recognizes, accepts, and even mobilizes the occult as an epistemological system for understanding, explaining, and bringing coherence to an unpredict-able and volatile world. For many Africans life is full of relationships, relationships that have to be stable in the community in order for one to live a fulfilling life. This may explain not only the prevalence of John Mbiti's "I am because we are" philosophy as an explanation of African religiosity, but also the place of God, ancestors, and other humans, who have to have a certain balance in their relationships for a good life to commence (see, McGill, this volume, for more examples of this phe-nomenon).[30] Sacrifices, curses, and blessings, all function to respond to this desired balance that is built in community, a community based on relationships that have to be constantly maintained.

Christianity and development, however, tend to emphasize indi-viduality and autonomy that, when combined with a disproportionate distribution of material resources visible in our world today, results in jealousies and an overt turn to the supernatural realm especially the occult. Scholars have argued that malevolent occult forces in Africa (and elsewhere) become most visible during periods of intense social change and instability, when social systems become imbalanced as has been witnessed in Africa in the last four decades. As incidents of disease, drought, malnutrition, and natural calamities increase so do cases of those Africans who seek solutions to their material pre-dicaments in the occult. This is the context within which the expansive growth of Christianity and corresponding socioeconomic and political unrest can be read and understood. Ethnographers such as Erica Born-stein who worked in Zimbabwe analyzing the work of World Vision and Christian Care in the 1990s detail the presence of witchcraft amidst a community self-identifying as Christian; so does the work of Birgit Meyer's work in Ghana and that of Harri Englund in Malawi. All these scholars show that Christianity in these parts of Africa is fraught with contradictions or continuities as traditional belief systems that place great emphasis on witchcraft and the occult still occupy a large part of the spiritual life of African Christians.

As stated above Terrence Ranger's work in Matopos, Zimbabwe shows how after Christian missionaries' introduction of better plowing methods as a way of attracting coverts did not work as such because the local people attributed their increased crop yield and better farming to traditional Mwali shrines that the missionaries had all along tried to discredit and dismantle.[31] Such a reality should not be regarded as a testament to the superficiality of Christianity in Zimbabwe but rather the reality of a coexistence of Christianity and traditional worldviews that are not discernible within a Western dichotomizing paradigm emphasized by enlightenment. One can be a Christian in Africa and still believe in the power of witchcraft just as one can believe in Christ's power over disease and still trust biomedical interventions that are primarily secular and often developed within a realm of science that negates the efficacy of religious faith. In a sense these practices have to be understood as projections of the cultural manifestation of religiosity where despite attempts by Christianity to produce new creations in its converts, erstwhile beliefs are hard to shake off. Birgit Meyer has argued from her extensive research in Ghana that contact with forces of modernity stimulates rather than diminishes beliefs in local spirits and demons. She shows, for instance, how spirit possession is a manifestation of social pressures brought by such tensions as those emanating from the conflict between Christian ideals, the nuclear family, and the autonomy of the individual on the one hand and the demands of extended families and collectivist worldviews of Ewe culture on the other.[32]

Interactions between local and externally produced ideas and practices about religious life also manifest themselves in development work and I would like to devote some time discussing development as mobilized by faith-based (Christian) organizations. I do so in order to highlight the value of analyzing how African cultural practices interact with notions and practices of development promoted in the continent in the last few decades. One common strategy used by both faith-based and secular NGOs to mobilize resources to African communities for economic development, for instance, is through child sponsorship. Compassion International and World Vision are cases in point when it comes to faith-based NGOs. Because child sponsorship in many African communities is for the most part a foreign idea, rooted in Western individualism and capitalist expectations, its actual implementation and mobilization in local contexts that are characterized by poverty and inequality, tends to reinforce perceptions of inequality that often inspire jealousy. Within a community built to depend on its members to produce and share resources for survival, a focus on an individual child challenges such a social arrangement. Sponsorship, while providing material benefit, draws lines between sponsored and unsponsored children, and also between sponsored children and their parents who are often unable to offer similar material resources that are brought by sponsorship. Furthermore, sponsor-child relationships, designed for the donor to be a personal way of giving, are facilitated through impersonal monetary exchanges mediated by staff from faith-based NGOs.

These arrangements of sponsorship like most forms of Western Christianity, tend to interact with local cultural practices to produce outcomes that defeat the initial expectations of those involved in the work. Child sponsorship then implicitly amplifies the social distance and difference between donor and child, making one sponsored child in Zimbabwe to ask "How can someone who doesn't know me come and take care of me? They never met me, yet they are saying how much they love me."[33] Material assistance in many African contexts exists between and among kin and individuals socially tied to the donor. The practice of assisting someone not known to one with whom no social relationship has been established is an unusual phenomenon. Assistance is often out of social obligation than a gesture of individual generosity.

Despite these challenges and disparate perceptions of giving, we cannot disregard the value of child sponsorship all together because individual sponsors and sponsored children do benefit from the arrangement and there are numerous sponsored children whose lives have been transformed by such programs. In a sense this takes us back to Max Weber's rendition of the Protestant Ethic[34] regarding capital accumulation that he argues is not inherently evil or immoral for Christians. Instead he chooses to focus on how such accumulation is mobilized, arguing that what is important is what good Christians *do* with the resources or "gifts" that are bestowed upon them by capital-ism. Tithing and redistribution of this wealth, as often exemplified in child sponsorship, for instance, allows for Christians to *do* good with their wealth. This ideology of distribution as some scholars see it, is no different from belief in the occult and witchcraft accusations in Africa.[35] Both systems encourage distribution but frame it differently: development projects function as a conduit for the transnational redis-tribution of capital (from wealthy Christians to needy Africans) while witchcraft provides a moral framework that prevents the immoral accumulation of resources and power.[36] However, what is at odds with these redistributive systems, and what then becomes a source of spiri-tual insecurity for many recipients of such assistance in Africa, is the emphasis on individuality and autonomy pushed by faith-based development and by Christianity's notion of development, often as cultural reflections of a Western ontology.

What then are the effects of Christian interventions in development on rural communities, especially in areas of success, inequality, and jealousy? An answer to this question is located around the Christian dichotomy of good and evil. Christian development came into Africa by defining poverty as evil and development as good. Along with it came Western capitalist economic systems that carried with them a system of inequality and individualized success. This arrangement clashed with an African system that values equal distribution of resources and one whose system of enforcement was through spiritual manipulation actualized in witchcraft. Protestant Christian conceptualizations of development are engrained and mobilized through the work and the structures of these faith-based NGOs that are quite numerous across many of the countries in Africa. A "holistic" view of human development often taken by many Christian NGOs such a World Vision tend to mean that religious and economic development are intertwined even though they hardly address systemic and structural problems that underlie the development needs being addressed.

"Development" and "salvation" when seen from a prism of faith are nearly equivalent. The right religious mindset is as important as anything else in development, both for development workers and for community members. Even though they are development organizations, many faith-based NGOs define themselves differently and see their mandate and practice as the sharing of the gospel by exemplifying Christian values and building long-term relationships through acts of physical kindness often termed "lifestyle evangelism."[37] Such an approach would not grapple with the question, of "what distinguishes a borehole sunk by a faith-based NGO and a secular NGO?" A faith-based NGO would say that its borehole is different because it comes not as an end in itself but as an expression of the salvific gospel that engulfs all other aspects of life of the individual and community. Through development, faith-based NGOs can accomplish two tasks simultaneously—economic development and evangelism. What is intriguing, however, is that the countries that are targeted for Christian missions and evangelism are the same ones that fall under the economic indices of underdevelopment.

What then is the relationship between Christianity and economic development? Given that Christianity often wears the cultural jacket of the place it inhabits it is not surprising to see that the Western brand of economic development brought by modernity and the age of reason is very much reflected in the brand of Christianity brought by Western Christian missionaries of any period. At times there is little separation between economic development and spiritual prosperity. This may account for the common practice among Western Christians to see their economic and material prosperity as a clear indication of God's blessings upon them and their societies. Such a simplistic explanation of their material success ignores the systemic and historical inequalities that have led to economic prosperity for some and not for others. To consider their prosperity a blessing is to downplay the role of unjust systems that tend to produce unequal societies where resources are not equally distributed.

THE CONTENT OF THE VOLUME

Clearly the shape, flavor, and magnitude of Christianity in Africa today are at the very least complex and astounding. No one can clearly state that he/she has a pulse on the entirety of Africa's Christian practice, experience, and expression. As the number of Christian adherents continues to grow so too will the complexity of their practices and experiences of Christianity. Taking both Andrew Walls' and Kwame Bediako's admonition that Christianity takes on the cultural jacket of the community in which it finds itself,[38] we can expect that African Christianity can best be regarded as an expression of Christianities, reflecting the cultural, historical, political, and economic realities of the specific times and places where it finds a home. What we lack, however, is a nuanced understanding of how Christianity in Africa is practiced and expressed in order to see these complexities. Where do we place, for instance, information from Uganda that shows families, which have converted to Christianity increasingly make positive steps out of poverty compared to their non-Christian neighbors even within a shared socio-economic and political context?[39] Where do we place Charles Banda of Malawi who when preaching to his community in 1995 saw two people carried in a stretcher dying of cholera and decided they also needed physical nourishment and started what became the Freshwater Project?[40] And where do we place a widely circulated opinion piece titled "As an Atheist, I Believe Africa needs God" that appeared in *The Times* at the end of 2008 by Michael Parris claiming that "Missionaries, not aid money, will solve Africa's major problems."[41] In view of these and other examples, it seems clear that there is not only a need for a theoretically grounded and research-based understanding of the place of Christianity in the social life of many Africans (beyond anecdotal information and trendy statistics) but also one that is multi-disciplinary and informed by various perspectives from different African countries.

This edited volume seeks to fill this gap by providing critical accounts by scholars and practitioners from different backgrounds—academic, social, cultural, economic, and political—that address the social impact and place of Christianity in Africa today. This volume draws on the contributors' own interactions and study of Christianity especially its role in providing a socio-cultural framework through which to understand various facets of contemporary African life. Blending theoretical and philosophical analyses with field-based experiences working in East, West, and Southern Africa, contributors to this volume provide an important scholarly exploration of the place of Christianity in contemporary Africa.

Divided into two sections organized around two different but related issues this volume weaves together three strands of the social role of African Christianity in Africa today: first is the issue relating to theoretical/theological ideas about African Christianity versus Western Christianity and the impact of culture on Christianity—the impact of African Christianity on Christianity itself and its unique manifestations on the continent. To support this theme are chapters by Caitlin McGill, Josh Kuipers, Ross Acheson, and David Hoekema. The second section focuses on empirical work, showing what the church is actually doing on politics and development issues and the changes the contributors have seen over time in observing Christianity's social engagement. This section is supported by chapters by Tibebe Eshete, Damaris Parsitau, Christine Bodewes, Njonjo Mue, and Johanna Kuyvenhoven. These two themes allow for an analysis of the cultural manifestation of Christianity found in Africa while drawing on the similarities and differences in the actual manifestation of the faith on the ground.

In his chapter on "Faith and Freedom in Post-Colonial African Politics" David Hoekema questions African post-independent leaders'

19

decision to divorce the road map for building their nations from the foundations of Christianity despite being trained in Christian schools themselves. Many African leaders articulated a vision of participatory democratic governance that would also adopt valuable elements of African traditional society that, as Hoekema argues, are very much aligned to Christianity. Today as African communities and their leaders seek to find a way forward in increasingly difficult economic and political contexts, recovery of the religious foundations of the founders' vision, Hoekema proposes, is an essential element.

Caitlin McGill's contribution titled "Culture, Missions, and Africa's Lessons for Western Christianity" is a personal journey into the world of missions and Western perceptions of Africa and African Christianity. The explosive growth of short-term missions for North Americans going to Africa and other developing nations has produced mixed responses. Using her high school experience as a participant in a short-term mission to East Africa, McGill discusses the positive and negative attributes of this expanding phenomenon. She specifically uses her own personal experiences in the short-term mission, a subsequent study abroad trip to East Africa, and images of Africa and African Christianity she acquired before the trips, to challenge not only her earlier assumptions about African Christianity but also the taken-for-granted notion of Western Christianity as the model for Africa. McGill charges that Africans, by virtue of their collectivist worldview, for instance, have a better grasp of what Christianity in the West ought to be and shows how such a worldview actually reflects the essence of ancient Biblical tradition. Such an understanding of African religious worldviews allows Western Christians to not only constructively enhance their own faith but also do better work when participating in mission trips in Africa. McGill concludes her chapter by sharing some specific examples of how individuals and groups can prepare for a more fruitful short-term mission in developing nations.

Ross Acheson's piece on "Charismatic Renewal in the Catholic Church in Ghana." What happens when Catholicism interacts with charismatic religious culture in Ghana? Acheson explores this interaction by focusing on primal religious culture, Pentecostalism, and Western tradition in Ghana to show how the axiom of Christianity taking on the cultural mould of its location is clearly expressed in the Catholic Church at the University of Ghana, Legon. As a participant in the church, he uses his experiences to show that charismatic spirituality has enabled the Catholic Church in Ghana to better address many of the popular concerns that arise out of a primal religious context prevalent in Ghana in order to make the church more relevant and responsive to the everyday spiritual and material realities of many Ghanaians. From this position Acheson is able to give a compelling contrast of how prayer and orientation towards the everyday in the Catholic Church he attends in the US and the one he attended in Ghana, is clearly informed by different sensibilities of the supernatural embodied by the subsequent congregations.

Starting his chapter titled "Missions, Charismatic Renewal, and Lessons Learned in Kibera" with a critique of the history of missionary work in Africa, Joshua Kuipers discusses lessons he learned about contemporary missions in a neo-Pentecostal church in Kibera, Kenya, that are very instructive of contemporary missions in Africa. From this experience in Kibera Kuipers concludes that the Western church and missionaries have many lessons to learn from the Kenyan church especially in the areas of holistic ministry and love, that promotes a different type of mission work, where the goal shifts to the promotion of a self-propagating, self- supporting, self-governing, and self-theologizing church. The resulting challenge to this process, Kuipers argues, is a relationship between the Kenyan and Western church that focuses on the strengthening of partnerships for mutual growth rather than as a one-way street with the Western church leading the Kenyan church in all aspects of growth and sustenance.

Tibebe Eshete's chapter "The Gospel for Ethiopia by Ethiopians" provides a good example of the rift between Christianity and political ideology identified by Hoekema. What happens when a population with the oldest roots in Christianity in sub-Saharan Africa interacts with Western higher education philosophies, Pentecostalism, and Marxism, in a period governed by a revolutionary government steeped in Marxist ideology? Eshete provides an answer to this question through a clear and well-informed narrative of the experiences of university students at the Haile Sellassie I University. He discusses the stiff ideological competition that raged between students in the Marxist camp, which he belonged to and those in the Pentecostal camp, which he later joined, to win the hearts and minds of fellow students in a period of great political volatility when Ethiopia was governed by a revolutionary government favoring Marxism. Eshete uses eyewitness accounts and historical data to argue that the cry of the Ethiopian Pentecostals encapsulated in the "The Gospel for Ethiopia by Ethiopians" was more than an evangelistic plea for reaching the nation; it was a militant effort aimed at launching a micro revolution from within to serve as a springboard to unleash a national renaissance. This revolution later prevailed but the ideological war started at the time continues to shape Ethiopia's politics and religious culture today.

Damaris Parsitau's chapter on the "Socio-Political roles of Pentecostal Christianity in the Public Sphere in Kenya in the period 1970-2009," challenges the once famous assumption of Pentecostalism's aversion to politics and public engagement. She shows that just as Pentecostalism has come to represent one of the fastest growing expressions of Christianity in Africa, it's growth and development have recently morphed into increased socio-political significance in the public sphere. She supports her discussion with specific examples of how Pentecostal pastors and their congregations have increasingly participated in politics and the shaping of political discourse in 21st century Kenya with up to twenty-three Pentecostal pastors and leaders vying for various political positions in the 2007 general elections. This she argues has not only changed the role Pentecostals play in public but also created what she calls "Pentecostal culture" that shapes not only other Christians' public culture but those of some Muslims as well.

Taking on the classic anthropological role of a participant-observer, Christine Bodewes analyzes a civic education program she carried out in Kibera through the Catholic Church, and carefully and reflexively outlines the small successes and challenges of teaching basic human rights to a community focused on the everyday politics of survival. Bodewes engages some of the literature on civil society that often asserts that civil society organizations have the power to perform multiple functions ranging from socializing their members into democratic behavior to mobilizing them to hold the state to account. She concludes that the civil society advocates are only partially correct in their claims primarily because the parish ministry was able to inculcate new democratic values, behavior, and skills in some parishioners but unable to mobilize them to hold local government officials to account for their corruption and abuse of power.

Njonjo Mue weaves his chapter on Church-state relations with vignettes of his own experiences working closely with Church leaders especially in trying to formulate a response to the post-election violence that engulfed Kenya in late 2007 and early 2008. From some of the ethnically-based divisions that he observed among Church leaders, Mue concludes that the Church in Kenya has yet to become the "salt and light" of the country. In critiquing the Church's response to the violence, Mue provides specific individual and collective strategies that Christians can use to uphold their critical social role in their communities. He concludes with examples of his personal experiences of speaking truth to power in an unpredictable and dangerous environment, through which he often found himself on the receiving end of police brutality and unlawful incarceration. In this regard he shows the difference that individual Christians can make in their communities were they to take personal responsibility not only to practice their faith privately and when it is safe, but also publicly and when it is risky.

Finally, Johanna Kuyvenhoven's chapter shows how teaching literacy not only provides materially deprived students an opportunity to navigate the global processes of change but also a powerful form of Christian witness than direct evangelism. Using personal experiences stretching over a decade working with local teachers to develop appropriate curricula and teaching resources in Sierra Leone, Kuyvenhoven shows that time tested literacy teaching skills can be critical tools for preparing students to live in full and intimate communion with others in the world. Through continuous assessment of comparative data she shows that Christian education can be a model for a nation's education system especially one coming out of a long tumultuous civil war.

This diversity of topics, experiences and approaches is a replica of the complexity of African Christianity as it is practiced and mobilized in contemporary Africa. These authors only scratch the surface of the many examples of how African Christians are living their lives of faith in the ways that they best can. One thing for sure, however, is the agreement among all these scholars that for anyone to think of Africa today, one has to consider the role played by Christianity. Christianity in Africa, unlike in the West, is very much a public religion and one that embodies the authentic realities of its place and time.

1

FAITH AND FREEDOM IN POST-COLONIAL AFRICAN POLITICS

David A. Hoekema

When Americans return home from visiting Africa, what is uppermost in their minds? Think back on the most recent conversations you have had with colleagues and family members and what overall impressions they brought home. Two broad themes are likely to come to mind, at or near the top of the list of topics that you discussed: first, the vigor and vitality of African religious life and, second, the bleakness and hopelessness of African political life. Many of the contributions to this collection address the first topic directly, highlighting specific instances of the churches' role in contemporary African society, the extraordinary growth of Christianity on the continent, and the growing importance of Africa to the global church not just in numbers but also in matters related to liturgy and theology. And there is much to be learned from the encounter between Christianity and Africa's two other major religious movements, Islam and the broad family of traditional religion.

The second topic has been the focus of several recent studies by historians and social scientists who have told the tale of foreign aid that never reaches its intended recipients, economic reforms that only preserve entrenched elites, elections whose outcome is predetermined or simply invented, and a persistent slide in country after country from democracy into autocracy. Any well-stocked bookstore has a shelf full of these volumes (Calderisi 2007; Moyo 2010; Meredith 2006). My focus in this essay is related to both of these themes, or rather on the relationship between them. I want to call attention to a troubling irony that links these two phenomena, the flourishing of the church and the withering of politics.[1] For if we turn the clock back a half-century to the era when African nations emerged from colonial rule, we find a highly unusual political environment, one in which clearly articulated and widely endorsed ideals guided the events of history. Moreover, these ideals reflected—to a degree seldom acknowledged even by their main advocates—the profound influence of Christian teaching.

It is difficult today even to remember how inspiring the vision of a newly independent Africa was not just to its own people but to observers around the world in the mid-20th century. In my own conversations with colleagues and friends in several regions of Africa, the founding ideals of that period were frequently invoked as a fond memory, but few regard them as exercising influence over contemporary politics. Their assessment of their own countries' prospects for the next few years varied considerably, from darkly pessimistic to guardedly hopeful. Some Kenyans see positive signs in the willingness of the two major parties to work together for passage of a new constitution, for example, while others fear that the outbreak of killing that followed the contested 2007 elections will prove to be only a small-scale rehearsal for the exploitation of ethnic resentment in the next presidential ballot in 2012. Ugandans give credit to the Museveni regime for fostering steady economic growth and resolving longstanding civil conflict in the north, but they do not believe they will see a restoration of genuinely democratic rule for a decade or more. South Africans find encouragement in their nation's economic growth and the global prominence brought by the World Cup even while they have little hope that the ANC government will ever be able to deliver on its promises to create employment and build adequate housing for everyone in the townships. And yet, when pressed, residents I have spoken to across contemporary Africa acknowledge that there are ideals still widely embraced that could give direction and help their nations move forward.

I will begin this discussion with a brief snapshot of the period when African nations achieved independence, and then against that background will outline the contours of the liberating philosophy of some of its founders. In the third section I will note briefly what impeded the achievement of this vision, and then in closing little I will outline some ways in which a recovery and reaffirmation of the church's witness to society might help to revitalize not just Africa's political ideology but also its political practices. My purpose is to examine the core elements of the new vision that was articulated by the leaders of Africa's liberation, to explore its relevance to African political realities today, and to consider the possibilities for a renewed partnership between church and state—a partnership of a kind unavailable in the Western world today.

AFRICA'S ABRUPT ENTRANCE ONTO THE INTERNATIONAL STAGE

Of all the regions of the world in which European powers established colonial rule in the modern era, sub-Saharan Africa stands out in several ways.[2] The history of colonialism was radically compressed, for example. English and Spanish colonies in the New World existed for several centuries before achieving their independence, while nearly all of the European colonies in Africa were established in the late 19th century and set free within six or seven decades. Areas of colonial control in South and East Asia arose by implicit agreement among the European powers as a result of a long history of trade relationships, control over shipping routes, and occasional wars of conquest; but the continent of Africa was parceled out around a conference table in Berlin in 1884 and 1885. Elsewhere in the world colonies of each nation were clustered together in the same regions of the world: Spain and Portugal dominated Latin America, France the Caribbean and most of Southeast Asia, while Great Britain and the Netherlands each held large areas of South Asia. In Africa a much more complicated patchwork was established. A voyager on the Gulf of Guinea at the beginning of the 20th century could have put in, in the space of just a few hundred miles of coastline, at ports located in colonies held by France, Great Britain, Germany, and Portugal.

Another way in which colonialism in Africa stands out is the rapidity with which it came to an end. Great Britain led the way, granting the Gold Coast its independence as the new nation of Ghana in 1957. Dozens more new nations emerged across all regions of the continent in the decade that followed. Alongside the political developments of this short period, the leaders of newly independent states were also engaged in a thorough reexamination of the nature of the state and its relationship to it social and cultural context. Africa's political trans-formation was also an intellectual revolution. As the Federalists and Anti-Federalists in the early years of the American republic engaged in probing debate on the basis and limits of centralized political author-ity, as Gandhi challenged his fellow colonial subjects and their British governors to rethink the relationship between violence, authority, and power—in similar ways the architects of the new African states sought to forge a new vision of how political authority can be most persua-sively grounded and most effectively applied.

The circumstances in which this discussion unfolded were far dif-ferent from what they had been in the English colonies two centuries earlier, and different too from the Indian context just a few decades prior to the creation of nations from African colonies. The end of colonial rule in sub-Saharan Africa came at a time of bitter ideological conflict between East and West. Leaders of the self-proclaimed "free world" in Europe and North America sought to enlist Africa's emerg-ing nations as their allies in the global struggle against communism. Their counterparts in the self-styled "democratic socialist" realm of Russian and Chinese influence countered with an appeal to join the worldwide ascendancy of workers over owners, common people over wealthy elites. Each side sought to win the allegiance of Africans with advice, technical assistance, and development aid. Each party offered assurances that, when the ideological battles had all been fought and won, it would emerge victorious, delivering the poor and downtrodden of the world from their suffering and ushering in a new era of peace and prosperity for all. Each side depicted the other party as deeply deluded and profoundly misinformed about what enables societies to function and individuals to find meaning. Choose this day, the developed world told the new leaders of post-colonial Africa, whom you will serve: the god of capitalism, free markets, and liberal democracy; or the god of socialism, mutual solidarity, and people's assemblies. Each is a jealous god, and if you choose one you must forsake the other.

The new generation of leaders in many of the newly independent colonies rejected this dichotomy, however. They acknowledged the appeal of each party and the accomplishments of which each could rightly boast: the commercial and industrial might of Europe and the United States and their commitment to political openness and human rights; the rapid transformation from pre-industrial into industrial economies and the revived sense of common purpose and mutual responsibility that could be seen in Russia and China and its allies. (The most heinous abuses and most abysmal failures of socialism—Stalinist purges of the 1940's, the Great Leap Forward of the 1950's—were only gradually coming to light, and there could still be some plausibility in Soviet and Chinese claims that these were only Western fabrications.) But many of Africa's leaders were unwilling to align themselves with either party. The path forward for Africa, they insisted, lay in a different kind of political and social order, one that would benefit from the example of East and West while avoiding their errors. In Kwame Nkrumah's words: "We face neither East nor West; we face forward."

THE FOUNDERS' VISION OF A NEW POLITICS FOR A NEW CONTINENT

The most forceful apologist for a new African order was Tanzanian president Julius Nyerere, who guided the formation of the new nation of Tanzania from the British protectorates of Tanganyika and Zanzibar. From the founding of the Tanganyika African National Union (TANU), in 1954 he campaigned vigorously for an independent Tanganyika, of which he was elected the first president in 1961. His dissatisfaction with British rule nudged him toward Moscow and Beijing, but as he took up the responsibilities of national leadership he formulated an ideal model of African political and social life that did not conform to any of the models he saw in the developed world.

The new order in Africa, Nyerere insisted, must be built on distinctively African foundations, and its institutions and policies must be tailored to the needs and priorities of the African people today, not to the assumptions of either capitalist or socialist ideology. To refer to this new form of social organization he adopted the Swahili word for "family" in the extended sense, *Ujamaa*. Relations between citizens and government officials, he insisted, must be characterized not by domination and suspicion but by mutual trust and shared responsibility. In the new African society there can be no masters and no servants but only fellow members of an extended political family. The new order must be socialist in key respects, Nyerere insisted: economic policies must be structured to diminish inequality and ensure the well-being of the worst-off. But socialism need not be a policy imposed from above by centralized authority. For in African traditional society, Nyerere observed, the principles of socialism already operate through networks of care and mutual concern. These practices and expectations can be adapted to the needs of African societies in the transition from colonialism to independence, Nyerere believed, if its citizens cease to see themselves either as victims or as competitors but as members of a unified nation (Nyerere 1998 [1966]).

To that end, Nyerere mandated one national language—Swahili—and implemented policies that minimized ethnic differences and highlighted national unity. He spoke of his ideals to audiences large and small, in major cities and in isolated villages across the new nations of Tanganyika, which became Tanzania with the annexation of Zanzibar in 1964. A teacher by profession, he regarded his political office as a means of advancing the nation's political education, and even while serving as president he was often addressed as *Mwalimu*, "Teacher."

The vision of a unified and prospering Tanzania was, unfortunately, never achieved. Many obstacles blocked the way, including international pressure toward liberalization and privatization and simmering internal conflicts, especially after the abrupt union with Zanzibar. Nyerere achieved remarkable success—unparalleled elsewhere on the continent—in establishing a single national language, and few other states have built as strong a sense of national identity.[3] But there were also catastrophic failures, including a policy of forced communal farming, undertaken in the name of the socialist future. Tanzania's already stretched national economy was also drained by Nyerere's unswerving commitment to freedom for other Africans, manifested in his support for the African National Congress in South Africa in the 1970s and 1980s and in Tanzania's war to oust the Idi Amin regime in Uganda in 1968. Tanzania never became the ideal model of *Ujamaa* of which its president dreamed.

Arguments and ideals similar to those brought to Tanzania by Nyerere were offered by his contemporaries in other regions of the continent. Kwame Nkrumah, first president of Ghana, set out his philosophy for a new Africa in speeches and writings, most extensively and explicitly in *Consciencism: Philosophy and Ideology for De-Colonisation* (1970). In this dense work, both a philosophical monograph and a program for political reform, Nkrumah advocates an "African socialism" that begins not with the revolution of the proletariat but with an acknowledgement of the interdependency of every member of society and the importance of personal as well as political and economic relationships. A society structured on the principles of African socialism, insisted Nkrumah, would build systems of electoral accountability that would seek consensus rather than factional competition, and it would encourage individual initiative while ensuring that the most vulnerable are not neglected. Such a society would draw on Africa's unique social and cultural heritage, without relying on Romantic fictions of an Edenic past where chiefs and their people lived in harmony and power was never abused. In a speech on "African Socialism Revisited" delivered in 1967 to a conference in Cairo, Nkrumah was careful to distinguish his vision of the future from an appeal to an imaginary past:

> Colonialism deserves to be blamed for many evils in Africa, but surely it was not preceded by an African Golden Age or paradise. A return to the pre-colonial African society is evidently not worthy of the ingenuity and efforts of our people.
>
> All this notwithstanding, one could still argue that the basic organisation of many African societies in different periods of history manifested a certain communalism and that the philosophy and humanist purposes behind that organisation are worthy of recapture. A community in which each saw his well-being in the welfare of the group certainly was praiseworthy, even if the manner in which the well-being of the group was pursued makes no contribution to our purposes. Thus, what socialist thought in Africa must recapture is not the structure of the "traditional African society" but its spirit, for the spirit of communalism is crystallised in its humanism and in its reconciliation of individual advancement with group welfare (Nkrumah 1967)

Other figures from the same period saw an even closer relationship between African traditions and renewal of socialist ideals. Léopold Senghor, for example, a leading poet of his generation who became founding president of Senegal after its liberation by France, linked the political future of Africa to the concept of *négritude*, which he understood as a distinctively African way of relating to others and to the world. The "Negro-African," wrote Senghor, "does not separate himself from the object, he does not look at it, he does not analyse it." Rather, he relates to the world through "pure sensation" (Skurnik 1965, 351-

20). For Africa there could be no question of adopting the political and economic systems of the developed world. The desperate grasping after wealth that capitalism enjoins on all only cuts them off from their neighbors and their culture, while the socialists' "dogmatic formulas," practiced not just in Russia and China but also in Scandinavia, have produced only "partial failures." In the end, wrote Senghor, "we will not be seduced" by any of these models but must develop a socialist political and economic order that fits the African context and advances the welfare of all its people (ibid. 354). Such a society, he insisted in a telling phrase, will be "a community-based society, *communal*, not collectivist" (Senghor 1998, 442).

Senghor's African socialism, writes Walter Skurnik, was both "a method and a myth" (Skurnik 1965:349). The same could be said of the political ideals advanced by Nyerere and Nkrumah. Socialism in the African mode was a method for governing the new states and advancing their welfare: it mandated certain economic and social policies intended to maintain a middle course between the fragmentation and alienation that prevail under capitalism and the homogenization and repression that too often result when socialism is imposed by political fiat. But behind the method there was always a myth, an ideal of a more fulfilling and more connected life as individuals and as nations. And this ideal that is deeply rooted in African history and experience. The myth was a powerful motivator to political change, and it helped propel its apologists to leadership in three of Africa's new nations. In South Africa, a similar vision of democratic socialism rooted in communal regard motivated the African National Congress in its struggle to overthrow the *apartheid* regime. Archbishop Desmond Tutu, looking back on the first five years of multiracial democracy in his country, summed up the underlying ideal in this way:

> [A] central feature of the African *Weltanschauung* [is] what we know in our languages as *ubuntu*, in the Nguni group of languages [such as Zulu and Xhosa], or *botho*, in the Sotho languages. . . . *Ubuntu* is very difficult to render into a Western language. It speaks of the very essence of being human. When we want to give high praise to someone we say, "*Yu, u nobuntu*"; "Hey, so-and-so has *ubuntu*." Then you are generous, you are hospitable, you are friendly and caring and compassionate. You share what

you have. It is to say, "My humanity is caught up, is inextricably bound up, in yours." We belong in a bundle of life.
We say, "A person is a person through other persons." It
is not, "I think, therefore I am." It is rather, "I am human
because I belong, I participate, I share" (Tutu 1999, 31).

Many in South Africa and elsewhere respond to language such as
Tutu's with impatience: isn't this just another appeal to an idealized
African essence, the flip side of the colonialists' conception of child-
like natives who need benevolent guardians to protect them against
the modern world? Such a charge cannot be laid at the feet of Archbishop Tutu, however, in light of his stalwart and courageous leadership of the struggle to uphold the dignity and secure the political rights
of all the people of South Africa. Tutu's language here is more pastoral
than analytic, but the point he makes is essential to the distinctively
African vision for a new politics that we are examining here: it must be
a politics whose fulcrum is not individual rights, nor the balancing of
opposing interests, but rather the flourishing of human beings in their
communities. This was the characteristic vision of African socialism
that we have seen in the writings of Nyerere, Nkrumah, and Senghor.
Tutu holds to it still.

THE VISION FOUNDERS ON THE SHOALS OF REALITY

Yet when we look back from the vantage point of the early 21st
century at a half-century of African independence, the record of
African socialism is far from inspiring. Indeed, we cannot escape the
conclusion that the founders' dreams of a new African socialism failed
on both counts, as method and as myth. What were the causes of this
failure, and what lessons can be drawn from it for Africa's often tumultuous political life today? These are the questions to which I devote the
remainder of this chapter.

I write as a philosopher, and also as a citizen of the United States
who has come to love and respect Africa and its people as a result
of extended visits to several regions of the continent and study of its
history and culture. My observations are therefore personal judgments
based on limited evidence and should not be taken as authoritative. My
goal is to articulate some issues and suggest some themes for further
reflection, both to those who are directly involved in Africa's political

and social life and to others who share a concern for its future. Why, first of all, has African socialism failed as a method? Why has it proven impossible for African economies to implement the vision of a society that is "communal, but not collectivist"? The shoals on which socialism has foundered as a method of political and economic reform are complex and cannot be enumerated in detail here. Some of them were external, for the end of colonialism was by no means the end of Africa's vulnerability to exploitation or to its dependence on former colonial masters. Only in rare instances did the European powers make a serious effort to prepare their colonies for effective independence and self-government; often they simply packed up for home and walked away without looking back. Aid designated to build domestic institutions and economies was offered sporadically and inconsistently. Demands from international banks and development organizations to enact "structural reforms" led to spiraling poverty, diminished state capacity, and massive wealth transfers to domestic and international investors in many African nations. Because African export economies are heavily dependent on agricultural products and minerals, the collapse of world markets in many such commodities devastated national budgets across the continent.

Internal factors, however, played just as large a role. When the populist leaders of liberation movements moved from the forests and the streets into the state house, they settled in all too quickly and granted themselves many of the benefits and prerogatives that their predecessors in the colonial regime had enjoyed, necessitating both high taxes and regular "contributions" from those who stood to gain from their official acts. Corruption and nepotism were common features of colonial administrations, but the newly independent African office-holders raised them to a high art. Where high government offices had been reserved for Europeans under colonial rule, under self-rule they were often effectively closed to all but the president's cousins and cronies. Stalwart defenders of free and open elections found it necessary to rethink their position when the prospect of leaving office drew nearer: so terms were extended indefinitely, and opposition parties were either banned outright or relentlessly harassed. Freedom of the press was rare, and fragile, and many a journalist paid for his or her contribution to open political debate by spending time in detention, or worse.

34

When socialist policies were put into effect, too often they were implemented by government decree, with insufficient consideration of how they would be received or of their prospects for success. The forced movement of Tanzania's farmers to agricultural communes in the 1970's is an especially telling example. Measured simply by population movement the policy succeeded, moving 90 percent of the rural population into newly established agricultural communes. But these produced only 5 percent of the nation's crops, and the disruption of traditional smallhold farming soon turned one of Africa's leading food exporters into one of its neediest importers, rescued from bankruptcy only by World Bank loans. Agricultural output plummeted, and Africa's leading exporter of food soon became one of its principal importers (Meredith 2006:249-59). Similar episodes unfolded across the continent. Socialist restructuring of fragile economies was attempted, but successes were rare.

The case of South Africa is unique in many ways, beginning with its history as an independent republic from the first decades of the 20th century. Where the demand for independence elsewhere in Africa was founded on the demand for majority rule, the Union of South Africa was established in 1909 largely for the opposite reason, to ensure the continuation of white control over native populations without meddling or interference from colonialist do-gooders. The African National Congress, bitterly opposed to the enforced separation of the races, invited multiracial membership from its earliest years, and it pursued the goal of a democratic socialist state for all South Africans unswervingly through the decades of struggle. And yet the ANC government, on coming to power after the 1994 elections, quickly retreated from many of the central aims of its prior socialist platform and, under intense diplomatic and financial pressure from its trading partners, enacted laws and policies far more friendly to foreign investment and to private capital than it would ever have condoned while still in opposition.

This is perhaps the clearest and most dramatic example of socialist ideology being vetoed by capitalist realities and forsaken virtually overnight, one that continues to drive internal conflict in the ANC and between it and various opposition movements in South Africa today. It is a story too complex to relate here—it would require, and has received, extensive discussion on its own. I set it aside here and turn once again to the way in which earlier socialist ideals were attempted, but abandoned, in countries in other regions of Africa. But it reinforces the point that was already clear from other examples: socialism has not become the organizing principle of the political or economic structure of any of the leading nations in contemporary Africa. As a method of achieving ethnic harmony and social unity, and a structure for sharing the fruits of development and limiting inequality, African socialism has been effectively abandoned.

WHAT SUSTAINED, AND WHAT CAN NOW SUSTAIN, A VISION FOR AFRICAN RENEWAL?

It is easy to cite failures, and difficult to identify successes, of socialist methods of economic reform in post-independence Africa. But what of its importance as myth—as an ideal that can motivate reform, a counter to the sense that Africa is doomed merely to languish in poverty while the developed world continues to exploit its natural resources and its cheap labor? Has African socialism fared any better as motivating idea than as practical method? In some respects the answer must surely be affirmative. Any government that set out to provide access to education at primary, secondary, and postsecondary levels for all, and to assure access to health care regardless of economic resources, would have placed itself firmly in the socialist rather than the capitalist camp in the Cold War era; but these are taken without question to be essential goals by most independent African nations today. In the United States, lingering fear of socialism ensures that education policies and standards are set locally rather than nationally, and the same fear has brought health reform efforts to almost a standstill even after the historic passage of the health care bill in early 2010. In the African context, national standards and central government funding for education at all levels, and universal access to immunization and medical treatment, are affirmed as goals by parties of left and right alike. International socialism lost its battle against capitalism with the collapse of all the major socialist states in the last decades of the 20th century (except in China, which has created its own blend of ideological rigidity and economic openness). But it won a signal victory in the hearts and minds of African leaders, who have not forsaken their commitment to a society that attends to citizens' wellbeing.

An important part of the reason for the durability of this vision is one that is seldom recognized: from the beginning, the ideals of

African socialism were deeply imbued with Christian ideals of mutual responsibility, brotherhood and sisterhood of all people, together with a sense of respect for the order of Creation. This element in the founders' vision was seldom made explicit, and indeed it was often intentionally obscured by those who adopted the vocabulary and the ideological assumptions of Marxist orthodoxy (Tibebe Eshete's contribution to this volume explores the tension between Christianity and Marxism in Ethiopia). The churches' complicity in the establishment and administration of colonial rule throughout the period preceding independence fueled the perception that Christianity was not an aid but an obstacle to liberation. So few observers of the liberation movements of the 1950's and 1960's would have discerned a significant religious dimension in their methods or objectives.

The intellectual leaders of the liberation era were strongly influenced by the official atheism of Russia, East Germany, and Cuba (after its 1959 revolution). They had chosen to play for that team in the Cold War contest between East and West, after all; and many members of the educated class had accepted invitations to pursue graduate study in socialist countries. In that environment, socialism was regarded as a new world order in which religion—like the state itself--would soon fade away, as the human needs that it once satisfied come to be met instead by new structures of shared responsibility and common ownership. Many African leaders were wary of putting their trust in the grandiose promises of Russian and Chinese socialism, and few anticipated the disappearance of either the church or the state from their renewed societies. But many of them adopted, all the same, the militantly secular language in which socialist intellectuals formulated their ideals.

And yet the rhetoric of militant secularism was laid over an underlying vision of society that was deeply indebted to Christian ideals and teachings. The new society envisioned by leaders such as Nkrumah, Nyerere and Senghor was closer to the "beloved community" of the New Testament writers than to the collective agricultural and industrial collectives that were being imposed on the people of Russia and China. In *Consciencism*, Nkrumah calls attention to Africa's "triple heritage," the convergence of Christian teachings coming from the West, Islamic practices coming from the East, and traditional African religious beliefs that continue to shape daily life for many. Indeed, he said of himself: "I am a Marxist-Leninist and a non-denominational Christian – and I see no contradiction in that" (Mazrui 1999, 117). The religious roots and resonance of Nyerere's *Ujamaa*, and of Mandela's *Ubuntu*, are equally apparent. These are not secular ideals drawn from analysis of the dialectical struggle of the classes; rather, they are translations into political language of ideals of community, mutual care, and human integrity that are integral to the liberating message of the Gospel.

It has been noted by historians that nearly all the leaders of the new African nations spent their formative years as students in Christian boarding schools, established by missionaries to raise up a generation of spiritual leaders but serving in the end to bring renewal, and sometimes revolution, to African political life. The influence of priests and pastors is readily evident, under the surface layer of Marxist analysis, in many of the writings of the independence era. The University of Fort Hare in South Africa is a public university, not a church-operated institution; but Desmond Tutu, one of its alumni, served for at time as its chaplain, and its motto even today is "In Thy Light We Shall See Light." Like most public universities in formerly British territories it had a markedly Christian character during most of the 20th century. Besides Tutu, its alumni include many leaders of the struggle for justice across the continent: not only Nelson Mandela, Robert Sobukwe, Oliver Tambo, Mangosuthu Buthelezi, and Govan Mbeki, major figures in South African history, but also Kenneth Kaunda and Julius Nyerere.

Unfortunately, the spiritual foundations of reform movements in Africa have too often been ignored or suppressed, and politics and religion have become largely disconnected from each other. The ideal of an inclusive and mutually supportive form of democratic socialism has been eclipsed by political imperatives, and too much trust has been placed in the ability of economic reforms to overcome inequality and strengthen communities. The vision of a new society that captured the imagination and won the support of Africans and of their supporters around the world was fundamentally a vision in which spiritual, economic, and political renewal would move forward hand in hand. But this vision was soon dimmed as new leaders adopted the same authoritarian stance, and brooked as little dissent or criticism, as the colonial authorities that they had displaced.

Courageous voices in the church have continued to call on Africa's leaders to affirm the close relationship between Christian belief and the reform of society. An eloquent example can be found in Cameroonian theologian Jean-Marc Ela's *African Cry* (originally *Le cri de l'homme Africain*). In this address to the Christians of Africa, Ela is highly critical of a church that demands conformity with European cultural norms even while insisting that the Gospel is a spiritual and not a political imperative. On the contrary, he writes:

> Faith is the demand for an incarnation of the gospel in a society in quest of itself, a society undergoing radical transformations. . . . In short, faith is verified and actualized wherever the future is striven for and invented, in all of society's tension spots. Unless it takes account of economics as well as the realities of power and the correlative realities of powerlessness, faith is disincarnate (Ela 1986, 91-2).

A true understanding of the gospel requires us to carry on the work of healing the sick and raising the fallen, not just in individual cases but in society as a whole. "The faith cannot be lived atemporally," Ela insists, but must address the historical context in which repression and dehumanization sustain the powerful in their status and voices for reform are stilled. "We can no longer understand and live our faith apart from the context of the liberation of the oppressed" (ibid. pp. 87, 94). The Gospel calls us to believe and therefore to act.

> The Christian task is clear: to allow the human being to be reborn to a life of freedom and communion. The option of ignoring this task is not open to us. Injustice and inequity, inequality and the perversion of justice, swell beyond all bounds in society today (pp. 98).

Looking back over the first two decades of African independence, Ela bemoans both the lack of economic progress and the tendency of post-colonial leaders to emulate the worst practices of the colonialists. He is a bitter opponent, too, of the cultural philosophy of *négritude*, which the translator, contrary to common practice, renders as "Blackness." This stance, writes Ela, is no more than "a system belonging to ivory-tower intellectuals" that has been used both in Africa and in Europe to rationalize injustice and infantilize Africa's people.

If Blackness had its way, Africa would be transformed into
one vast reserve for the ethnologists, where they could preserve the past and keep anything from changing. . . . The
European tourist trade must have its virgin territory where
it can refurbish the tired old tropical paradises of its technological civilization. For all its vaunting of cultural speci-
ficity, Blackness only promotes the values of the past, thus
espousing a dead view of society, creating a mystique of vain
expectation, and doing its best to check the revolt of the
hungering masses by feeding them soporifics (pp. 124-5).

In place of romanticization of the African past, Ela calls for a bold
encounter with its present—with the avarice, graft, and cruelty that
have characterized so many of Africa's post-colonial leaders. The
churches must speak the truth and act in faith that justice can be
restored and human dignity upheld.

The church of Africa is faced with a serious choice. Swept
up in the mutations of African society, It finds itself before
two inexorable alternatives: slip away into anachronism
and become a stranger to the real questions of today's
Africa or else become prophetic and daring, but at the
price of a revision of all its language, all its forms, and all of
its institutions, in order to assume the *African* human face.
. . . We shall have to leave the beaten path, the trail blazed
beforehand, to undertake an apprenticeship of Christian
freedom, with all of the implications of that freedom in
terms of risk and daring (pp. 134).

I have quoted Ela at length, even though he wrote these words three
decades ago, because he articulates so forcefully the challenge that faces
Africa's Christians today: to renew the relationship between Christian
faith and contemporary economic and political life. Ela's scorn for the
négritude ideology is not a renunciation of every appeal to African
traditions and practices: it is simply a rejection of any conception of
African nature as unchanging and fundamentally "other." African ideals
and values must be upheld, not cast aside. But they must be affirmed
for what they are—distinctive strengths of many of the communities
and cultures of contemporary Africa—and not misconstrued as features of an idealized past. The political import of the Gospel message

is after all deeply congruent with some of these characteristic features, such as the emphasis on mutual care and responsibility in communities and the conviction that each individual's identity is closely bound up with the identity and the expectations of others.

How might the church in Africa today undertake the "apprenticeship of Christian freedom" that Ela calls for? I believe it is possible to answer this call by returning to the ideals that motivated the first generation of African independence, including the ideal of a judicious hybrid between prevailing capitalist and socialist models for the organization of society. The once dominant powers in the socialist world have nearly all collapsed, destroyed by their inability to sustain the hopes and welfare of their people. But the leading adherents of free-market economics and liberal democratic politics have failed to deliver on their promises, too, as inequality widens, poverty persists, and economic catastrophes periodically wreak havoc both within and outside their borders. The imperative to find another way, a middle path between the established models of the developed world, is as timely in 2010 as it was in 1960.

The extraordinary capacity of the churches to mobilize and focus pressure for political reform was demonstrated dramatically in South Africa's struggle for freedom. Theological arguments once provided an essential intellectual support for a system of racial division and domination, but today the churches of South Africa work side by side to address that nation's seemingly intractable challenges of urban and rural poverty, social division, and crime. In many of the most repressive regimes that have existed in post-colonial Africa, such as Uganda under Idi Amin and Zimbabwe under Robert Mugabe, the churches have offered a brave and persistent witness for justice. A renewed call by leaders of Africa's churches to build a political and economic order that will "allow the human being to be reborn to a life of freedom and communion" may be just what is needed to catalyze the demand for accountability, political liberty, and social support in many of the nations now suffering under corrupt and self-protective political dynasties.

Yet in many instances the church has muted its demand for a just and compassionate order in order to focus on issues that bear only a tangential relationship to the core imperatives of the Gospel, and it has encouraged its members to judge their leaders by their adherence to a checklist of specific social policies. I will mention two examples that received some coverage in the Western press in 2010: the campaign by Ugandan pastors to enact legislation declaring homosexuality a capital offense, and the efforts of Kenyan clergy to defeat the proposed new constitution because it does not embody their position regarding abortion and Muslim family affairs. I have written elsewhere (Hoekema 2010) voicing concern that church leaders have chosen opportunism over public education, and have characterized opponents of such draconian laws as advocates of unrestricted sexual and social license. In the period leading up to August 4th 2010 Kenyans were engaged in a wide-ranging and probing debate over the provisions of a proposed new constitution; but the public comments of most Christian pastors often passed over fundamental issues of justice, fairness, and representation and focused almost exclusively on two minor and highly questionable demands: that the constitution define human life as beginning at conception, and that there be no recognition of the operation of Islamic courts, the *Kadhi* courts, in matters of family law when requested to render a ruling. These demands if met would represent a new intrusion of specific religious agendas into constitutional politics: there is no prohibition against abortion in the current Kenyan constitution, while the provision to defer to Islamic courts in family law matters has long been included in its provisions. Abortion is already highly restricted under Kenyan law, and these laws will continue in force until changed by legislative action, regardless of whether a new pro-life clause is introduced into the constitution. Submission to the jurisdiction of the *Kadhi* courts is voluntary, and their availability appears to have helped to promote amicable resolution of matters of family law in a small minority community that has not always received equitable treatment from public institutions. Nevertheless, leading Christian pastors, including the Anglican archbishop and the head of the National Council of Churches, have urged rejection of the proposed constitution unless these matters are addressed in the way that they advocate (Gekara 2010).

Nearly 90 percent of Kenya's people identify themselves as Christian, and the notion of a strict separation of church and state matters has never been embraced in Kenya, nor in many other African nations. A call by the nation's pastors to address fundamental issues of justice in society in the constitutional debate would have considerable influence, and it would be regarded as an appropriate contribution to the national debate. Instead of taking this high road, however, many church leaders have drawn the battle lines in ways that promote division and mistrust rather than unity. Can we imagine a way in which religious voices might be raised in the public arena as advocates for renewal and reform, not for a partisan political agenda? I believe there is great potential for more constructive and more effective engagement of Christians in issues that affect the future course of Africa's independent nations. Let me close this essay by suggesting four features that might characterize such advocacy.

First, church leaders could lead the way in recovering the founders' vision of a distinctively African form of socialism, not imposed by fiat or based on abstract economic theory but organically rooted in central features of African family and community life. Christian leaders are in an ideal position to explicate what it would mean to build a society that is "communal, not collectivist," a politics of inclusion, mutuality, and equal regard. Such a social order would be entirely compatible with flourishing markets and vigorous competition, but it would insist that economic development bring benefits to all, particularly to those unable to meet their own needs without the help of others. In the United States today, entrenched political prejudices would immediately nullify the effect of such an appeal from church leaders. In the African context, it would be taken much more seriously. The problems facing contemporary African nations are so daunting, and the commitment of African Christians to live out their faith in every dimension of life so deep, that church leaders would gain a much more attentive hearing in sub-Saharan Africa.

Second, Christian pastors and lay leaders could argue for—and exemplify—a mode of critical engagement in society that departs sharply from the "wall of separation" model of American constitutional law. Certainly there are risks of meddling and moralizing that must be avoided, and political authority has sometimes been misused for sectarian purposes. But in African political life the idea of a strict separation between politics and religion has never prevailed. Prayers at public events, religious language in parliamentary debate, and inclusion of church leaders on government commissions are examples of the openness to religious perspectives that has characterized African political life. When clergy undertake to implement their own agenda in matters of public policy, as in the Ugandan and Kenyan examples cited above, neither the church nor the state benefits. But if church leaders would strive instead to call their societies to reaffirm and nurture core values that are shared by

Christians and by responsible office-holders—values of mutual regard and care, of fairness and accountability—they would show how religious voices can play a constructive role in political debate.

Third, leaders of the Christian churches could acknowledge honestly, and seek forgiveness for, their complicity in past and present injustices. The Dutch Reformed Church of South Africa, long a stalwart supporter of *apartheid* policies, showed a commendable spirit of humility when it renounced its past errors, both theological and political, and—equally important—launched major initiatives to share its resources with black and "coloured" sister churches. In other contexts where church leaders have either supported or simply acquiesced in the actions of corrupt and repressive governments, fearing of persecution or exclusion from the corridors of power, similar measures of repentance and restitution are necessary. The church is an imperfect human institution, its leaders fallible and sometimes themselves corrupt. To gain an appropriate measure of influence in seeking societal reform, church leaders must first acknowledge and make amends for their own wrongs.

Fourth, in the contemporary African context it is essential that churches build effective collaborative relationships with partner organizations that, like them, stand outside governmental structures but exercise considerable influence over the nation's political life. These partners include Western sister churches and non-governmental organizations that contribute to church-supported efforts in health care, education, and economic development. Too often outside aid is linked to unfounded assumptions of external expertise and local incapacity; the churches can help donors avoid these pitfalls. This has little to do in a direct sense with the reform of national politics, but in an indirect way it makes an important contribution by building networks of communication and trust that can contribute to renewal at all levels of society.

The partners with which churches build strong relationships must also include non-Christian religious communities, especially— in nearly every African nation—the community of Islam. This goes deeply against the grain for many church leaders in Africa, who have seen Islam as an enemy, not an ally. But in the call for a renewal of the founders' vision of a society of mutual regard and common purpose, support can be found in Moslem ideals of justice, fairness, and mutual support no less than in Christian concepts of brotherhood and human dignity. Christian-Moslem relations have more often been characterized by mistrust and mutual suspicion than by a sense of common purpose; but there are exceptions to this pattern. South Africa's ruling ANC party has at various times included Christian, Moslem, Hindu, and Jewish adherents among its leaders, and the divisions within that party and between it and its challengers—deep and bitter as they have been—have never fallen along religious lines. In Ghana, in several presidential contests, parties have nominated a Christian from southern Ghana as president and a Moslem from northern Ghana as vice-president, or vice versa. Both in the subsequent actions of the winning candidates, and in Parliamentary and regional politics, a high degree of interreligious cooperation and respect have prevailed. There are too few parallels across Africa to this level of harmony, but it is essential for Christian leaders to find common ground with leaders of the Muslim community, for the benefit of both religious communities and the entire society.

The call I make on church leaders is bold, and my authority for issuing it, admittedly, is dubious. But I issue it all the same. In the history of Africa's era of liberation we can find an inspiring vision of a new form of politics that is socialist in its fundamental understanding of the importance of common purpose and mutual support, deeply African in its conception of persons as rooted in families and communities, and democratic in its structures. That vision has never been achieved. But it is a vision with deep roots in Christian values, and it is a vision that Christian leaders in Africa today can revive and help to implement—if they will call attention to its coherence with Christian teachings, seek an active and constructive role in their nations' political life, acknowledge past wrongs done by Christians, and build partnerships both externally and internally, especially with Moslem communities. The result could be the transformation of both church and society envisioned here by Jean-Marc Ela:

> In wresting free of its historical, contingent constraints, Christianity here rediscovers its radical, basic capacity to educate women and men to the freedom to which God calls them (Gal. 5:13). A gospel that causes persons to mature engages faith. A gospel that opens people's eyes, that asks the real questions of life and society, seems to be the thing that will respond to the expectations of today's African youth. In order to understand these expectations,

however, we may well have to be willing to emerge from our defensive apologetic attitude, and accept the concrete challenge addressed to the church in Africa by our changing societies (Ela 1986, 102).

2

CULTURE, MISSIONS, AND AFRICA'S LESSONS FOR WESTERN CHRISTIANITY

Caitlin McGill

I think many American Christians that I've met overseas cannot distinguish between things American and those that are Christian. Where I see them uncompromising many times are on things there is little Biblical warrant for while they are compromising on core Christian principles. I also have witnessed the "institutionalization" that occurs because American deep pockets and short term energy keeps ministry work alive and the locals are content to sit back and be served and think that the funds are inexhaustible.

– The Puritan Board

For some people the phrase [short-term missions] brings to mind memories of a beautiful trip overseas, getting to know other members of God's family, and serving them with God's love. For others, it is a poor use of the resources God has placed in the church's hands because the more affluent members of Christ's body spend huge amounts of money on overseas travel while others are dying form malnutrition or disease. Some even find it a counterproductive reinforcement of the negative habits of ethnocentrism and cultural insensitivity.

– Lundy Scott

INTRODUCTION

Most of Western media's capitalization on Africa as a continent filled with plights and trials has often created an image of a needy and undeveloped continent with nothing but war, disease, and famine. While there are enough examples to support such images there are equally enough images to show Africa's successes and development but these latter images are very hard to come by. This preponderant negative image of Africa has shaped how most Westerners have talked about and dealt with Africa. Missionaries, development workers, volunteers, and travelers alike often see or seek out this Africa that supports their preconceived notions. Over the past few centuries, for instance, some Western missionaries have followed these images and aggressively visited Africa and its people groups in an effort to help materially and even "save souls" assumed to be plagued by spiritual need. Such a mission of helping/saving Africa quite often involves individuals and church groups that are convinced that Africa's problems lie in its people's traditional belief systems that rely on another spiritual world that challenges the ultimate authority of the Christian God. Even when this perception is not the main driving force, there are often cases of Western Christians going to Africa for short-term missions and framing their trips on the same assumptions of Africa's need for Western saviors. These "saviors" may come in the form of visitors to orphanages or rural communities where such activities as feeding the hungry, clothing the poor, and constructing shelters for the needy take place. Amidst all these activities are opportunities for evangelism as Western Christians share the gospel of Jesus Christ with local hosts. Quite often the assumption of some short-term missionaries, as it was with many earlier Western missionaries, is that the target communities not only need material assistance but spiritual enhancement as well. Such marrying of material and spiritual assistance is nothing new; David Livingstone is best remembered for insisting that Africans could be elevated to the level of White people through commerce and Christianity.

In this chapter I want to analyze how I came to understand African Christianity first through the common Western narrative that quite often follows the "spiritual darkness" motif and later from interacting with Christians in East Africa. I show that a better understanding of the African worldview would have saved the hundreds of years of pouring a significant amount of money into missionary endeavors to spread a "superior Western Gospel," that could have been carried out differently and probably provided better results. It is clear that Western ethnocentrism has blinded the West to the lessons that Africans as well as African traditional religious systems have to offer even to the Western church and way of life today. I then use my own experience in East Africa to critique the new kind of missionary work that is mobilized through short-term missions, arguing that care must be taken not to repeat the same mistakes that were made by earlier missionaries. Rather than serving evil gods as many Western missionaries assumed, Africans through primal sensibility take on the concept of Christianity that leads them to a greater understanding of salvation than the Western church has imagined or provided. Instead of the Western Church and missionaries condemning African beliefs, I propose that the West first understand how the two vastly different worldviews of Western individualism and African collectivism play a part in the religious life of their practitioners. This would then lead Western Christians to reflectively consider how their own cultural orientation has shaped (and even distorted) their view of faith.

AFRICAN WORLDVIEW AND WESTERN CHRISTIANS

In Africa, the interdependence of all community members, whether they are past or present, shapes the identity of the individual. Therefore, transitions such as those brought by death are not a barrier to communication but rather a fellowship with ancestors that allows for a continuation of the earthly conversation. While some Western Christians are threatened by this communication, claiming it to be idol worship and unbiblical, one can clearly see that the African collectivist worldview and communication with ancestors not only help to better explain human relationship with God, but also a collectivist lifestyle is much more in line with Biblical principles than Western individualism. Instead of immediately molding African Christianity to model the one developed through Western culture, Western Christians would be better placed if they were to recognize that Christ meets people where they are, no matter their religious beliefs and that, as Andrew Walls has convincingly argued, Christian faith finds expression in the culture it inhabits (Walls 1982).

For many decades Christianity has been seen as the "White man's religion" because we as Westerners have confined our understanding of faith and the global notion of God to a Western worldview and cultural orientation. Because our brand of Christianity is shaped by our Western culture, we worship a White Christ in European style buildings with Western music styles; we discuss issues amongst ourselves that affect our Western individualized world such as personal daily devotions or how to rely on God to help us make big decisions, but often ignore greater global issues such as poverty and AIDS and the value of depending on others for our survival. As Christians we must determine whether Christ has dominion over all culture and areas of the world or if his Lordship is limited to one culture (ours) only. If Christ is Lord of the entire world then our practices and interactions with other cultures and communities have to reflect that reality. Unfortunately the way we relate to other cultures seems to say that we consider ourselves more Christian than others and our lives as more "blessed" than those of others. We tend to regard material prosperity as a sign of blessings, completely disregarding the historical processes that lead to material prosperity. When we make some progress materially even if it is, in part, a result of some historically generated structures of inequality and exploitation, we consider it a blessing from God. To avoid all this conflation of material prosperity with spiritual growth we have to follow the example of Jesus Christ and heed his basic call. John Taylor, an anthropologist that lived in Uganda, explains our call as Christians as one that requires us to

> ...go with Christ as he stands in the midst of Islam, of Hinduism, of the primal worldview, and watch with him, fearfully and wonderingly, as he becomes—dare we say it?—Muslim or Hindu or Animist, as once he became Man, and a Jew. (Taylor 2001, 74).

For this to happen and for there to be a clear understanding and spiritual growth, the Western Church should seriously consider acknowledging and appreciating the African worldview as a legitimate Christian heritage in order to better understand Christ's global power and relativity. By so doing, the Western church will start an important exchange or dialog that allows for positive aspects of African culture to not only inform their engagement with Christianity but also to positively influence Western Christianity. Without such mutuality and attention to the difference between faith and cultural expressions of it, there will be some divisions and misunderstanding in the worldwide body of Christ. Such divisions would most likely be felt in traditional (African) communities oriented towards collectivism when we, as Westerners with our individualistic approach to Christianity, try to convert their community members to our individualistic brand of Christianity (Taylor 2001, 75). As some scholars have argued, such conversion is often confused for salvation, while indeed it is for the most part a Western worldview imposed on the Africans instead of bringing Christ to inhabit the lives of Africans within their own worldview and molding their lives from the inside out (see, for instance, Bediako 1995). Western Christians would do well to heed Andrew Wall's explanation of Christianity's belief in the incarnation when he states, "Christians' central affirmation is that God became human under particular conditions of time and space. Christ is formed in people [as] Paul says in his letter to the Galatians" (Walls 2000, 792). Christ inhabits a people and community as they are. Western Christians have to continually understand this reality and meet Africans in their own cultural element. This call is applicable to all Christians but I am here specifically focusing on Western Christians.

INDIVIDUALISM, CHRISTIANITY, AND AFRICAN COLLECTIVIST ORIENTATION

The first step to understanding Africans in the realm of their worldview is to see beyond Western individualism and provide room to embrace African collectivism, which I will argue reflects biblical views on Christianity. A sense of community and serving others according to one's blessings is one of the key elements of the early Christian church. In Acts 4:32-35, for instance, we see a clear call to Christians being attentive to the needs of others and not recoiling into their own individualistic realms:

[32]All the believers were one in heart and mind. No one claimed that any of his possessions was his own, but they shared everything they had. [33]With great power the apostles continued to testify to the resurrection of the Lord Jesus, and much grace was upon them all. [34]There were no needy persons among them. For from time to time those who owned lands or houses sold them, brought the money from the sales[35] and put it at the apostles' feet, and it was distributed to anyone as he had need (Holy Bible, NIV).

The African philosophy of collectivism that is often expressed in the statement "I am because we are," resonates with this early Church configuration of Christian communities and is closely tied to an African's social and spiritual existence to his/her community (Taylor 2001, 60). From this perspective of being part of a larger community and one's own identity being formed and guided by such an orientation, scholars then start to say that other aspects of African identity are also to be understood from a collectivist perspective. Ugandan cultural critic and social scientist, Okot p'Bitek argues that the individual and the self or even their mind is best seen as a byproduct of external elements beyond an individual's control, contrary to the Western model where the self is contained in the brain. The African self is beyond the physical body, and memory is derived from spirits, spells, and other influences, which are considered elements to be countered. Anger and jealousy enter from the outside world like diseases or curses would, and are the causes of certain behaviors (p'Bitek 1964, 34). These external actors conflict with the Western view that memory is explained through Freudian terms such as psychosis or neurosis (Taylor 2001, 43).

The Western notion of self deals solely with the single person, diminishing obvious outside influences that are key in self-actualization (Taylor 2001, 44) and in return contribute to the knowledge of the future. But in Africa, people acknowledge that they are products of knowledge of the past. People's identity is derived from various relations to "those who brought [them] into the world" (McCall 1995, 258). The African self does not exist independently of other influences, whether they are past or present. Therefore, as Taylor emphasizes, "until we have felt our individuality vanishing and our pulses beating to collective rhythms and collective fears, how can we guess what the Lord looks like who is the Savior of the African world?" (Taylor 2001, 15).

This African worldview can, for instance, offer a different perception of the family compared to what we mostly uphold in the West. The family unit illustrates the interconnectedness of all of humankind, and identity is found in those connections. A human being exists as a family, and this understanding is revealed through the pattern of village life throughout most of Africa. John C. McCall, who studied familial ties in Africa, explains that the "compound" that villagers live in is more than a grouping of buildings or huts. The specific array of buildings is a way to physically represent the important influences of this family from the past or present that have shaped the current community. Even the compounds are named after the founders who cleared the area and established the ground as their cultural space (McCall 1995, 259).

In these communities, the responsibilities are shared because a human being realizes his/her being through his/her family. The duties of raising children are shared, as are trials and blessings, all playing a key role in unifying and securing the village. Community members surrender their individualism to the larger family, recognizing that they cannot exist apart from the family, and a greater sense of security results. Africans recognize that the living and deceased kin are inextricably tied together out of a need for each other. Now consider many Western missionaries who have been socialized to consider the individual as the most important unit of existence. When such a missionary lands in an African location, some misunderstanding and even harm results when the two cultural perspectives (African and Western) clash.

In the African collective family, the past members are just as important as the present ones because there is no real distinction between physically present members or members that are deceased or distant. In some situations this cultural phenomenon has led many missionaries to believe that Africans worship their ancestors instead of seeing such a relationship as one of dependency that is always continuous. Dependency on other community members evolves as one matures starting at birth with one's socialization, then into youth for food and shelter, and later in adolescence for bride wealth, among other benefits. This interdependence creates a social structure that gives different members purpose and creates connections as these new members enter into relations of social obligation to other community members. Mark you these relations are not limited to life on this earth but also include those departed who are often considered to be physically absent but spiritually part of village life. As Taylor argues, "the family is a delicately poised and interlacing organism in which each member knows to whom he owes particular duties, from whom he can expect particular rights, and for whom he bears particular responsibilities" (Taylor 2001, 70). In such a reality those who are recently deceased join the world of the living dead and have as much say in the structuring of daily life as are those living. When the living dead are invited to be active participants when decisions are being made regarding the living some Western observers conclude that those present are worshiping their ancestors.

ANCESTORS AND CHRISTIANITY

One of The differences between the African worldview and the Western worldview, therefore, is in the value Africans place on their dependence on deceased family members often referred to as the living dead. Africans maintain links with the dead because there is power in that relationship. As clearly stated by Pikkert, "the living relies on the dead and maintains links with them because when an ancestor dies, he is freed from the physical world and thus obtains greater powers of influence" (Pikkert n.d., 2). The reliance on these deceased members can be exemplified variably by present members of the community including the practice quite often observed among many West Africans that involves pouring wine onto the earth or making other offerings to maintain social and spiritual relations.

In contrast to the relationships that living Africans have with their deceased ancestors due to Africans' sense of collectivism, Westerners have a tendency to fear and over exaggerate the African belief in the supernatural world. Hollywood and popular media have further mystified these seemingly strange cultish acts, relaying a savage like stereotype of Africans to the Western world. There is a misconception that all African traditional religious practices require evil sacrifices and worship to ancestors. Rather, African's high regard for ancestors is not a form of worship but simply respect, just as elders in the community are respected (Ubah 1982, 100). Africans include the dead in their thinking of "we are because we participate." Africans view the living spirits of ancestors as means to better the community. The ancestors are "both objects of honor and tools or agents which can be manipulated to achieve competitive goals" (McCall 1995, 257). Relationships are maintained and respect is given because the ancestors, who were once human, understand the needs of their descendants (Ubah 1982, 101). This respect and emphasis on ancestors is not very different from the notion of Saints in the Catholic Church.

In the African worldview God is distant, and ancestors play a key role in mediating between humans and God; they become the bridge that completes the God and human cycle. While some Western Christians feel that this shows a lack of dependency on God, for others it is no different than asking for other living people to pray for you or for you to pray for other living people. We pray for each other in this life, so asking those living in another life to pray to God, on our behalf, should not be regarded as wrong. Yet, from a Western view of Christianity, communicating with ancestors and the notion of a tenable spiritual realm is frequently criticized because it is seen as diminishing the power of God. One can argue, however, that if the concept of death and the eternal soul is indeed what Christians believe it to be, then having direct access to the dead should be natural and confident (Taylor 2001, 114). In the Bible, death is not final, as Christ promises that our spirits will live on. With Christ's death and resurrection, we are reminded that there is not only life for the dead, but power within that life; and the present state of life is not the end of one's story. Communication and interaction with ancestors is essentially fellowship with living persons, for death has not separated the living and the dead more than sleeping would (Taylor 2001, 112). This relationship with the ancestors is merely an extended form of fellowship.

My argument here is that there is a lot we can learn about the relationship God has with the world through Christ by paying attention to the importance of ancestors and lineage expressed in African spiritual life. The continuity that we find between the New and Old Testaments in the Bible is primarily because of the relationships that attend between individuals and communities in both. God made the first ancestor, Adam, but then the human, as a result of sin, experienced distance from God and became "self contained and self sufficient in his absence." But through Christ (sometimes regarded as the second Adam), God is no longer separate from humans, for we are a result of Him and He takes responsibility for us just as ancestors do in the African religious world. In this regard, therefore, Christ is the ancestor that links us to God because "Every branch and bud of the human tree...is answerable directly and constantly to God" (Taylor 2001, 80). This idea of God as our ancestor and the family of believers echoes the collective worldview existing among Africans. Even the illustration that depicts us as "children of Israel" creates a unity and follows the patriarchal pattern of a common ancestor (Taylor 2001, 78) and connects Christians to humans who are no longer living but who shape much of Christian living and expression today.

Because Christ is the common Christian ancestor, Christ is seen as the "second Adam"; he is the new father of descendants of Abraham. To many Africans, the ancestor is the ideal of humanity, for he or she is wise and has experienced life. God entered humanity through Christ, experiencing human trials and being initiated into humanity through common rituals such as birth, circumcision, sacrifices, and baptism when God became human through Christ, therefore, he embodied the ideal human and union with this ancestor brings them closer to the life-giving power of God (Bujo 1992, 1). The belief in one common beginning leads to faith in one common destiny.

Finally, the African notion of Christianity includes a greater appreciation for what "being in Christ," or the Christian body, means. The African collective worldview, which explains human's continued connection with ancestors, is also more in line with Biblical principles of being there for others than the Western emphasis on individualism. In the Bible, there is very little to no reference of a man or woman existing only by himself and for himself, and there is also little attention given to a person's individual relationship to God. The Bible teaches that our value and identity is found in the role we play in our community. Paul, in 1 Corinthians, demonstrates humanity's interconnectedness through the metaphor of the body; each person makes up a different part that contributes to the overall function. The body could not exist without each part, and each part could not function without the body. Accordingly, "The Christian can never truly say 'I am man', but only 'I am in Man'; he exists not of his identity but in his involvement" (Taylor 2001, 77). Africans are more familiar with what it means to have common blood, be part of the same, living and continuing organism, and share a common destiny. Now, with the help of African collective nature, Western Christians can fully understand what it means to be "in Christ." This understanding prepares us well to carry out today's version of earlier missionary work as mobilized through short-term missions. By appreciating that Africans have a lot to teach us about our faith changes the way we approach missions abroad. We come not as superiors coming to show them what it is like to live a Christian life but as partners learning from each other how to live a life of faith.

SHORT TERM MISSIONS AS THE NEW MISSIONS

Now that I have spent quite a potion of this chapter showing the value and legitimacy of African worldviews and the compatibility with Christianity, I want to share my own journey and relationship with African Christianity when I visited East Africa while in high school. I will show how I initially had brought with me the common assumptions about Africa and African Christianity that I have critiqued above and how my experiences interacting with local Christians totally transformed me. Before I visited East Africa, I believed that Christianity in Africa was inferior to Christianity in the West. Now after years of in-depth studies of religion and interacting with Christians and traditions from around the world I have become a little averse to short term missions and have come to view my own experiences in East Africa with a new set of eyes. When I was in high school the word "missions" used to excite me, imagining myself in some far away place helping people and getting a chance to visit some remote villages and see some wildlife. I am sure I am not alone in this view. Indeed, as some scholars have noted there are an estimated 1.5 million or more participants in short term missions each year (VerBeek 2008, 475 and Wuthnow 2009).

Reading Western textbooks in school written with an imperialistic mindset, I had fallen into the familiar mode of thinking that depicted Africa as lacking many of the things I had grown up with in the US. This mindset is not isolated and may be shared among many of my peers and fellow North Americans who participate in short term missions in Africa as the following example shows. When asked to comment on a program that was set up to allow North American university students spend six weeks in Zimbabwe, a local builder, who was in charge of the project, explained

> What the Americas didn't know is that we here in Africa also know how to build buildings. It isn't that they didn't work hard. The trowel was too slow to put mortar between

the bricks so they used their bare hands to speed things up. But they must remember that we built buildings before they came and we will build buildings after they leave. Unfortunately, while they were here, they thought they were the only ones who knew how to build buildings. Finally things got so bad, we had to ask them to leave (Glenn Shwartz).

This episode happened in 1961 and yet such an attitude towards Africa endures. Before going to East Africa myself I particularly thought that Africa did not have a good knowledge concerning Christianity. Besides, I had never heard of African Traditional Religion and the specific worldview that shapes African's social reality. I had just assumed that Western Christianity was superior to all other religious practices. The Church and Christian organizations that I was familiar with made Africa a continent in desperate need of our saving, constantly showing pictures of children in poverty and "cruel" practices such as polygamy and circumcision. Interestingly my home church did not speak much of Africa. Poverty, AIDS, or the spiritual condition of Africans was never addressed from the pulpit and such topics were rarely discussed in any gatherings organized by our church. This has changed with time as noted by Wuthnow (2009) who talks about many American churches now becoming transcultural due to intense globalization. Without this transculturalism, I was left with my impressions of Africa emanating from the media and texts to which I had been exposed. There were random drives at my church, however, that asked us to donate to causes such as Samaritan's Purse's Christmas gift drive, which ended up perpetuating the mindset of the "West" aiding the "rest." None of these activities ever provided a forum to discuss what was causing poverty or how we could work along side African people to overcome many of the challenges they were facing. Instead we were asked to give because it was the right thing to do as Christians. Now in retrospect I see that there was need for some analysis and some asking of questions that would have helped my young mind better understand poverty in its right context.

My first encounter with African Christianity was on a short-term mission trip to Mfangano Island, Kenya during my senior year in High School where our team worked alongside a local church to build some homes. That one week I spent in Mfangano Island introduced me to local religious practices and changed my perceptions of Christianity and African Christians forever. I was particularly amazed by the local people's faith in the power of prayer. They submitted every want and will to Christ, no matter how big or how small. Nothing was done out of one's own desires, but every request was brought to Christ by prayer. I had never experienced such dependency on prayer and walked away from the trip surprised that the people I had come to minister to actually ministered to me. I saw their thirst for the will and blessings of God, and realized that they experienced a deeper Christianity than I was experiencing living a life of relative luxury in the United States. This experience was an important milestone in my own faith. I returned to East Africa and studied with fellow student athletes at the Uganda Christian University in Mbale.

Initially I went to study abroad in Uganda because I was interested in being a missionary. I wanted to get a taste of what living abroad would be like before making a full commitment. While in Uganda I trailed some missionaries during the weekends to see what they were doing around the country. But after studying the work of different missionaries and different development theories, I was struck by the amount of harm missionaries may inadvertently have done in Uganda and all over Africa. When culture is disregarded and missionaries and development workers impose Western traditions and practices, systems break down. Just because Africans do things differently does not mean they are wrong. And by spending time to listen and learn first before judging or changing, I found myself learning more from the Africans I interacted with than I could have taught them.

SHORT TERM MISSIONS AND EXPANDING WORLDVIEWS

My worldview was widened and as a result I decided not to pursue my earlier goal of being a "missionary" in the traditional sense. I was overwhelmed by the damage some past missionaries may have caused to different people groups in Africa due to cultural insensitivity. It was a harsh realization that my own faith had entirely been interpreted through Western cultural eyes. What I had thought to be the authoritative interpretation of Biblical text was actually influenced by Western culture and not history or reality. I began to question many of my beliefs that were derived from my teachers' interpretation of the Bible and what I was taught in Sunday school. If people on the other side of the world could prove their beliefs were Biblical, who is to say who is right or who is wrong? I decided to observe and learn from the Africans before trying to alter their beliefs or behaviors through my intended missionary work. I realized how our brand of individualism that gets expressed in our Western brand of Christianity clearly limits the "White man's religion" from fully comprehending the collectivist nature of Biblical Christianity that I experienced in East Africa.

Are all mission trips ill advised? There are certain aspects of short term missions or missions of any nature that make them popular and acceptable. Proponents of short-term missions, for instance, claim that the services that guests provide to hosts are life changing, as is the gospel the Christian missions groups bring. Moreover the effects of the trip on the people going to serve are innumerable with claims of spiritual growth, learning more about the world around them, and coming home with new habits of service and monetary giving (VerBeek 2005, 445). Without challenging these claims or undermining them in any way I would like to offer some critique of the stated outcomes of missions. Given that when I left for East Africa I had not done any sufficient academic or cultural preparation for it how much effect would my visit have on the local people? Without the grasp of the local language and a clear understanding of the workings of local culture, how effective would I be in bringing about change to the community I visited? Was I not guilty of what David Livermore has termed the uniformity of work that assumes that cultural differences do not matter in missions abroad (Livermore 2006)?

As Livermore states, "in our obsession with making the Bible the end-all rather than a means to an end, we've imported far too much Western Culture into understanding the purposes of the Scriptures" (Livermoore 2006, 79). As a result mission groups are unable to do effective evangelism because they don't understand the language or the culture of the people they are trying to reach (Van Engen 2000). Ironically, in many of the countries where such missions take place, Christianity is already present and as I found in Mfangano Island, I was the one who was gaining more spiritually than the local people were gaining from me. Kurt VerBeek's extensive research in Honduras on the spiritual impact of mission groups on Honduran beneficiaries is very much applicable to many trips in other parts of the world. VerBeek's research shows that no notable spiritual difference can be seen after Short-term missions groups leave (VerBeek 2009, 449). According to his research whether or not these people met short-term missionaries, they still had faith in Christ. Instead of changing lives spiritually, many groups go to a country and "meet articulate poor people who often believe in God more than they do and who want a world where North- South relations are characterized by justice rather than charity" (Jeffrey 2001, 6). This very much defines my experience in Mfangano Island.

It is the notion of justice that rekindles my interest in missions and has been instrumental in shaping my own vocational trajectory. While I still plan on doing missions work I am more interested in the "outreach" sense of doing missions than being a missionary. I would like to do missions a little differently—focusing on the larger structural level. I am particularly interested in working for the US State Department and addressing issues of national security, peace, and conflict resolution. These I believe are the critical issues that underlie some of the many socio-economic and political challenges that we sought to address in my short term mission trip in East Africa. I believe that many developing countries require such structural support in order to provide a stable environment for the citizens to get the kind of services and privileges I have received in my growing up. With all my travels as well as from courses taken on various aspects of politics and development, I have learned that stable environments and honest governments encourage citizens to be productive, safe, and enjoy many aspects of a prosperous life. Justice becomes a reality in such contexts and ultimately the West benefits from prosperity and stability abroad.

WHAT IS GOOD ABOUT SHORT TERM MISSIONS?

When embedded in short-term missions justice is often mobilized through "hands on" tasks such as building structures (classrooms, clinics, or houses), digging wells, or running a week-long clinic (Jeffrey 2001). Not surprising my first trip to East Africa was a short-term missions trip with Mission Discovery. A team of seven of us went--five students and two adult leaders. Before we left, we did the typical Vacation Bible School preparations (which were actually in vain because we arrived in East Africa during the local children's school year, not realizing they would not have the same "summer vacation" as we did in the US). We also took a personality test and discovered different ways we would be able to contribute to our small team. Before our departure we met with a Kenyan family from our church in Illinois who showed us pictures of the area we were visiting, gave us a typical Kenyan meal, and briefed us on cultural items such as dress and customs. Someone from Mission Discovery who had made a few trips to Kenya coordinated our trip. He, however, had not spent any substantial time in the same area in which we would be working. Consequently, there was poor communication between him and our group in the planning stages, and upon execution of the trip, it was the local pastor on the island who gave us most of the directions. When in Kenya, we did not end up doing Vacation Bible School, instead we helped make cement bricks and then transport them to two different work sites, where we started to assemble two single room houses for two widows.

This approach to missions is commendable but it is not without its own challenges. After interviewing numerous beneficiaries of a home-building project in Honduras after hurricane Mitch, for instance, Kurt VerBeek found that while many people appreciated the effort of the short-term mission groups, they would have preferred that the often-exorbitant costs of the trip be used differently. "It is better for them to send the money in order to help more people who are in need" (VerBeek 2005, 453). Likewise, even when people bring professional skills such as those of doctors and nurses, it is hard to justify the expense and trouble taken to host them. JoAnn Van Engen argues that the money used to bring a medical team to a community in a developing nation could hire the numerous doctors often unable to find appropriate remuneration for work in their own countries. If anything these doctors already understand the culture, language, and specific health problems their fellow citizens face. Even when brigades are supplementing preexisting clinics, one doctor from Nicaragua admits that, "he spends over a year preparing for and hosting U.S. medical brigades. He admits that the brigades accomplish very little (visiting doctors mostly hand out aspirin for headaches and back pain), but hesitates to complain since the U.S. organization funds his clinic" (Van Engen 2000, 23).

There is also the danger of using North American cultural practices to engage local people as reported by Steve Corbett and Brian Fikkert who argue, "the individualistic cultural value of STM teams can undermine local knowledge in a collectivist context. For example, as STM team will tend to assume that treating every individual in the community the same way is obviously the right thing to do and may give out, say, food, in equal amounts to everyone" (Corbett and Fikkert 2009, 170). Corbett and Fikkert go on to say that this kind of practice fails to acknowledge local practices where large amounts of food are disproportionately given to some individuals whose acumen then enables them to accumulate resources that in turn become important sources of livelihood for the community in times of need.

In terms of the goals North Americans hope to achieve, research does not provide much more promising results. Kurt Verbeek conducted surveys and phone interviews with 127 people who had returned from a short-term mission trip through the Christian International Development Organization (CIDO). Verbeek used a "Life Change Scale" that asked participants to quantify time spent in prayer, volunteering, giving of money, knowledge of CIDO, financial report of CIDO, home church involvement, interest in poor countries, advocacy for the poor, interest in short term missions, interest in long term missions, and time spent learning and reading more about missions and poverty (VerBeek 2005, 459). In short, the Life Change Scale looked at all the goals mentioned by Livermore as those participants found important in STM programs. Only 11% of those surveyed reported significant positive change in time spent in prayer, volunteering, or level of financial giving (VerBeek 2005:460). While 66% indicated a slight or significant rise in interest for poor countries and missions, VerBeek points out that according to Babbie in *The Practice of Social Research* (2001), "whenever we ask people for information, they answer through a filter of what will make them look good" (VerBeek 2005, 460). Adjusting the statistics for this bias, it would appear that the change was very slight indeed.

MAKING SHORT TERM MISSIONS WORK

With little positive impact (and indeed some of it negative) on receiving countries and only slight change reported among those who go on mission trips, one might wonder if they are worth continuing. I would argue that they are but under the right conditions. As the population grows and our world shrinks, curiosity and a sense for adventure are only natural, and I do not think this is a bad thing in the right circumstances. Indeed, these very factors have led to the increased globalization of many congregations in America where they are much more aware of the world far away from them and spend quite some substantial resources to support missions abroad (Wuthnow 2009). As

Christians, I think it is important to appreciate the cultural diversity God has created. Furthermore, we are called to "walk humbly and do justice" (Micah 6:8) as well as to "love our neighbors as ourselves" (Mark 12:31). Missions can be an opportunity for human relationships and learning, if they are placed within the correct context. Mission trips may also open our eyes to various career paths we can pursue. Indeed, this is what I learned on my trip to Uganda Christian University while I was a student at Calvin College.

While at the Ugandan University, I joined the track and volleyball team as a way of carrying on with my own athletic interests and to interact with local students. I, along with other students, also participated in the University's daily chapel and various extra curricular activities such as choir concerts. I can state that it was my experience in this second trip that shaped the career path I have taken. I am currently pursuing graduate studies in International Affairs focusing on national security and American diplomacy with an eye to working in a context where I am able to participate in the drawing up and implementation of US international and political policies that have direct influence on the lives of many people in Africa. Based on my experience in Uganda I would suggest that instead of short-term trips focusing on building houses, they should start focusing on building relationships. By coming to a country with an intention to learn, mission participants may have the opportunity to start genuinely caring about the people they meet. In turn this could create advocacy in North America for the kind of long term sustainable justice partnerships that impoverished countries need.

4 goals ⁝ If a team really wants to serve, they might focus their project around four goals: empowerment, capacity building, equity, and sustainability (VerBeek nd., 64). At the root of all development and all relationships is the need for human dignity as image bearers in Christ. By ensuring that the project focuses around local skills and knowledge and can continue after the service team has left, mission participants would be able to both give and receive the gift of cultural interconnectedness through service and love. Again Cobbert and Fikkert advice is appropriate here: "a good first step is for the mission trip to be done as part of a long-term, asset-based, development approach being implemented by local ministries" (Cobbert and Fikkert 2009, 170). The key question to consider is how mission teams fit within the existing local development strategy, what are the local goals and how can short-term missions fit into those goals?

In order to achieve this sort of result teams cannot just pack their bags and hop on the first flight to some far away place. They need good preparation. Such preparedness involves something Livermore calls "Knowledge CQ," which refers to knowledge about cross-cultural issues and differences (Livermore 2006, 115). While this includes things like language, history, and the cultural stereotypes of a specific culture that are sometimes mentioned in short term mission orientations, knowledge CQ must move beyond this in order to be effective. "The most important part of knowledge CQ is gaining general information about how cultures vary. Explicitly and implicitly, how does culture affect the way people view the world?" (Livermore 2006, 116). Preparing for a trip by studying things like intercultural communications and basic anthropology, the effects of the participant's own ethnocentrism can be diluted to allow for more genuine connections and understanding. Admittedly not many mission team members have the time or interest to do all this preparation and not all well prepared teams end up having successful trips. To respond to this I would suggest that at the minimum a mission team undergo some basic orientation to cross-cultural engagement and read relevant literature for the target community. Further, the team may be well served by engaging the services of a local person conversant with cross-cultural issues and is able to "teach" on the ground as relationships develop and work is carried out.

Before planning a trip there is need for careful preparation on the ground, finding individuals who can work closely with the North American team to broker the cultural barrier and create a bridge that would enhance better relationships between the guests and hosts. Such a relationship calls for a lot of reflection on the mission team, knowing about their own cultural orientation and worldview and how that shapes their thoughts and action. When this is done well we might avoid the common faux pas we often see or hear about from mission team members. How often have team members come back and all they could say is: "Oh they were so poor but so happy"? A careful analysis of such a statement will say more about the person uttering it than the person or people it is supposed to describe. Asking why one would be equipping happiness with material possessions.

Once prepared for the trip, it is important to use the short time available to make the most out of the sacrifices it has taken to get there. Van Engen points out that "short-term missions are expensive. They spend money that third-world Christians could desperately use. But short-term missions can be worth every penny if they mark the beginning of a long-term relationship" (Van Engen 2000, 23). Kurt VerBeek suggests arranging for local leaders in the community to talk to the group, or have the group take time to visit local historical sights and learn the community's perspective about their importance. "Before trying to fix poverty in Honduras, students need to meet the poor; listen and talk with them..." (VerBeek nd., 67-8). Perhaps most importantly, many short-term mission groups tend to put goals above relationships. North Americans are raised in task-oriented cultures that often differ with the many relationship-oriented cultures served by short-term missions. Consequently many mission participants go with good intentions, wanting to show "poor people" that they are loved but the short-term mission trip groups' notion of love is very much framed in their own cultural context. Overall missions should aim to create relationships and lessons that will last far longer than the photographs. And when we take photographs to bring home we would be better served to actually know the names of the people in our photographs, otherwise what is the difference between them and the buildings and animals we find fascinating?

3

CHARISMATIC RENEWAL IN THE CATHOLIC CHURCH IN GHANA

Ross Acheson

INTRODUCTION

In the past hundred years Pentecostalism has become a major force within Christianity worldwide. Its emergence was by far the largest Christian movement of the 20th century, going from zero to over 500 million adherents, according to one study.[1] Today the number of Pentecostals in Africa is 107 million and growing.[2] Many Pentecostal churches have emerged on the global scene and Pentecostalism itself has inspired charismatic movements within many of the historical mainline churches worldwide. What may have been regarded earlier as a peripheral expression of faith has today become a major force within the larger Christian body. Indeed, the now well-established nature of these churches has made charismatic spirituality much more influential primarily through the interaction of strong Pentecostal experiences with long-standing church teachings, traditions, and spiritualities that were initially developed in the West. As Parsitau shows (this volume) Pentecostal practices are even shaping the public presentations adopted by some Muslim groups in Kenya. In much of Africa and other areas that retain their strong primal roots, Pentecostal practices contribute to a fascinating interchange between traditional cultural frameworks, Western traditions, and charismatic spiritual experience within everyday practices of Christianity. The charismatic renewal movement in the Roman Catholic Church in Ghana provides an excellent case study for this dialogue.

The word "charismatic" is generally used in Ghana to refer to a set of fast-growing, mostly-urban, independent congregations that stress healing and tend heavily toward prosperity gospel preaching. In academic parlance, these are better termed "Neo-Pentecostal" churches. I will use the word in a different and more universal sense. "Charismatic" is an adjective meaning "Of, relating to, or being a type of Christianity that emphasizes personal religious experience and divinely inspired powers."[3] Thus charismatic spirituality is "characterized by a quest for [or occurrence of] inspired and ecstatic experiences such as [sensing God's presence,] healing, prophecy, and speaking in tongues."[4] Adherents to charismatic spirituality, whom I will henceforth call "charismatics," place emphasis on the active presence of the Holy Spirit in their lives and on the use of the gifts of the Holy Spirit mentioned in the Bible, especially those spoken of by Paul in 1st Corinthians 12.4-11: words of wisdom, words of knowledge, faith, healing, working of miracles, prophecy, discernment of spirits, speaking in tongues, and interpretation of tongues. The term "charismatic" refers to this emphasis on spiritual gifts, as the word is derived from the Greek word χαρισμα (charisma), which means "a gift freely and graciously given."[5] This definition does not differentiate "charismatic" from "Pentecostal." The terms are closely related, but in general usage they refer to the same sort of spirituality but connote a difference in doctrine and affiliation, with charismatics generally being more moderate, and associated with mainline denominations.[6] "Charismatic renewal" refers to the revival of charismatic spirituality in mainline churches. Mainline churches are defined here as "the older, and generally larger churches instituted as the result of European Missionary endeavours in Ghana in the 19th century."[7]

BACKGROUND

The missionary activity that introduced Christianity to Ghana was conducted by persons heavily influenced by the rationalistic worldview of the West. The newly established churches tended to be "unable to sympathize with or relate to the spiritual realities of the traditional world-view."[8] This made their growth initially very slow, having most of their impact on children and youth through education initiatives. In the case of the Catholic Church, missionary activity in Ghana began taking root from 1880 onward. It expanded fairly quickly, showing the significant appeal of the liturgical, sacramental, ritual, and communal life of the Church. The Catholic Church remains the largest single denomination in the country. However, Western idioms, question-and-answer memorization as a primary form of catechesis, and moving very late both to use the vernacular in worship and to recruit indigenous persons for ministry, all contributed to a lack of depth in the Christianization of Catholic converts. Similar lack of ownership and depth characterized many of the other mission churches as well.

It took the emergence of lay African prophets from 1914-1937 for Ghanaian adherents to begin having the confidence to make Christianity their own. These prophets received direct calls from God to preach the Gospel of Christ to their fellow Africans, and were given spiritual powers for healing, exorcism, and miracle-working to accompany their message. Their demonstrations of God's power[9] showed that the Christian God could hold his own among the gods and spirits with which West Africans were familiar, and could even supersede them. These few individual prophets were responsible for the conversions of tens of thousands of people. They operated on the periphery of the mission churches, referring converts to them for further discipleship. They did not establish formal ties, however, and in fact many of the church establishments outright rejected them on account of their independence and eccentricity, while still being glad to receive the influx of new converts. The ministries of these prophets initiated what could be considered the first Christian charismatic movement in Ghana. In the wake of their ministries, many people came into the mainline churches, but there were also many who decided that these churches were not meeting all of their needs. They had seen that there was more to Christianity than the foreigners were serving them. This led to the start of the African Independent Churches (AICs), many of which continue to today. These are vibrant, charismatic, ritualistic, and very much African. They had the independence and the indigenous social capital to enable them to develop their own approach to the Christian faith that is relevant and appealing to Africans. As they developed they drew away many members of the mainline churches into their own folds.[10]

Meanwhile the Pentecostal movement that had begun in the United States at the beginning of the 20th century was developing and spreading quickly. It too started at the periphery of the established churches. Generally, adherents formed or joined new churches, which we now refer to as "Classical Pentecostal" churches. They tended to have a strong missionary orientation, and quickly sent missionaries all over the world. The first Classical Pentecostal fellowship in Ghana traces back to a number of people's experience of the "baptism of the Holy Spirit" in 1927. However, the Pentecostal movement also made its way towards the center of some of the mainline churches, and finally began to show itself in the 1960s.[11] Committed members of these churches started to have Pentecostal-type experiences, and wished to share them within their own church context. Charismatic renewal in the Catholic Church is traced back to the experiences of a number of American Catholics in 1967. The Renewal quickly spread worldwide. Already by 1971 it had begun to take root in a few cities in Ghana, and soon the various streams merged into an organized unit called the Catholic Charismatic Renewal (CCR). The CCR is headquartered in Kumasi, and oversees and supports the numerous local CCR groups within Ghanaian parishes. A good example of this Charismatic renewal is Bishop Peter Kwesi Sarpong, a pioneer in making the Catholic Church Ghanaian, and Bishop of Kumasi Diocese.[12] Bemoaning the negative perceptions Christians have of those who follow traditional religions, Bishop Sarpong says that growing up he noticed a sense of deep religiosity and fear of the Lord among people practicing traditional Ghanaian religions, who he says fear God more than Christians do. In this regard he tries to see how being rooted in a specific cultural tradition directly interacts and bonds with being Christian, stating "you cannot be Ashanti at the expense of being Catholic or be Catholic at the expense of being Ashanti." When he introduced drumming in his church some older male members of his church called him aside and told him he was going to spoil the church. He responded by wondering how he could spoil the church by using something Ghanaian, something Ashanti in the church. This was the beginning of making his church more in tune with local cultural practices. He gives as example of earlier mass liturgy where the congregation would be stating, "I am sorry" as it repents its sins. Accompanying that repentance was a gesture of striking one's chest. Bishop Sarpong says that such a gesture (inherited from the European tradition of mass) went contrary to Ashanti culture because when, for instance, a man strikes his chest he is symbolically saying, " I am a man, I am strong and I am going to fight you." How could such a gesture be used among the Ashanti to honor and surrender self to God? How could Catholicism make sense to Bishop Sarpong's congregation without being aligned with its culture? He slowly incorporated aspects of Ashanti culture into the worship services and gradually made his congregants at ease with being both Ashanti and Catholic. Many other Christians across Africa have done the same and have done so in many aspects of their spiritual life as we see in the following example of services I attended in Ghana at the University of Ghana in Legon. I specifically focus on how Catholic Charismatic renewal unfolded to me while in Ghana. Having attended Catholic mass in my home church in the US for many years, my experience in Ghana was more than an intellectual journey, it was also a personal entry into a different way of being Catholic.

PARTICIPANT OBSERVATIONS

In September through November of 2008 I participated in some of the activities of one local renewal group, called the Legon Catholic Charismatic Renewal (LCCR), based at St. Thomas Aquinas Catholic Church in Legon. Legon is a small suburb of Ghana's major city of Accra and is best known as the home of Ghana's premier university, University of Ghana. Because of the university's centrality to this space many have come to associate Legon with the university. Indeed, the word Legon in the Ga language denotes a hill of knowledge, which appropriately symbolizes the identity of the university. During my time at Legon I attended a number of weekly Sunday night meetings and as much as possible carried out a few informal interviews with persons involved in the group. While these observations and interviews did not constitute enough data for an in-depth understanding of charismatic renewal in the Catholic church in general, they allowed me a window through which to make some informed analyses of charismatic renewal in a university setting in Ghana. Using these observations and drawing from Cephas Omenyo's book *Pentecost Outside Pentecostalism: A study of the Development of Charismatic Renewal in the Mainline Churches in Ghana*, I show that charismatic spirituality has enabled the Catholic Church in Ghana to better address many of the popular concerns that arise out of a primal religious context.

A non-charismatic Westerner drifting into a Charismatic Renewal meeting in Ghana might feel very odd, confused, or out of place. Right at the outset of the meeting, the majority of people begin expressing themselves freely, praying rapidly in a strong outdoor voice, swaying bodily, dancing, clapping, and singing. Many people also pray out loud in unintelligible languages. Little greeting occurs before or during the meeting until part way into the meeting when the programmed greeting time comes and people start to dance around singing, "I love you with the love of the Lord," offering handshakes or an embrace. During a lull in the music and dancing someone might cry out a message from God, spoken in first person and with overpowering emotion. A collection is taken, but it is not clear what it is for, where it goes, or whether one is to participate. One needs to be an "insider" to figure out the nuances and norms of participating in the meeting.

Despite having seemingly chaotic elements, meetings of the LCCR are quite structured. They follow a general pattern and keep close to their two hour time limit. The Sunday night meetings begin with a time of intercession, during which one member, who has been appointed to the task for the night, gets up in front and leads those gathered in praying out loud and in praying in tongues for various intentions. The leader has ways of directing the gathering's flurry of simultaneous prayers through subtle signals to pipe down while directions are given, and oral flags, such as, "in the name of Jesus... Amen." Part of the intercession leader's role is to set the tone for the meeting and to introduce a heightened energy for prayer by offering loud, impassioned petitions and words of praise over the microphone in a quick cadence and in rapid succession. Next comes the aforementioned greeting time, during which three or four minutes the people share a hug or a greeting with as many people around them as possible; friends share familiar greetings, acquaintances acknowledge one another, and members welcome new faces. This is followed by musical worship, which a soloist leads, backed up by a choir, keyboard, bass guitar, and drums.

Music plays an important role in every meeting, offering a mode through which everyone present can participate. At St. Thomas' masses, the greater portion of songs come from the Catholic Hymnal, which is mainly comprised of relatively old, imported Roman Catholic hymns in English; but at Renewal meetings most of the songs are local choruses, usually in the predominant local language, or international (especially US and UK) contemporary worship hits. Both sorts of songs tend to be well-known and popular across church and denominational lines. The songs I recognized, having heard before in the US, stand as testimony to the globalization of Western Christian worship culture. After worship, a collection is taken in classic African style, with a song playing by which to dance forward and deposit one's offering in the basket. The money goes toward the facilitation of the group's programs—buying musical instruments, funding special events, and advertising. Then comes time for the music ministry to *perform* another worship song, during which the rest of the people usually sit and listen. This functions as a precursor and a preparation for the second major division of the meeting, which has less to do with music and more to do with the spoken word – I call it the Word Element. The Word Element of a meeting most often takes the form of a talk or exhortation delivered by a guest speaker or a leader in the group. Occasionally the time is set aside for members to share impromptu testimonies to God's work in their lives. The Word Element might also be used for a Bible study, during which members read a scripture passage in small groups and then discuss it. Finally, after the Word Element the meeting concludes with announcements, a final song and prayer, and the communal recitation of a parting blessing/benediction, spoken by all while holding hands. Most of the testimonies regard answered prayer, or God showing his blessing through remarkable coincidences, but some of them also stressed God's help through personal struggles. At one meeting one woman spoke about God blessing her with all Christian roommates, after being worried about being negatively influenced by university life. Another woman talked about God helping her get a B+ on an exam after having extreme difficulty studying late into the night. A philosophy student shared about the pain and struggles he had been experiencing since having been rejected from seminary.

Leadership in the Charismatic Renewal is also very structured. A Coordinator, Assistant Coordinator, and Secretary comprise the core executive team. The parish priest and a set of older, experienced members of the CCR group function as an advising council. Then there is the service team, or parliament. This is made up of the leaders of the various ministry teams operating within the group. Ministry teams include Music Ministry, Choir, Shepherding Ministry, Teaching Ministry, Prayer Ministry, Outreach Ministry, and others. Each of the ministries has a team leader. All members of the CCR are strongly encouraged to join one of the ministries that suit their gifts and interests. All leadership positions in the group are volunteer positions filled by lay leaders who are passionate about doing God's work.[13] This leadership structure while reflective of the Catholic Church in general, is also a function of the local Ghanaian culture that greatly values structure and authority, especially along age and social status. The fact that the CCR is a lay movement is a significant thing for a Church whose leadership has historically often been dominated almost exclusively by the ranks of clergy and religious leaders. The fervor of lay devotion demonstrated by members of the CCR has given some credence to the movement's claim to be a renewal movement for the whole church.

The normal course for membership in the CCR involves going through a "Life in the Spirit Seminar" course that seeks to ground members in the faith[14] and prepare them to receive the "baptism of the Holy Spirit." Emphasis is placed on Bible study and Bible teaching. The course usually takes nine weeks, and always concludes with each participant being prayed for to receive the Holy Spirit in a new way, followed by a final commissioning by the pastor. In October 2008 at the Legon CCR the parish priest commissioned twenty-two people. Each person received a cross to wear, a lit candle to represent the light of Christ, and salt on his or her tongue. These symbolized their call to "be salt and light for the earth." The priest told the people that just as the salt had a distinct flavor in their mouth, they should have a distinctive presence in the world. He also reminded them that "apart from [Jesus] you can do nothing."[15] Because the priest ran the show, the commissioning service seemed to lack much of the characteristically charismatic ethos of a normal meeting, and instead had a distinctively Catholic feel—the ceremony was silent except for the priest's words, and focused on the use of sacramental objects to communicate spiritual realities. Clearly there are certain areas of the CCR that allow for creativity and spontaneity but others that strictly follow the traditional Catholic structure.

Charismatic renewal in the Catholic Church extends beyond the formal organization called the Catholic Charismatic Renewal. In many places charismatic-style prayer and expression has become commonplace within normal Catholic parish life, depending in extent on the area of the country and on the priest in charge of the parish. At the St. Thomas Aquinas parish on the Legon campus the charismatic movement has clearly generalized into parish life, though by no means does it dictate all or even most of the church's direction. The priest, Reverend Father Ebenezer Akesseh hopes that in the time they have at his parish, students will come to understand and appreciate different spiritualities within the Church, and for this reason opposes having the church only express itself as charismatic. At the same time he wishes that all of his parishioners would live in the presence of the Holy Spirit, which he regards as the most basic definition of charismatic spirituality. Each year he holds a "Holy Spirit Mass" for the incoming freshmen, and he would also like to begin running Life in the Spirit Seminars as a whole parish, rather than leaving it just for the CCR group, since "the Holy Spirit is for everyone," and since some members are leery of the CCR. Pax Romana, the Catholic student organization on campus, tends to have a charismatic ethos, even though it does not specifically designate itself as charismatic. It incorporates many different Catholic spiritualities and associates them together, but at big events like the Pax Crusade charismatic spirituality is the most pronounced.

The theme of spiritual warfare is a very important one in the CCR. Western Christians tend to discount Satan and evil spirits as either symbolic or unimportant, but Ghanaians tend to discern a much more active and formidable host of spiritual enemies—evil spirits, and persons influenced by them, that are opposed to God, his truth, and his people. This awareness can make for very different and very interesting dynamics. During my study the Catholic student group Pax Romana organized a "Pax Crusade" event to reach out to the student body on campus. Though Pax Romana is not officially charismatic, the Crusade nevertheless had an extremely charismatic ethos. The event was entitled "Whoever fights against you shall fall," taken from Isaiah 54:15b. To me, this theme felt unnecessarily violent and essentially irrelevant, so I was slightly put off when I saw posters for it; thus I was surprised when the Crusade drew more than three hundred people to its Friday Night all-night prayer meeting. At the event, a great deal of time was given to subduing evil forces affecting peoples' lives. During the deliverance portion of the night, which was the climax of the program, the speaker gave much attention to being free from witchcraft, and from any and all residual associations or entanglements with traditional deities or devotions, whereby evil forces might have gotten a foothold in peoples' lives. There was a whole terminology surrounding these associations, most of which I did not understand. The speaker methodically introduced every major kind of satanic foothold she could think of, and proclaimed God's deliverance over each. People for whom these footholds resonated were encouraged to accept this deliverance and declare it for themselves in prayer. In addition, all through the night except during the mass, it was a frequent occurrence for people (mostly women) to lose control of themselves. Generally they would scream and cease to be able to stand on their own, sometimes beginning to convulse. Most of them were carried to the back of the church where a prayer team, including the parish priest, was there to minister to them. When I spoke to the priest, Reverend Father Ebenezer Akesseh, he referred to these as instances of people "manifesting," but was unclear about whether they were manifesting the Holy Spirit or demonic spirits, even when I pressed the question. The sense I got was that either way, it denoted God's powerful working in situations of interior battle. He said that the Holy Spirit's fruit of self-control in Galatians 5:16 refers to moral self-control, and does not preclude God's spirit temporarily overpowering one's person.[16] Compared to the Pax Crusade the LCCR meetings are comparatively gentle and moderated, but similar themes and deliverance methods are present on a smaller scale at the CCR meetings, especially as part of the intercession time.

The most important part of general Catholic parish life is the mass. Charismatic spirituality can be incorporated in places in the mass, but in most Ghanaian Catholic churches including St. Thomas Aquinas it is not the dominant norm. I spoke to a nun, Sister Constancia Atachie, who is a member of the St. Thomas Aquinas parish and is involved in the CCR. She said that the mass has room for all of the different Catholic spiritualities, including both the charismatic and the contemplative. She mostly equated charismatic spirituality with the loud singing, dancing, and clapping that characterize charismatic meetings.[17] Fr. Akesseh pointed out that charismatic spirituality is expressed here and there within the mass at St. Thomas Aquinas. Sometimes the bidding prayers are offered by CCR members or other students in an impromptu style common to charismatic spirituality, and other times the CCR choir leads the music, with its local choruses and international worship anthems. He said that he desires to keep the expressions in the mass varied, and also emphasized that it's hard to keep charismatic expression to the time limits the mass requires.[18] Some parishes in Ghana may have more fully charismatic masses, in most places charismatic expression is an occasional addition rather than the norm.

Catholic charismatic renewal presents a number of challenges in the Church. CCR groups face internal challenges, and they also pose challenges to the broader church. Within the group, despite the high energy that seems to come naturally to the leaders and members, it can be difficult to keep up the novelty and the excitement of it, especially when meetings become predictable and overly limited by time constraints. It can become monotonous.[19] There is also little room for quiet devotion or the possibility of members experiencing spiritual dryness. Because the group is mostly made up of students, time limits are held to be important, but this also makes it difficult to spend enough time to allow for the Spirit to shape the meetings or let people listen for God's voice together.[20] Leaders in the Catholic Church sometimes worry that CCR groups do not emphasize traditional Catholic doctrines and devotions enough. Fr. Akesseh expressed sadness that some charismatics do not appreciate Sacred Heart devotion, the Rosary, or even the Mass, but said he is encouraged when he does see people bridging these devotions. He also said that if there was one excess of the charismatics in his parish, it was that they sometimes lean too much toward Pentecostalism. He gave an example from the Pax Crusade, during which a woman felt like she wanted to physically throw up as a way of spiritual purging. He felt like that was taking things a bit far. Charismatic groups also tend to alienate some church members who have not had the same ecstatic experiences, or who place more emphasis on other devotional traditions practiced by the Church. This is illustrated by the fact that, as mentioned before, Life in the Spirit Seminars would reach more people if they were put on by the parish, rather than the CCR, since the parish is seen by many as more legitimate. Charismatics sometimes also espouse pompous attitudes, regarding their way of approaching the faith as superior and intended for all. This has sometimes caused quarrels between CCR members and clergy (especially clergy members who do not personally sympathize with the movement) or other parishioners. Finally, from a more secular perspective, one might question whether there is not a certain degree of emotional manipulation driving people's charismatic experiences—loud music and dancing, energy-infused atmospheres, group/crowd dynamics, and playing on areas of strong human feeling.

The fact that Catholic charismatics do not tend to place emphasis on distinctively Catholic devotions is very interesting. On the one hand it is reason for Catholic leaders to worry that Charismatic members will move out of the Church. On the other hand it makes a place within Catholicism where interaction, dialogue, and spiritual fellowship with Protestants can occur much more naturally, and participation in the Renewal keeps some people in the Catholic Church who would otherwise leave for a more Pentecostal church. Charismatic Catholics sometimes feel they have more in common with protestant evangelicals and Pentecostals than they do with the more traditionalist members of their own Church. In the LCCR group, I noted evangelical-style views on conversion, accepting Jesus as Lord and Savior, altar calls, personal prayer/quiet times, and Bible study. Meanwhile the Rosary, prayer to saints, and Catholic contemplative traditions were mentioned only occasionally, and were discussed in depth even more rarely. On the whole a charismatic protestant could walk into a CCR meeting and feel pretty comfortable. Thus charismatic renewal in the Catholic Church has opened new lines for ecumenism in Ghana, a door through which Protestants may lose their anti-Catholic prejudices and be able to draw on the heritage of the Catholic Church. Also through these lines, Catholics have been able to learn from the good emphases of Protestants that have become lost in the Catholic Church.

The charismatic movement in the Catholic Church is a worldwide phenomenon. There are aspects of the movement that are common throughout, but as with any global movement, some aspects also vary by region and culture. Having my background in the renewal in the US, I felt fairly well at home in the CCR group at St. Thomas Aquinas, but there are some ways in which the CCR in Ghana is rather different from the CCR in the United States. Firstly, it is more prevalent in the Church in Ghana. Only a small percentage of churches in the US have charismatic groups, while the numbers in Ghana are greater. In 2002, there were over 1000 organized groups, over 100,000 members, and over 100 priests involved in Ghana, and these numbers were increasing steadily.[21] Secondly, charismatic ministry seems gentler in the United States than in Ghana. On the whole Ghanaians pray harder, sing harder, dance harder, preach harder, and even prophecy harder. They do all of these things with more energy and more boldness than most of their American counterparts. Thirdly, there are different emphases according to the different needs of the people. Witchcraft and entanglement with lesser gods are not much on the minds of most Americans, but they are significant concerns in Ghana. In addition, "manifestation" of evil spirits is more frequent and more dramatic in Ghana. Monetary and academic concerns are also less often expressed in the United States, or are expressed in different ways that put more emphasis on the individual's responsibility. For example, in the US one might hear someone pray for diligence to study or for help to find a job, more often than hearing someone ask directly for a good grade or a job offer. These variations make every bit of sense when put into the context of the cultures within which they operate, and show that charismatic spirituality is adaptable to meet different needs in different contexts.

Primal religious culture in Ghana is still a strong influence on the mentalities and lifestyles of Ghanaians, including those who no longer practice African Traditional Religions.[22] Most Ghanaians take spiritual power very seriously. Deities are valuable inasmuch as they are able to help provide for the well-being of people in the here and now. Beliefs are shared and passed down orally. The spiritual and the physical are deeply connected. When Christianity came to Ghana, it was carried by people who only made room for one main spiritual power in the world, the Supreme God whom Ghanaians had considered too distant and powerful to approach directly. They emphasized spiritual and future salvation only. They passed down their faith largely through the written word and rote memorization. They made greater distinction between material and spiritual realities. To most socialized Ghanaians the message was interesting, but lacked power, except to the extent that conversion made for a good position with respect to the colonizers. However, when more charismatic forms of Christianity arose, many Ghanaians flocked to them. In the AICs and in the Pentecostal churches Ghanaians developed ways of doing Christianity that they could own, and that were compelling within their primal worldview, because the "fundamental aspects of Pentecostal/charismatic spirituality [were] analogous to basic African spirituality."[23] Charismatic spirituality offered "an authentically Christian solution to questions emanating from realities in their context."[24] When charismatic spirituality caught on in mainline churches like the Catholic Church, it enabled them too to better address concerns that arise in this cultural context. Charismatic renewal in the Catholic Church empowers people by allaying spiritual fears, offering deliverance, and providing avenues for continued participation. At the same time, the Catholic Church and other mainlines churches are at the cutting edge of a new project of establishing a balance between centuries-old inherited traditions and orthodoxy and the culturally adaptable and ever-renewing charismatic ethos.

4

CHARISMATIC RENEWAL: LESSONS IN MISSIONS FROM THE KENYAN CHURCH

Joshua S. Kuipers

INTRODUCTION

Talking about missions and missionaries in the 21st century can at times be challenging given the many negative images that have come to be especially associated with Western missionaries working in non-Western locations. Images of White missionaries arriving in a village in Africa with a Bible in hand and ill-prepared for effective cross-cultural engagement may have come to form the foundation for some of the critiques leveled against missionaries in general. Overall missionaries are often assumed to be culturally insensitive to local communities, some of which may have had negative encounters with colonial administrators. There are stories of missions going sour and at times involving some differential power relations between missionaries and local people. Indeed, the continued presence of missions and missionaries in many African countries, at a time when Christianity is growing faster there than in the West, is often surprising and probably only justified by a discourse not framed in the language of saving souls and being Christ to the rest of the world as it was in the 19th century but rather by a language of development and paternalistic notions of "helping." Because of clear material differences between missionary-sending nations and missionary-receiving nations some present day missionaries are more likely than not to be involved in some type of development work that centers on material resource sharing.

Despite some of these negative images of missionaries, however, there are some beautiful success stories coming out of the mission field in Africa as well. Quite often these are not stories of Western missionaries suddenly changing their mode of operation and letting the work of Christ affirm and transform what is on the ground (even though there are such cases) but rather stories of local pastors and fellow Christians rising up, using local and international resources, to reach out to their own people with a gospel of Christ-like love and of truth even in some of the most economically trying contexts. Far away from television cameras of news reports are everyday Christians sacrificing to bring hope and wellbeing to their own. There are mothers taking in orphans and raising them just like their own children; there are communities coming together to raise funds for hospital bills of fellow brethren; and individuals leaving their well-paying jobs in order to serve their communities. Such stories are best appreciated by being there. I had the opportunity to witness one such story while living in Kenya in 2005 shadowing a pastor in a neo-Pentecostal church. This is the story I want to share in this chapter as I develop a discussion of what I consider "good missionary work" in today's changing world. How can missions today be carried out differently and with more relevance to the communities served than in the past? I will use Kenya as my frame for this discussion.

For the purpose of this chapter I will refer to the church I worked with and others as neo-Pentecostal. There seems to be so many terms used interchangeably to describe the charismatic churches of Africa, so to clarify, what I mean by neo-Pentecostal is a charismatic church that was not formed through a mission endeavor of a Western or classical Pentecostal church. Some prefer the term "Independent," "Modern," or "Young Pentecostalism" but I don't believe their proper identity is in its relationship as the independent, modern, or younger sister to Western Pentecostalism, but as a new strand all together. Kenya, like many other African countries, has many examples of missions, and even though the journey of the neo-Pentecostal church has not been easy or short, it has produced abundant fruit that could change the way the world participates in, and views missions in the future. Missions today are also quite diverse in terms of sending and receiving locations. Joel Carpenter provides a good sense of this when he states

> The great missionary movement is not over, but it has become omnidirectional. There are 400,000 missionaries in the world, and before too long, the majority of them will not be from Europe and North America. I visited Nigeria in 1990 and met with some American and Canadian missionaries. They lamented that instead of the 500 comrades they had in 1960, now there were only 100. Many of the enterprises they had started were fading. The next day the missions director of the Nigerian sister church of this mission, now 2 million strong, told me about its 900 missionaries, serving sacrificially in rural northern Nigeria, and in Niger, Cameroon, Chad, Burkina Faso, and darkest London.[1]

My own interest in African Christianity began almost as a self-serving endeavor, and has turned into a point of excitement and wonder. My moments of thinking critically about Christianity and the role of missions was sparked, however, when I began brushing shoulders with professors at Calvin College including Mwenda Ntarangwi, Tebebe Eshete, Diane Obenchain, Todd Vanden Berg, Nyambura Mpesha, Johnathan Bascom, and Paul Freston. Pursuing an interdisciplinary major I was lucky to take courses with them in a way that was not only beneficial to my own learning but my major as well. Being in their courses provided me with multiple perspectives that helped me to engage with my own faith and experiences in Kenya. Clearly I had had a good experience living in Kenya but I needed to think clearly about it and process some of the experiences I had in Kibera as a way to travel the road of discernment for my future calling. I knew I wanted to get into Church work at some point and that my experience in Kenya had something to do with that trajectory, but I needed more clarity.

CONTEXTUALIZING MISSIONS IN KENYA

Word Impact Center may be a small church in a large slum, but it does not stand alone, it is interconnected through centuries of Christian History in Kenya. In 1498 the Portuguese explorer Vasco da Gama set anchor on the coast of Malindi bay on the Indian Ocean and his contact with local people were followed by evangelistic works. By the 16th century, there was a small wave of missionary movement consisting of missionary priests in Lamu and Augustinian friars in Mombasa who witnessed to over 600 Kenyans who converted to Christianity (Barrett 2001, 427). At this point Europe's colonial reign began to spread over the entirety of Africa, and with it came the Western Church. In 1844 the Anglican Church landed in Kenya on the back of Dr. Johann Ludwing Krapf, a German Lutheran attached to the Church Mission Society (CMS), and concentrated in the central region of the country inhabited mostly by the Kikuyu. As an accomplished linguist, Krapf began translating excerpts of scripture into local Kenyan Languages, and setting up a permanent missionary base (ACK). By the late 19th century, Catholic missions were established and pushed forward by the Holy Ghost Fathers. At the same time, the British and Scottish Presbyterians had arrived on the scene, and African Inland Missions, currently Kenya's largest denomination, had set up camp on the east coast. As the 20th century commenced, a railway from Mombasa to Kisumu allowed the rapid growth of the protestant mission in the west (Barrett 2001, 427).

Throughout the rest of Africa a similar story was being written. Along with Christian witness from Western Missionaries came Western culture and the two were instantaneously attached. Conflicts came as African leaders began to rise up in the church and express a desire for a contextualized Gospel. Mojola Agbebi, a Nigerian preacher in the early 20th century, argued that Africans should have their own version of the English Book of Common Prayer. Agbebi's proposal was refused, however, because imperialist missionaries often saw a desire for a contextualized gospel as a means for political gain and as a break from colonial reign. Agbebi responded by saying that, "the joys of the Christian life are one; redemption is one; Christ is one; but our tongues are various and our styles innumerable" (Sanneh 2008, 165). He suggested that there were different standards in play as Europeans professed their Christian faith and remained in their Western customs while not allowing the same of their African brothers and sisters. Agbebi's words have now been realized as many Africans, beginning with such renown scholars as Mbiti and Bediako, have continued to insist on highlighting the role of culture in the expression of the Christian faith irrespective of the location and calling for Africans to reclaim their Africanity as they embrace Christianity.

An inevitable response at the time came in the form of East Africa's charismatic revivals in the 1920's. This was their attempt to merge Christian faith with their own cultural worldview, while paying close attention to their desire to remain true to the word (Sanneh 2008, 167). Such revivals were usually inspired by Kenyans who were involved in classical Pentecostalism. Whenever I use the phrase Classical Pentecostalism I do so in reference to churches established by a Western Pentecostal missionary. In Kenya this was largely the Pentecostal Assemblies of Canada, which today is known for its work in establishing Nairobi Pentecostal Church (which has one of the largest congregations comprising membership from over five member churches). The student movement and fervent missionary activities spurred by these initial revivals are often referred to as neo-Pentecostalism in Kenya (Mwaura, 2005, 247) under which World Impact Center falls. Charismatic followers of such revival meetings started to diverge into their own strand of Christian expression and were soon known as the *balokole* ("saved ones," in Luganda, the language of the Baganda of Uganda) and the *Ahonoki* ("saved ones," in Gikuyu, the language of the Kikuyu of Kenya) (Mwaura 2005, 248 and Kalu, 2007, 19). This movement had some profound influence on Christianity in Kenya in the 1930's as the East African Revival, emanating from Rwanda and focusing primarily on personal salvation, swept across Kenya (Gifford 2009).

In the beginning, the neo-Pentecostal *balokole* suffered much persecution from the Mau Mau, an anti-colonial movement primarily composed of Kenyans whose land had been annexed by the British settlers with the help of the colonial government in Central, Eastern, and Western Kenya. Members of the Mau Mau assumed that since the neo-Pentecostal churches were also fighting for (religious) independence they would join in the fight being waged by the Mau Mau. But the *balokole* were looking for a harmonious contextualization of their beliefs and were not willing to take up arms against the British colonialists, especially because many were benefiting from mission education. Often the *balokole* would refer to themselves as "obedient rebels" (Kalu 2007, 19) because even though they desired independence and contextualization, it is said that at their meetings "nobody [was] asked whether he or she is Anglican, Catholic, Lutheran, 'A.M.E.' or Zionist, all [were] alike" (Sanneh 2008, 168). Following these non-combatant responses from the church, the Mau Mau resurgence ended up creating a rift between the neo-Pentecostal churches in Kenya and their Western counterparts (Sanneh 2008, 166), with the Christians being seen as "sell-outs" especially because many of them ended up taking up positions of influence in the colonial system as well as missionary-ran institutions.

Despite this rift, the neo-Pentecostal church grew rapidly during the 20th century and even faster in the wake of the 1963 Kenyan Independence. This movement had become an interdenominational, interracial, and interethnic movement that began to attract attention from around the world. In the 1960's and 1970's, for instance, American evangelists such as Billy Graham and T. L. Osborne had visited Kenya and popularized the emerging global Pentecostalism that was gaining ground in the USA (Mwaura 2005, 249). In Kenya the often young, neo-Pentecostals "were on fire for the Lord – they expected to experience miracles in everyday life – supply of needs, healings, raising the dead, and especially a moral change in lifestyle" (Kalu 2007, 20). As Ogbu Kalu argues, this strong evangelical zeal and a committed heart to the actualizing of missions, allowed the neo-Pentecostals to carry out missions across Kenya and throughout Eastern Africa, seeking to not only convert their own people but also to demonstrate the need to live lives of transformed individuals filled with the spirit (Kalu 2007, 21). The spirit of independence and of the charismatic renewal in Kenya were not limited to the neo-Pentecostal churches alone because charismatic elements trickled into many of the mainline Western denominations as well (Sanneh 2008, 169) just as Ross Acheson (this volume) has also shown in the case of Ghana. Neo-Pentecostalism and the entirety of the Kenyan church became an important facet of Christian identity and continued to develop to date. Certain periods also recorded specific trajectories in Christianity's shape in Kenya. In the 1980's, for instance, the American Pentecostal prosperity gospel came to Kenya in full force, while the 1990's saw the introduction of ideological issues surrounding modernity and media in the church (Kalu 2007, 21). Not surprising the neo-Pentecostals have remained strong and continue to be one of the fastest growing Christian denominations in Kenya.

The current growth of the church in Kenya is an encouraging one, to say the least. In 1900 Kenya was home to approximately 5000 Christians comprising 0.2% of the population. By 1970 that number had grown to 7,299,800 or 63.5%, and currently there are 23,859,800 Christians living in Kenya, which is 78.7%. The largest Christian affiliation in Kenya is "independent" and "Pentecostal/Charismatic," totaling nearly 30% of the population (Barrett 2001, 426). This makes Kenya one of Africa's most statistically Christian nations along with Rwanda with 94% and South Africa with 80% of their population listed as Christian.[4] The number of American missionaries in Kenya is equally staggering. According to the Mission Handbook of 2007-2009, there are 843 missionaries from the United States in Kenya. This is extremely high, especially when compared to other countries within Eastern Africa except Rwanda, which has a higher percentage of Christians than Kenya. Ethiopia, for instance, has a population almost double that of Kenya and there are only 159 missionaries from the United States currently. Mozambique has only 105 missionaries from the United States. Granted most missionaries like other Western travelers to Africa often visit and stay in some African countries and not others. This pattern is often a result of internal government policy on foreigners, climate, political stability, level of infrastructural development, and language use, among other factors. In this regard North American missionaries are more likely to go to Kenya than Mozambique because the latter has had a volatile political history and uses Portuguese as its official language. Ethiopia has strict rules for foreigners coming into the country for various tasks and activities and hence the smaller number of missionaries present. With a more welcome and often lax codes for foreigners to enter and stay in the country Kenya continues to be a favorite destination for many Western visitors including tourists, study abroad groups, and missionaries. This high presence of foreigners into the country has opened up opportunities for collaboration and resources sharing among Christians in the country. There are many communities and congregations that continue to use both local and external resources while others entirely depend on local support.

A DIFFERENT KIND OF MISSIONARY?

In 2005 I joined a team of college students from around North America as a missionary intern in Kibera Kenya, through Adventures in Missions (AIM), an interdenominational missions organization that focuses on discipleship, emphasizing prayer and relationships working amongst the poor.[2] Poking around AIM's website one can see that in crafting their notion of doing missions they combine the lure of the exotic with the desire to have practical applications of one's faith. A description of a five-month trip to Kenya in 2011 for college-aged individuals reads, in part, "This trip begins in Mombasa where you will work with orphans, participate in service projects, do door to door evangelism and everything in between."[3] I had a slightly different experience even though I am not quite sure I was not enticed, like many of my peers, by the lure of doing service in a far away place and helping spread the Gospel. I lived inside the Karanja Road district of Kibera for eight months, and during that time I was connected with a local pastor, Sheth Oguok Otieno, as my partner and mentor. I was exposed to the church of Kenya, life inside Kibera, and the dark political side that engulfed Kenya in 2005. I was in Kibera through the constitutional referendum of 2005, which as Christine Bodewes has noted (this volume) was marred by violence mobilized along ethnic divisions. Looking back I was largely unprepared and undertrained for what I encountered in Kibera. I had left home with a yearning to serve alongside Christian brothers and sisters in Kenya and quite open to what God placed in my way. Little did I know that my life would be greatly shaped by that time in a neo-Pentecostal church in the slum.

Sheth Otieno is the Pastor of Word Impact Center, a small neo-Pentecostal church in the North West corner of Kibera (see figure 1), which, while serving a small monoethnic congregation, aspires to be more outward looking at least if the church's name is anything to go by. Kibera is an informal settlement that was established as a small settlement for Sudanese soldiers that assisted the British colonial army in East Africa (De Smedt 2009, 586). Kibera has changed from a small Nubian (decedents of the Sudanese soldiers who most likely came from Nubia) settlement to a large slum in which all ethnic groups of Kenya are represented (De Smedt 2009, 586). As Christine Bodewes has shown (this volume) Kibera is often considered the largest slum in sub-Saharan Africa, with an estimated population of over 600,000. However, from locals on the ground estimations draw much closer to 1 million, especially during the week as people want to reside closer to their jobs often located in the industrial sector of Nairobi. The slum is unofficially divided into villages that are often occupied by a specific ethnic group. The Nubians now represent a small minority within Kibera because Kenya's largest ethnic group, the Kikuyu, now own the majority of rental homes (De Smedt 2009, 586). Today, the largest population of Kibera dwellers is the Luo. They often reside in, but not restricted to, Gatwikira, Kisumu Ndogo, Shilanga, Lindi, and Kianda (see figure 4.1).

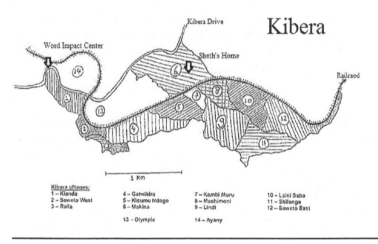

FIGURE 4.1. KIBERA (DE SMEDT 2009, 588)

As it is with many of the small neo-Pentecostal churches within Kibera, World Impact Center is mostly made up of a single ethnic group, in their case Luo. This is an unofficial divide that used to be rooted in linguistic differences, as pastors would preach in their ethnic language, but now most neo-Pentecostal church pastors preach in English or Swahili. World Impact Center falls into this latter category as Sheth often preaches and prays in English, sometimes with a translator into Swahili even though majority of the members in the church speak Dholuo (language of the Luo ethnic group). In a sense this language choice by Sheth is a symbolic representation of the identity of his church, not least, a cosmopolitan one. Sheth's cosmopolitan gestures notwithstanding, ethnic divisions have kept neo-Pentecostal churches within Kibera from growing in numbers by attracting members from groups beyond the specific ethnic population in close proximity to the church. Because many ethnic churches remain reasonably small, often having less than 100 members, many congregations have struggled to unify and provide a much larger presence in the culture of Kibera. This reality is not restricted to Kibera, however, because even in places such as the US there are many churches that have continued to struggle to attract and maintain a multiethnic and multiracial congregation. In Kenya many denominations have tended to be associated with specific ethnic groups because when missionary churches were founded in the early 1900s, colonial administrators allocated specific missions to particular territories occupied by communities that were ethnically homogenous. This may explain why, for instance, the Methodist church is dominated by the Meru while the Presbyterian and Anglican churches are dominated by the Kikuyu.

This constitution of churches along ethnic lines has dwindled especially in urban areas where populations are becoming more and more multiethnic. As more independent churches emerge, this multiethnic identity in churches will grow but only in areas of mixed ethnic residential patterns. Kibera is yet to become one such area. As a pastor of an independent church, Sheth brought a very unique flair to his work as a pastor in Kibera. He is charismatic in practice, but completed part of the requirements for an undergraduate program in theology at Carlile College, an Anglican college of Theology and Business Studies based in Nairobi, and was at the time working on his masters degree in Urban Missions through the University of South Africa (UNISA). In a slum of undereducated pastors, and a religious context that often favors personal charisma over doctrinal or theological training, Sheth brought together aspects of Western theology and neo-Pentecostalism in a harmonious contextualization. During my time with him in Kibera I participated in open air evangelistic services, mercy ministries within the church family, youth driven rallies, church renovations, and simply shadowing the daily walk of a pastor in Africa's largest slum. The sense of family, the fervent worship and prayer, and the impact the church had on individuals and the community at large was like nothing I had ever experienced, and has caused me to still be reflecting four years later. As with any attempt to identify a phenomenon I cannot typify all neo-Pentecostal churches by the experiences I have had with just a few.

I understand that my experiences were greatly shaped by the fact that the church was inside Kibera and not a large church such as Winners Chapel International, Nairobi Chapel, or the Redeemed Christian Church of God (RCCG), all of which are based in Nairobi in close proximity to Kibera but attended by a more multiethnic, wealthier, and more educated congregation. Given these specific differences in congregation types based on class, ethnicity, and location, among other factors, I will now provide a brief historical context that has helped me place Word Impact Center into the broader picture of the church in Kenya, then attempt a reflection on the neo-Pentecostal church's strengths and impacts on society, and finally take a brief look forward in the realm of mission partnerships. My goal is to look at how contemporary practices in a small neo-Pentecostal church under a pastor trained in one of the mainline denomination seminaries informs our understanding of current and future partnerships between churches in the West and South. I specifically argue that 21st century mission work looks very different from the negative images mentioned above regarding many perceptions of missions and missionaries. Missions today are complex and have variety but I favor those that allow for "outsiders" to learn from "insiders," specifically for North Americans to learn from Kenyans.

WORD IMPACT CENTER IN CONTEXT

Word Impact Center, is a small neo-Pentecostal church of approximately 60 people, most of whom are Luo. The congregation consists mostly of hand laborers that are employed or often self-employed within Kibera. However, there are a handful of families that could be considered working professionals such as a high school teacher in a Nairobi school district, three nurses for local clinics, as well as a restaurant manager. These families are the primary financial supporters of the ongoing costs of Word Impact Center. There is also a group of extremely poor members in the church such as young single mothers that try their hand at sewing to make a minimal income and youth that are often unemployed.

Word Impact Center gathered regularly for prayer, study, and worship. Sundays consisted of multiple services. As the sun rose, approximately 7:00 AM, a handful of members would meet at the church with Sheth for prayer. These gatherings had a contemplative feel to them as individuals quietly prayed on their own and occasionally joined in vocalized corporate prayer, often for the church and the greater community. By 8:00 AM other members, often the core adults in the congregation, gathered and Sheth would lead a Bible study. This usually lasted an hour and consisted of Sheth teaching on a specific biblical text that fit into a larger series that the church was in the midst of studying. This was a very effective way to use time for teaching and learning because members of the congregation also had a chance to call out questions relating to worldly situations that they had found themselves in over the past week and then seek biblical counsel from Sheth.

The official worship service began at 10:00 A.M. during which the children would go to a side room and be taught biblical stories and sing together. The main service began with at least 30 minutes of impromptu singing and prayer. The songs were usually led in Swahili by a couple of members of the church. The songs were not predetermined or accompanied by instruments but rather a call and response format kept the service flowing. Scattered throughout the songs were also impromptu sessions of prayer where everyone would individually pray out loud until the last person, usually Sheth, had finished their prayer. Sheth would then get up from his seat and begin preaching. He would passionately weave together scripture with localized examples of what a Christ-like life would look like in Kibera. He would usually conclude with a call to salvation or for an opportunity to come forward and be prayed over for physical, emotional, or economic healing. Outside of the activities of Sunday members of the congregation had opportunities to meet. On Wednesdays, for instance, core members of the church would meet at each other's homes, on a rotation, for a Bible study and worship. They would share food together and build relationships that resembled that of a family. Sheth would visit member's homes throughout the week as well as spend a significant amount of time evangelizing and bringing new people to the church.

REFLECTIONS ON NEO-PENTECOSTAL MINISTRY

While participating in the activities of Word Impact Center I observed several things that in part contribute to the continual growth of such a fervent neo-Pentecostal church. Even though some of these things are specifically reflective of local culture, they inevitably hold lessons for us all. There are five points coming out of my analysis of World Impact Center, which instruct us about 21st century missions. First, the neo-Pentecostal church has the ability to bring a sense of community that might have been lost during urban migration. In many rural settings the lifestyle often reflects that of a polychronic community in which the spontaneity of relationships often veto the structured demands of industrialized production. As neo-Pentecostalism has grown the most in urban centers it has proven to bring order, stability, and a renewed sense of community to its members who may feel out of place in the productivity driven hustle and bustle of urban centers. Word Impact Center was able to do this through multiple prayer and worship meetings every week, as well as shared meals throughout the week. There was a deep sense that the Church body became the peer group of its members. They were not co-attendees of church but were best friends, brothers, and sisters. They were family in the truest sense, celebrating holidays together, mourning together, and sharing all aspects of life together. Here church became the glue that bound individuals into a tight community in an otherwise anonymous and individualistic life that urban centers are famous for producing.

Second, and possibly the most obvious characteristic of the neo-Pentecostal church is its focus on worship. Pentecostalism has been characterized as having highly emotional and personal lyrics that encourage a full-bodied experience (Miller and Yamamori 2007, 23), something that has been critiqued as missing from the liturgical mainline denominations not only in Kenya but other parts of Africa as clearly shown by Ross Acheson (this volume). Physical healing and a release from spiritual oppression also find themselves intertwined with the entirety of the worship experience. At Word Impact Center there was an expectation for God to act in the members' presence. A new song that made the connection between scripture and God a very present reality in all of the lives of the congregants, was being sung almost every Sunday I attended church. A song like *Mambo sawa sawa, yesu akiwa enzini, mambo sawa sawa* (Things are already better; when the Lord is on the throne; things are already better), sung frequently in church, spoke to the neo-Pentecostal understanding that life is better now, because God is actively working in the present. Such a spiritual embodiment of the now left little need for the "escapism" previously taught by Western missionaries who emphasized the afterworld instead of the here and now. As Paul Gifford has argued, many of the missionary churches were pietist and focused more on personal salvation and less on the social order (Gifford 2009). At World Impact Center, Bible studies, worship services, and counseling sessions rarely finished without at least one impromptu time of fervent "Daniel-in-the-lion's-den" type of prayers in which participants shared a personal challenge they were going through and the rest of the group prayed fervently, often "delivering" the evil cause of the challenge out of the "victim." Such intense worship and prayer experiences align themselves very well with African religious philosophy and practice (Bediako 1995; Sanneh 2008).

Third, there is a large focus on Christ-like love that was also critiqued as missing from many missionaries who brought Christianity in Africa in the 18th century (Sanneh 2008, 170). David Kasali paints a good picture of this practice by Western missionaries to Africa when he write, "Typically, they [missionaries] would build their homes on the top of a hill and the health clinic or church down the hill. They would come down to minister to the people, then retreat to the hilltop to live in the security of their homes. This was not discipleship; this was not modeling, identifying, and living with others as Jesus did."[5] The Pentecostals often view "[Christ-like] love as listening, sharing, sympathizing, an understanding in depth between equals" (Sanneh 2008, 170) whereas historically some Western missionaries had practiced more of a paternal love with the Western missionary acting as the quintessential leader and knowledgeable intermediary leading people to God. Within the church this focus on Christ-like love actualizes itself in holistic social ministries such as mercy ministries (where members of the community, especially women are offered programs to support their livelihood and give them life skills to build self-reliance), emergency services, education, counseling, medical assistance, and economic development (Miller and Yamamori 2007, 42). Word Impact Center used its pre-school, pastoral and occupational training center, as well as constant financial and medical assistance programs to minister to its congregants. Such practices provided the sort of care that would be common among families in a rural setting. During the unrest in Kibera following the controversial 2007 presidential elections in Kenya, Sheth constantly made the trip out of Kibera to bring food back in for the church. Those shared meals during times of fear and desperation strengthened the church, and they spoke thereafter of the time as representing a small local revival.

Fourth, there is an aspect of personal development that is a byproduct of all of the above. Within the community driven, worship focused, and holistic ministry of the neo-Pentecostal church, everyone is encouraged and even expected to be involved. This includes reading scripture, leading worship, cooking meals, preparing Bible studies, translating, teaching, and even preaching. For some this is their only exposure to literacy, while for others it is an opportunity to develop public speaking and critical thinking skills, leading to confidence in themselves, which in itself is immeasurable. In the small congregation that I was a part of I can think of several members whose lives were dramatically enhanced solely from being active members in the church. Eunice joined the church in her early twenties and eventually began to lead worship and sharing testimonies. She then would assist as a translator during some services, and finally began to prepare and teach the congregation. She believes that the skills and confidence that she developed while engaged in Word Impact Center prepared her for the political position she now holds in Nairobi. Ben would tell a very similar story of how just being active as a leader in the church gave him skills and confidence he uses in his political position in Kisumu. Many others like them have benefited greatly from the call of the neo-Pentecostal church to be active leaders and not only attendees. This model of leadership, while developed due to limited resources and opportunities for theological training in Kibera, reflects a more appropriate and even Biblical model that is solely homegrown through mentoring and discipleship.

Finally, neo-Pentecostalism resonates with many traditional African cultures and worldviews, because both highly value the work of the Spirit world among many other things. The Christian church, however, is able to take it one step farther as there is no longer a need to gain the acceptance and blessings of a plethora of spirits, but there is free grace and love from One. Kalu spoke to this stating, "African Pentecostals have equated principalities, powers, and demons with various categories in their worldview and as enemies of God and man" (Kalu 2006, 119). It is this ability to align Christianity with an African worldview that allows congregations such as those at the World Impact Center to not only localize the Gospel but also make Christianity relevant to the socio-economic and political realities of its followers. In a sense neo-Pentecostalism makes Christianity truly African.

A MOVE FORWARD

As I reflected on both the tremendous growth of Christianity that has already taken place in Kenya, and the strength of the neo-Pentecostal church to mission to the people of Africa, there is a need for a new model of partnership between the Western church and the African church. This partnership must reflect a change from a previous paternal love to a brotherly or sisterly love between equals. When addressing and defining the partnership, or relationship, I have combined the work of Rufus Anderson, Henry Venn, and Line Onsrud by calling for the establishment and supporting of a "self-propagating, self-supporting, self-governing, and self-theologizing" (Onsrud 1999, 425) church in Africa.

A self-propagating church is one that calls its own members to take responsibility for the spread of the gospel witness instead of relying on the mission endeavors of foreign missionaries. This is to the betterment of the ecclesial community itself, and it has also proven to be a very effective form of evangelism. As a case study, the Redeemed Christian Church of God (RCCG) is one of the fastest-growing neo-Pentecostal churches in Nigeria, and has become so through their fervent self-propagating missional focus (Mwaura 2005:250). In 1995, through a connection with a Kenyan woman, two pastors moved to Nairobi and planted the first RCCG church in Kenya. It began as a house group that focused on physical and spiritual deliverance, as well as prayer and Bible study. Within a year they had grown to the point that multiple building upgrades were needed, and a Bible school had been established. This first RCCG church became the headquarters for the entire RCCG in Eastern Africa, and within the first seven years they had already planted over twenty churches in Kenya alone.

RCGG's membership continues to grow at a consistent state and they have set themselves apart as a self-propagating church with a "commitment to reaching the unreached and thus venturing into the rural areas" (Mwaura 2005, 251). The RCCG may be one of the stronger examples but it is by no means the only. Winners' Chapel International and Victoria Faith Assembly are other great examples of Kenyan churches committed to outreach, and seeing great results (Mwaura 2005, 251-254). One can argue whether or not the prosperity gospel being taught in church like Winners Chapel International is a proper means of spreading the church, and if it contributes to the growth of the denomination. Either way a bountiful life on earth in addition to eternal salvation has always been integral to the good news shared through Christianity. In African religious life God is involved, directly or through intermediaries, in every aspect of life including and especially material prosperity and protection for deliverance from disease. Consequently prosperity makes sense in an African context. Many of the churches in Kenya that are seen as promoting a prosperity gospel do not operate in a vacuum as their founding fathers are often thought to be American charismatics Kenneth Hagin, Kenneth Copeland, and Frederick K. C. Price.

A self-supporting church is free from the dependency of Western church donations to survive. The word "partnership" seems to be the fad in missional discussions, but a partnership can only find fulfillment where equality is found, and this can be very difficult when one of the partners provides the majority of financial resources and also when partnership is primarily measured by financial support. Scott Moreau, Gary Cowin, and Gary McGhee have argued that, "Money is to missions what fire is to the human condition: God's gracious provision for our survival, empowerment, and even our enjoyment. Like fire, however, it is also capable of wreaking havoc." (Moreau, Cowin, and McGhee 2004, 225) This havoc may take the form of Western power in the decision making of the local church, based on their financial contributions. It can also become a crutch to local churches that keeps them from learning the joys and responsibilities of Christian stewardship (Ibid., 226). A self-governing church is a family of believers under the stewardship and leadership of people within the culture who comprise its membership.

Finally, a self-theologizing church is one that is free to explain God for its congregations in accordance with scripture, an explanation that mirrors what Andrew Walls terms contextualization – expressing Christian faith in ways appropriate to the particular context. This is not to say that Western church history and literature should be discarded, but rather that each church should be allowed the freedom to discern for itself its specific needs and practices while of course trusting the Holy Spirit to preserve truth. There are two major missionary contributions that have and will continue to be key to a self-theologizing church such as the World Impact Center. First, in order to produce a contextual theology based on scripture each people group needs the Word translated into their mother tongue. Lamin Sanneh says, "If the Christian Church in Africa is to be really African and really Christian, it must be built upon the basis of the indigenous peculiarities and gifts of the people, it must become part of the African genius, and these will forever be embedded in the mother language" (Sanneh 2008, 179). This is an important proposition because unless people can learn to express themselves in a way that is authentic and fits their very basic circumstances then the result might be the case of Christianity being "a mile wide and an inch deep."

Second, a self-theologizing church needs to be encouraged by missionaries and national church leaders to recall, record, and reflect on its Church history. "For a young Church it is necessary to gain self-confidence and build a strong identity to be able to produce good contextual theology" (Onsrud 1999, 444), and since a strong sense of history creates strong identity the recalling, recording, and reflecting on local church history is imperative. Tibebe Eshete, is an excellent example of such work. In 2009 Eshete created a breakthrough in African publishing with his book *The Evangelical Movement in Ethiopia: Resistance and Resilience*. It is a comprehensive history of the evangelical church of Ethiopia by an Ethiopian historian and scholar. Future mission endeavors must include both the translation of the Word into the mother tongue, and the encouragement of local leaders to be self-historians.

The neo-Pentecostal churches within Kibera and across Africa are growing in numbers and have the vision to continue to move forward and shape the life of communities in which they are located. It is my prediction that they will not only continue as a dominant force within the religious tapestry that makes up Africa but will surely impact global Christianity as African Christians continue to have notable impacts in global Christianity through immigrant church planting and partnerships with existing Western congregations. Cross-denominational and cross-cultural partnerships must be a part of their move forward for the benefit of both parties involved. A remaining challenge for many neo-Pentecostal churches, especially within Kibera, is the need to unite in the hopes of becoming a larger voice in the culture and politics of the area and the country. A blending of ethnically divided congregations and improved communication between the local pastors will most defiantly assist churches, such as Word Impact Center, and become a larger impact in a world starving for fervent Christian leaders.

As historian Barbara Cooper notes in her book *Evangelical Christians in the Muslim Sahel*, Western Christian missionaries have a lot to learn from their predecessors' experiences. She captures this in a paragraph that I find befitting here as I reflect on how much I learned in Kibera. She states

> Being a protestant Christian in Niger means more than adopting a certain set of beliefs or attending a certain church. It means seeking out and sustaining a community in which one can tell jokes and they will be appreciated.

CHARISMATIC RENEWAL: LESSONS IN MISSIONS FROM THE KENYAN CHURCH

> It means celebrating playfully the knowledge that it was
> the Hausa who taught the hapless missionaries the lan-
> guage of belief, not the reverse. It also means enjoying
> the secret knowledge shared by Hausa Christians that the
> social practices of the early missionaries (and their current
> employers)—the eating habits, the dress style, the Anglo-
> phone performance of piety—are not the same thing as
> Christianity itself.[6]

I know I learned a great deal from a Church that by Western standards would be considered in great need of missionaries. It is time to rethink missions especially in Africa as Western Christians sit at the feet of African pastors and fellow Christians to learn what faith means in their context.

5

THE GOSPEL FOR ETHIOPIA BY ETHIOPIANS: MAPPING THE CONTESTED TERRAINS BETWEEN PENTECOSTALS AND MARXIST RADICALS

Tibebe Eshete

INTRODUCTION

An Ethiopian evangelist once compared Jacob and Esau, the two sons of Isaac, to Marxism and Pentecostalism, radical albeit conflicting movements that emerged within the Ethiopian rising intelligentsias of the 60's, but did not identify which stood for which son. The two movements have struggled bitterly to capture the souls and hearts of Ethiopian youth in the throes of bewildering socio-political changes and have thus left delineable marks in the history of the nation along different trajectories. The cry of the Ethiopian Pentecostals encapsulated in the "The Gospel for Ethiopia by Ethiopians" was more than an evangelistic plea for reaching the nation; it was a militant effort aimed at launching a micro-revolution from within to serve as a springboard for unleashing a national renaissance. The encounter between Marxism and Pentecostalism, which started in pre-revolutionary Ethiopia continued all through the period of the military government (1974-1991) turning into a vicious scuffle between the seemingly "powerless" and the "powerful" groups, and paradoxically ended up as a losing fight for the latter. This chapter situates the rise and development of Pentecostalism within the crucial years of modern Ethiopian history, namely the period of the 1960-1990's, and examines its role in introducing a radical Christian faith that engaged Marxism using the Scriptural truth as a source of power through literature, aggressive evangelism, and protest songs.

SETTING THE BACKGROUND

The Pentecostal movement in Ethiopia had a number of precursors that influenced its initial growth and persistent place in both the public and private lives of many of its adherents. The movement had a particular presence in the Haile Selassie I University (HSIU) where students from both the Pentecostal and Marxist camps often interacted, honed their ideas and even expanded their political thinking. Some of the notable factors for this setting include youth focused urban ministries; The Mekane Yesus Youth Hostel; The emergence of Christian Students' Fellowships; and the role of Radio Voice of the Gospel (RVOG), among other factors. Let me discuss each one of these factors individually.

Youth Focused Urban Ministries

A Youth Center that was set up in 1960 by the Sudan Inland Mission (SIM) in a strategic area located between Arat Kilo and Sedest Kilo campuses of HSIU played a crucial role in providing a neutral space for all sorts of Christians. The center run multi-track activities such as recreational, library and counseling services to students who were facing some adjustment problems and needed guidance. They also held lecture series in which they invited distinguished guest speakers on topics most pertinent to university students including faith and science.[1] There were many students who embraced the evangelical faith through the services of the Youth Center. The center also attracted students from other faith persuasions, albeit for some other reasons. These were student radicals, mainly from the Crocodile group (a radical group of students with secretive activities believed to have been instrumental in planting Marxism and engineering the student movements in the university), who were openly hostile to the activities of the Center and who often came there with the intention of disrupting the programs.[2] According to informants interviewed for this project, some of the members of the Crocodile group would choose a song from the hymn book titled "America is beautiful" every time they came to the Center not because they liked the song but with the sinister intention of blackmailing the Center which they regarded as a CIA project. Manzke, who later understood the intention of the Crocodiles, tore that piece out of the hymnal.[3] Moreover, the Center created a common associational forum for Pentecostals and Christians coming from non-Pentecostal backgrounds to interact with each other ecumenically.

Lij Kassa Wolde Mariam, one of the former Presidents of the HSIU, told Harold Fuller that the Center's work has been one of the greatest contributions to the spiritual life of the students.[4] Evelyn Thompson, a missionary involved in the foundation of the center, reports that in her later travels in the various parts of Ethiopia she was surprised to be greeted by several "government teachers, clerks, medical personnel who confided to her that they had found salvation" in the Youth Center.[5]

One of the most enduring legacies of the activities of the Youth Center is the birth of *Hebret Amba* a fellowship of Ethiopian evangelicals, which first emerged as an independent church and later joined the larger Qale Heywet church. This charismatic church was founded entirely by Ethiopian students mostly from Haile Sellassie I University. It was the upshot of the outreach program of the SIM launched through the Youth Center. This "indigenous" church, attracted top-level students from the national university who actively participated in organizing the new church. Shiferaw Wolde Michael, Getachew Chiku, Yohannes Yegzaw, Seyum Weissa, Alemu Biftu, Berhanu Negash, and Mulatu Belachew, were among those students who actively served the church and significantly contributed to its growth. Some of these men later became university professors, prominent church leaders, and evangelists with international standing.[6] Shieferaw, in particular developed a distinguished career as a law school professor in the university and served as the Minister of Justice during the difficult years of the military regime while continuing to provide much sought after leadership for the beleaguered church and later became director of Compassion International for Africa.[7]

The Mekane Yesus Youth Hostel

Another development of major significance that occurred in the 60's was the establishment of a Youth Hostel in the heart of the national university under the auspices of Ethiopian Evangelical Church of Mekane Yesus. The Mekane Yesus Church (MYC) played a vital role in rallying young Ethiopians as a pioneer of the only evangelical national church registered under the government. It had attracted a small elite group from Eritrea, Wellega, and Addis Ababa who inspired many young Ethiopians around. The Youth Hostel was founded in 1966 through the support of the Lutheran World Federation (LWF) and other Lutheran churches.[8]

The hostel hosted programs that extended beyond providing rented rooms for students from the university. It opened its facilities to Christian students who were arranging various evangelistic and revival programs. In fact, after the establishment of the Haile Sellassie I University Christian Fellowships, the student leaders effectively used its facilities to conduct workshops and conferences.[9] The hostel provided various training programs in connection to evangelism and the systematic study of the Bible. According to Tekeste Teklu, a leading member of Christian youth activist in his time, the various academic and faith related activities given by the hostel significantly helped students meet the challenges of life as young citizens and university students.[10] The lessons they learned from qualified professional speakers on various subjects, like the relationship between science and faith, or creation and evolution and spirituality and rationalism and logic, had an empowering influence because they provided the students with rich sources of information that had practical applications for their lives. The greatest contribution of the hostel was what it accomplished during the period of the Ethiopian Revolution whose story will be reported at great length below.

The Emergence of Christian Students' Fellowships

It is not precisely clear, at this stage, when the fellowship of Christian students of the Haile Sellassie I University was founded.[11] The Youth Center, which significantly contributed to the strengthening of fledgling ties among the Christian students, provided one of the most influential sources of Christian learning and supplied a strong impetus for the creation of a Christian Student Fellowship.[12] The student fellowship, in turn, played a critical role at the evangelical movement in the university and elsewhere. It was from this Christian organization that leaders emerged during the military rule (1974-1991) and which provided cutting edge leadership to the church in difficult times.

Perhaps, it was the desire to counter the growing influence of Marxism among the youth that created the need among evangelical groups to set up an inter-denominational organization, which later evolved into the Ethiopian University Students Christian Fellowship (EUSF).[13] The Fellowship played a decisive role in bringing ecumenical awakening among believers and in recruiting new converts through its various outreach programs such as retreats, drama shows, revival meetings, and seminars.[14] The student's fellowship, undoubtedly, became one of the few and most powerful associations, openly challenging the new Marxist ideology that was making inroads increasingly into the university system. The Pentecostal group, which was very active, daringly confronted individuals who were promoting Marxism by taking time to study its philosophy and the position it took on religion so that they could task the student radical both at the intellectual and spiritual front.[15] The student activists who embraced the Marxist ideology saw the Pentecostals as a danger to the student movement and feared that the vigor they displayed for their faith left no room for participation in student politics.

The Role of Radio Voice of the Gospel (1963-1977)

The establishment of a modern radio station constituted another major development of immense significance to the expansion of the evangelical movement in Ethiopia. The first of its kind in Africa was the Lutheran World Federation's station named, Radio Voice of the Gospel (RVOG). RVOG, with a broadcast coverage of one billion people, was one of the most important ventures LWF had ever undertaken. It was set up with the purpose of countering the influence of Islam and atheism, and particularly the varieties of communism that were engulfing many Third World countries during the Cold War.[16] The station was established in Addis Ababa, Ethiopia's capital city, in 1963 after years of negotiations with the government. Emperor Haile Sellassie, who strongly supported the project, gave permission for its establishment, despite opposition from the clergy and some members of his cabinet.

While Haile Sellassie's support was important it also came as a liability because the station was nationalized by a decree of the Marxist government in 1977. The pretext given by the military officials for its confiscation was that imperialist forces were using the station as an instrument of subversion against the popular revolution. The government accused the RVOG of polluting the national culture and propagating a viewpoint contrary to the improvement of the broad masses.[17]

THE RISE AND DEVELOPMENT OF THE PENTECOSTAL MOVEMENT IN ETHIOPIA (1960s-70s)

I would like to propose that the Pentecostal movement in Ethiopia was a manifestation of a deep religious yearning demonstrated among young Ethiopians whose faith and religious convictions were being challenged by the modern secular thinking that engulfed their generation. As David Hoekema's chapter (this volume) shows this secular thinking was widespread in Africa in the 21st century. For Ethiopia, however, this thinking came with an interesting twist because of the enduring presence of Christianity in the country. Members of that generation were made to feel something was wanting in their inherited religious traditions as the result of the influences of modern education and the advent of Protestant missionaries, who had introduced an alternative variant of Christianity. The failure of the historic church to be proactively relevant to its adherents provided the soil in which the seeds of the movement nourished. Given the fact that more than 90% of the Pentecostals came from the Orthodox Church, it is tempting to characterize the movement as reformation from without. Yet there were factors for both internal and external influences for the movement.

External influences

Two Pentecostal missionary groups arrived almost simultaneously in Ethiopia in the 1950's. The first were the Finland Pentecostal Missionaries (FPM), who arrived in Ethiopia in 1951 and set up a station in Mercato, the commercial hub of the capital city. Mr. Sanfrid Mattson, the first missionary from the FPM, used to visit and hold comforting prayer with Emperor Haile Sellassie I while he was in exile in England as a result of the Italians' invasion of 1936.[18] It was his previous acquaintance with the Emperor that gave the missionaries the entrée to open up a station. The Swedish Philadelphia Mission (SPM), which arrived in 1959, was the second company to make its way into Ethiopia.[19] To a certain degree Pentecostal literatures that were slowly percolating from the US through books by Oral Roberts and T. L Osborn also left their marks of influence.

Revival movements in East Africa also had their influence in the rise and development of Pentecostalism in Ethiopia. Its wave began to splash through the Kenyan charismatic preacher, Omahe Cha Cha. Most of my informants were unanimous concerning the contribution of the Kenyan preacher, who gave the Pentecostal movement solid ground and articulation among its young Ethiopian adherents. He gave free expressions of the exercise of the works and the power of the Holy Spirit, which the young Ethiopians were using guardedly under the restraining influence of the Swedish missionaries.

Internal Dynamics

A closer scrutiny of the rise of the Pentecostal movement in Ethiopia reveals that it arose out of the interplay of several factors. Both pioneers and participants of the Pentecostal movement in Ethiopia emphatically state that the movement was spontaneous and would not favor an interpretation which links the movement's rise to impersonal forces such as existing socio-economic conditions of their society. For them, it was a revelation of the special power, the "fire," of God from above. They contend that the movement had its backdrop in the depth of their past spiritual consciousness which had been profoundly stirred due to the fresh inspiration they received through reading the Bible and related Scriptural literature and their earnest search for an authentic spiritual encounter.[20]

The Rise of an Independent Pentecostal Church (1963-1966)

Pioneers of the Pentecostal movement felt a sense of urgency to communicate the faith to the Ethiopians, which they seemed to carry out with a commitment level bordering the messianic. Pentecostals, especially converts from the historic Orthodox Church, claim that they redoubled their efforts to "reach" others who in their views were still "bound" by traditions, habits and rituals, which, from their perspective, simply made people become prisoners of fixed religious practices, instead of having "personal relations with Jesus." The redoubling of commitment drew from the bridge burning act of the Pentecostals and "the ideal-reality gap" they noticed between creedal values and actual practices. In their views, the only way to "redeem" their fellow Ethiopians was to give them a chance to receive their salvation and the experience of the power of God by helping them to make personal decisions to "trust" Christ and accept the gifts of the Holy Spirit.[21] This sense of calling to "reach out" to one's "lost" fellows, turned converts into bona fide missionaries and preachers. Partly explaining this gusto for reaching out, what the Pentecostals describe as their "lost" generation, was the rising influence of secularism and agnosticism in their times and the inadequacy of the traditional equipment of the national Church to innovate new approaches to save them from falling victims of these forces.

The motto, "The Gospel for Ethiopia by Ethiopians," the unwritten manifesto of the Pentecostals, proved to be the driving force behind this new spate of interest to go out and reach others, just like, "Land to the Tiller" (1965), was the driving slogan of the radical students of their generation in the national university. The Pentecostal movement developed a compulsion to create a contagious community of faith, which they sought to bring about with great zeal and consuming passion. According to its original founders, the movement was not devoid of social purposes. There was an embedded conviction among the pioneers that Ethiopia needed a religious revolution that invoked the power of God, through the Holy Spirit as a *sin qua non* for its socio-economic and political transformations.[22] Their zeal approximated that of the ebullient generation of American evangelicals in the early 20th century who were inspired by John Mott's slogan, "the evangelization of the world in this generation." As a result, the Pentecostals expanded their sphere of missionary activities from the capital city to the rest of the nation.[23] They accomplished this by mobilizing local missionaries, mostly men and women serving as government employees in different parts of Ethiopia by organizing self-supported revivalist meetings, which they called "spiritual conferences; and by establishing prayer homes, called chapels.[24] This "geographical peel off," to use Gerlach's expression, is one of the most important key elements in the dynamics of the expansion of the Pentecostal movement in Ethiopia.[25] The church comprised disparate groups, mostly students, who did not have solid leadership with strong theological foundations. Most of them, being well-informed people, made up for that weakness by assiduously reading the Bible and applying what they considered basic Scriptural principles to guide their fellowships in the context of their times, and by further deepening their commitment to their call to serve.[26] They also effectively utilized their social networking skills both to maintain their solidarity and expand their spheres of influences to propagate their newfound faith.

There are various perspectives on the development of Pentecostalism in Ethiopia. According to Dr. Tilahun Mamo, more than the failure of the Orthodox Church to adopt itself to change, the rise of Marxism and its growing influence constituted a very important context for the ascent of Pentecostalism in Ethiopia and the evolution of an autonomous church. His argument is that, unable to challenge the new atheist philosophy that was slowly creeping into the youth without a strong spiritual foundation, the youth clung to a more assertive, more definitive, and more radical faith that could be defended collectively on a more rational basis through experiences and the Word of God as written in the Bible.[27] It is difficult to establish the link between the rise of Marxism and the beginning of Pentecostalism in Ethiopia. Most participants of the Pentecostal movement were aware of Marxism and its growing danger to their faith and the future of their country, but did not necessarily see their movement as an intentional reactive or proactive step to challenge Marxism.

Afework Kebede, a former Marxist, now a church leader in the US, puts an interesting spin on the connection between Marxism and Pentecostalism. He agues that the rise of the Pentecostal movement, in fact, was a factor that gave further cause for the hardening position taken by the small Marxist groups and their increasing influence among the youth, at least, in the university. According to Afework, the embracing of the Pentecostal faith by the Ethiopian youth, its aggressive expansion and the apolitical tendency that the followers were perceived to display, gave the student radicals occasion to rally against followers of the new movement. They even enlisted the support of the *Haymanote Abew*, a reformist group from the Orthodox Church hostile to the Pentecostals, to join their ranks in outflanking the Pentecostals and in curbing their expansion.[28] Tilahun's view and that of Afework may look contradictory, but the significance of their insights lies in what they reveal concerning the linkage between the two radical youth movements with conflicted agenda yet co-existing at the same time, living more or less in the same space.

The student radicals were equally zealots in their pursuits of reaching and influencing their generation and redeeming the nation from socio-political ills albeit relying on a different source; the invocation of Marxism as a total panacea. The student radicals suspected that the Pentecostal movement was of a foreign origin promoted by westerners who wanted to use the new religion as a tool for a neo-colonialist agenda.[29] The radicals saw the growing attraction of the students towards Pentecostalism as a great obstacle to the spread of Marxism. The 1967 resolution of the student movement condemned what it considered the growing influence of foreign activities, in reference to Pentecostalism, as it was feared that it might arrest "our political consciousness and obscure our national goal."[30]

According to Solomon Lulu, a serious point of departure between the two groups that held opposing visions of the future of their country, was the Pentecostal's philosophical and theological contention that only a spiritually self-transformed individual had the moral justification to call out for actions that would bring an all-out community transformation. The Pentecostal's idea of revolution, which in their perception, began with the self, to be more precise, with the individual heart, as micro-model of revolution, definitely clashed with the student radicals' macro-historical model that took Marxism as it centerpiece.[31] For the Pentecostals, the value/spiritual factor or the moral revolution held primacy over all other transformations sought after.

This position tallies well with the main intention of the Pentecostals to spread "the Gospel for Ethiopia by Ethiopians," a form of messianic "Ethiopianism," which could be seen as a kind of nationalism couched in religious terms in contradistinction with the heavily loaded radical slogan, "Land to the Tiller" to which they were not against but had a guarded caution in its veiled political agenda as espoused by the student radicals. Prior to the 1974 Ethiopian Revolution, Pentecostals and student radicals contested along several religious and political fronts, whether they were explicit or implicit. Randi Balsvik points out that as of the late 1960s, radical university students were lodging scathing criticism of the role of the national church by asserting that it contributed to the under-development of Ethiopia and hence was no longer a useful institution.[32] She further explains, "Student criticism of the church was profound, whether it came from the minority that supported it, students of the College of Theology and the Haimanote Abew Association ...or from the majority who were estranged from the church."[33] Sandra Rickard, who conducted a survey of student attitudes in 1966, also observes that students found "the Church not only irrelevant to their generation, but a political block to progress."[34] This was the time when radical university students began to officially pronounce the view that religion was the opiate of the people, a cliché that became increasingly pervasive among many activists. This was a radical leap considering the fact that religious faith permeated vital aspects of social life and provided ultimate guidelines for behavioral norms for the most part of the elite of the 50's. Most of the pioneers of the Pentecostal movement in Ethiopia admit that political discourses were not within their immediate circle of concern, and as such, they did not exhibit expressed commitment in political engagements for politics per se.[35] Perhaps a major exception to this is the political contestation of the Pentecostals with the student radicals in 1971 presidential election of University Student Union of Addis Ababa (USUAA).

Solomon Lulu, now chairman of Ethiopian Christian Business Men's Association, and a key person behind the creation of the fellowship, recalls that Pentecostals were at loggerheads with the "small but pernicious" group called the Crocodiles. He observed that this articulate Christian group conducted a highly organized campaign to foil the plan of the Crocodiles and other student radicals who were working hard to make the late student leader Tilahun Gizaw, the President of USUAA. The Pentecostals were deeply offended by the radicals' open censure of God and hence were determined to make a dodged effort not to allow the radicals to succeed in getting their choice candidate elected.[36] According to Randi Balsvik, most of the candidates during the student election of 1971 vigorously attacked the church, but the statements which received the most spontaneous and loud applause was: "We, the students teach the Ethiopian mass that there is no God."[37] The Pentecostal students collaborated with those who campaigned for the election of Mekonnen Bishaw, a relatively more liberal candidate, who at the end of the day won the contest.[38]

Whatever their level of engagement/disengagement with politics at the time, most of the Pentecostals admit that they were trying to turn the country towards a new era and move along a new direction, albeit on religious terms. As a professor from the Faculty of Science and a former active participant of the movement noted:

> We were filled with a new wave of consciousness, purpose and destiny, we were messianic in our new ventures and endeavors, we did not want to let go of things; we wanted to be involved in the country's fate in the way we saw fitting, for us religion was the most fundamental issue on which all other things hinged upon.[39]

The participants of the Pentecostal movement, aware or unaware, were anti-establishment. By moving away from their traditional religion and creating an alternative expression of Christianity outside established Orthodox Church, they challenged the system from another angle, choosing the path of religion, unlike their counterparts who opted to revolt against the whole system with the ideological tools provided by Marxism.[40] Both groups viewed the national Church, pillar of the old system, as an institution that had not kept abreast with the time, and hence, left it aside and opted for new routes one in denial, the other in a new venture to re-engage the faith by making a new space.[41] Thus viewed from this perspective both camps represented waves of revolutions, spiritual and political, depending on one's perspective. At the risk of stretching the argument too far, the Pentecostal movement may be seen as one of the thrusts breaking through the traditional patterns of the Ethiopian society and discursive resistance to established order legitimated by religious codes.

Contexts of Radicalization

The 1960s were a period where the Ethiopian society was in some ways experiencing cultural, social, religious, and intellectual awakening, albeit in its nascent form. The transformations, which carried with them significant demographic, social and cultural shifts, allowed the emergence of a new social force that favored exploring new ideas and experimenting with new faith. The new social force that came to exist as a result of the combined effects of urbanization, a measure of industrialization, the expansion of modern education and state bureaucracy, sought to develop a new way of self expression, new ethos and sensibilities that resonated with the changed temper of the time. Caught up in the cusp of the old and the new, the rising Ethiopian intellectuals encountered the daunting challenge of what can be described as the "open predicament" virtually alone unaided by their resources of the preceding generation. Marxism that promoted radical political discourse in Ethiopia found grounding in the midst of cultural dislocation and the resultant loss of interpretive power suffered by casualties of modernization.[42]

The Encounters of Pentecostals with the Marxist State:1974-1990

The next major event that accentuated the spread of Pentecostalism in other evangelical churches was the 1974 Ethiopian Revolution itself. During the Revolution, the Pentecostal groups played an influential role in the underground church, drawing on their past experience and their presence in almost all denominations due to their experiences of persecution in the previous regime. Brian Fargher rightly asks, "What would have happened to the church of Ethiopia during the seven tough years of the revolution (1974-1980) if the renewal movement had not already effected many beneficial changes by that time"?[43] The fact that participants of the Pentecostal movement were largely men and women with a higher level of education coupled with their active involvement in various inter-denominational Christian fellowships in the past, helped them to network skillfully and play a key role in providing a tested model for the evangelical churches to adjust and withstand the challenges they faced during the revolution.[44] In this respect, it can be stated that their persecution experience in the past, though biting, served as a spiritual capital that was invested during the revolution.

During and after the revolution the Pentecostal movement entered into a new level. From being an elite oriented, virtually homogenous unit, it transformed itself into a mass movement, embracing new members from all walks of life.[45] Conditions contributing to this metamorphosis according to some informants, include the socio-political developments that had transpired during the period of the Ethiopian revolution and the decade that followed it. The political upheavals that Ethiopia faced over the last quarter of the 20th century, the dramatic transitions the society experienced and accompanying traumas, not only had a disorienting impact but increased people's level of insecurity that pre-adapted them for a faith encounter. Though Ethiopians had recourse to diverse outlets to circumvent these unsettling experiences, some found in Pentecostalism a place to feel at home.[46]

As Peter Berger aptly conveys, " It is in worship that the prototypical gesture of religion is fulfilled again. This is the gesture in which mankind, in hope, lifts up its arms to reach transcendence."[47] Pentecostals teach that their faith is also the here and the now, that God intervenes in human situations in multiple forms and is able to change the circumstance surrounding people' life. The Pentecostals provided a much needed counter-culture that convicts and indirectly attacks the Marxist paradigm by providing a secure zone of faith in an existentially perplex world marred by violence of White or Red Terror.[48]

The Pentecostals constituted one of the foremost intellectual task forces of the evangelical Christians during the period of the revolution. The young Pentecostals, who mainly came from the elite force of the Ethiopian society, made their presence felt among various evangelical churches resulting from their previous persecution experiences. Some of the young Pentecostals had already gained influential leadership positions in the denominations they had joined. They drew on their former friendships, trust and networking skills, key ingredients of social capital, to share experiences and information needed in the collective effort of confronting the challenges of the revolution.

The history of the Ethiopian revolution is a complex subject that would require a serous inquiry of a multi-disciplinary nature. However, a major backdrop of its unfolding is the Cold War, where competing ideologies contested to win the minds and hearts of an embittered youth questing for a direction and a roadmap of national progress. As mentioned above in the Ethiopian situation, instrumental to the expansion of radical Marxist thought was a group known as the Crocodiles, established by student radicals in 1964.[49] Little is known about the history of the group and its overall "agenda," for it was a somewhat clannish and furtive organization, with its membership being strictly based on dedication to its "cause."[50] Sandra Richard, who visited the national university in 1966, observed that the crocodiles represented communist organizations, "who are apparently receiving support from either the Yugoslavian or Czechoslovakian government or both."[51] Most informants, who were contemporaries of the group, confirm that members of the Crocodile seemed to have a hidden agenda. They also claim that they were the main actors behind the activities of the student movements.[52] The lure of Marxism was that it promised scientific technological progress, i.e., modernization with a perfect community, the overcoming of divisions such as class, ethnic group, religion, gender, etc. "In a country as diverse as and non-homogenous and as backward as Ethiopia, this was fascinating. No wonder that many Ethiopians became followers of socialism."[53]

Contested Terrains

Once the military came to power in ending the Solomonic Dynasty whose last representative was Emperor Haile Sellassie, it embarked on the road to socialism by openly declaring its official policy to be scientific communism. The Pentecostals who had suffered persecution in the previous government initially greeted the change with enthusiasm. According to some Pentecostals, the event of the fall of the regime had already been foretold prophetically. Informants reminisce that when the Emperor curtly dismissed delegates of the Pentecostals during their 1971 plea for religious freedom, a prophecy came immediately that Haile Sellassie's reign was doomed to collapse soon.[54] Whether this claim is to be believed or not is not the issue. What the story mirrors for us is the Pentecostals' anticipation of a change of government and their welcoming attitude to the revolution. There were even some gestures by some Pentecostal intellectuals to cooperate with the government by professionally identifying themselves with the concerns of the Ethiopian Revolution.[55] However, the leaders faced a serious dilemma of choosing to defend the faith while at the same time expressing support for the popular aspirations.[56]

When the Pentecostals got the full picture of the new state of affairs, they took the challenge seriously and engaged it accordingly. They countered Marxism and its damaging influences along several fronts, openly when the situation allowed and discursively, when otherwise. Very importantly, however, the Pentecostals fought Marxism and the state that showed unqualified hostility to their faith by building intricate network of house churches, a form of social strike in itself, where they were able to distance themselves while at the same time nibbling at the system from a hidden corner. The Pentecostals used their house churches as spring board to catch "souls" in their nets by increasing their evangelistic initiatives across any space available, some times at considerable risk. I will briefly consider areas of contestation between Pentecostals and the Marxists of their own generations:

1. Battling with Marxism in the various centers of the newly launched government program--Development Through Cooperation--popularly known as *Zemecha,* inaugurated in 1975. It was a strategy applied by the government to re-educate the population and bring about changes in their worldviews through a calculated indoctrination program using the Ethiopian students as the chief vehicles. In fact, *Zemecha,* according to the *Ethiopia Herald,* was unleashed basically to redress the problem of a religiously oriented thinking especially in areas where mission education was prevalent.[57] The Pentecostals relentlessly fought the radicals in all the *Zemecha* centers. In this contested terrain informants report that there were both losses and gains. While a few lost their faith unable to stand the pressure of the student radicals in the *Zeemecha* camp, who formed the majority, there were also some from the radical side who were won to their faith. By all accounts, given the numeral disadvantages of those who identified with the student radicalism, the battle was uphill for the Pentecostals.

2. Using open spaces: There were some available open spaces such as the student's Christian fellowship, the University Student Christians Fellowships (USCF) that the young Pentecostals could make wise use of. In this respect the role of the Mekane Yesus Church (MYC) deserves special mention. The church, which was spared from being closed because of its international stature as a member of the World Council of Churches, not only provided an office for the students' fellowship but also employed a full-time coordinator to galvanize and direct the various youth initiatives. Qes Gudina, Secretary of the church, who was later murdered by the government, supported the fellowships by encouraging the Christian student leaders to be fully prepared to stave off the growing influence of atheism and engage in aggressive testimonies of their Christian faith in word, life and deeds. Among the great accomplishments of the fellowship were the inter-Christian links it established among Christian students who were forced to participate in the *Zemecha program.* Evangelical Christians separated from their parents and their churches and bombarded by communist propaganda faced formidable challenges in maintaining their faith in their assigned

isolated rural camps. Since Marxism was in vogue among the youth, evangelical Christians, who constituted minority groups, became obvious targets of Marxist ideologues that ridiculed them and branded them agents of the CIA.[58]

The MYC invited a Korean-American missionary from the US by the name of Mildred Young in 1974 to use her expertise to lay the groundwork for a useful strategy of handling the new challenge. Miss Young gave training for young Christians on how to effectively read, interpret, and use the Bible for their Christian living. She networked with the students in their respective *Zemecha* centers through letters and other communication channels. She was primarily engaged in preparing a resource manual on how the Christian youth in the *Zemecha* stations could stay grounded in their faith and gain strength in their changed locale. She facilitated the preparation and circulation of weekly newsletters containing testimonies of courage and perseverance, words of faith, and encouragement, and exchanged useful information among the students. She also arranged and distributed a daily Bible study guide, including articles dealing with spiritual matters and selected news items.[59]

3. Organizing seminars with contemporary relevance: Leaders of the student fellowships, most of whom came from the Pentecostal background, organized seminars for the university students at the MYC compound on diverse interrelated topics such as Socialism and God, Creation and evolution, God in History, Christianity and politics, ethics and morality, and a host of other issues related to the youth and their existential challenges. The seminars were intended to anchor the students in their faith tradition and equip them with the basic ideas of Marxism so that they would not be enticed to its popular appeal. According to Professor Alem Bazezew, this was a great investment in the youth and an asset whose importance proved to be invaluable for the church at a time when it was forced to operate clandestinely and beyond.[60]

4. Resisting shouts of slogans: The government organized parades and marches to galvanize public support from the general population and raise the visibility of the revolution and its champions. In these organized parades participants were coerced to shout slogans

in support of the government and its ideologies. The Pentecostals did not want to participate in such exercises and refused to chant the pro-government chants often at considerable risks. One of the main reasons for the intensification of the plight of the Pentecostals youth was their refusal to salute the revolution with their left hands and chant slogans. They reasoned that raising the left hand was unbiblical. The youth abstained from shouting slogans too, not to show disrespect to the state, but to demonstrate fidelity for their faith as some of the slogans were found to be affronts to the basic religious tenets. The young Pentecostals, in particular, were known for refusing to stretch their hands and to chant slogans like "Foreword with our leader Mengistu," "We shall bring nature under our control," "Death to the enemies of the Revolution," "Religion is drudging the mass," and " Above all is, the Revolution." The last slogan, in particular, was found to be offensive to their core Christian values. According to some informants, the crux of the matter was that endorsing the slogan was tantamount to denying what is written in the Gospel of John 3:31, which says, "The one who comes from above is above all."[61] Several young students who adamantly refused to chant slogans were thrown in jail for years, accused of being anti-revolutionaries.

5. The Production of literature: the Pentecostals produced clandestine literature and distributed them, to their best capacities, to their members. Though it has not been possible to find sufficient documents of the clandestine literature there are some secretly kept, examples of which include: *Fitret Yemeskir* (Let Creation Speak), *Enkadene?* (Shall we Deny it?), *Eyesusen Meketel (*Following Jesus), *Emenet Sifeten* (When faith is tested), and *Metsehaf Qidus Men Yilal?* (What does the Bible say?).[62]

Allied with local production was the circulation of literature that came from abroad and which was avowedly read. Since the Pentecostals had experienced persecution in the past, most of its members, especially its leadership, were familiar with the stories of Christian persecutions in other communist countries. For instance, *Tortured for Christ,* written by the Romanian pastor Richard Wumbrand, was a popular book, which had been circulating amongst Pentecostals. Some of the Pentecostals were also familiar with Mel Tari's, book, *Like a Mighty Wind,* and the works of Dietrich Bonhoffer, such as the *Cost of Discipleship,* and his suffering and death under the Nazis for his faith.[63] As Alem put it, "we knew the price of suffering and the blessing entailed both theoretically and experientially."[64]

The new rulers feared the Pentecostals more than the other Christians because they knew that they were very bold and aggressive in communicating their faith, as their record in the past had shown. The Pentecostals were outspoken for their unflinching oppositions to Marxism and their leaders had combated the ideology long before the outbreak of the Ethiopian Revolution. Leaders of the Pentecostal movement had in the past counterbalanced Marxism right from its inception in the 1960's while they were university students. Moreover, Pentecostalism had been embraced by the rising elite in Addis Ababa and other urban centers, and demonstrated a high capacity to expand into other sectors of the society. This was a strain that the *Derg* (the communist military junta that ousted Haile Selassie) and its intellectual backers could hardly accommodate. For that reason, some of the leaders in the *Derg* and in the left wing opposition parties, both in the camp of the Ethiopian Peoples Revolutionary Party (EPRP and the All Ethiopia Socialist Movement, commonly know by its Amharic acronym, MEISON, were very hostile to the Pentecostals. It is no wonder that the persecution against Mulu Wongel Church (MWC) an independent Pentecostal church and other Pentecostals began earlier than other evangelical groups. The new rulers could not use their anti-evangelical Christian rhetoric in connection with the MWC, for it was entirely an indigenous church with no external backings. *Qebele* (Urban Dwellers' Associations created by the government) cadres used to say *"Be pentewoch kerse meqabir la'ay abyotachinen engenebalene"* (We shall build our revolution on the death yard or graveyard of the Pentecostals.)[65]

6. Building home churches: The Pentecostals built extensive networks of house churches that operated clandestinely with amazing complexity of security system no less than their radical counterparts, the EPRP, a major political contestant of the government. The home churches provided some kind of safety zone for many Ethiopians experiencing some sort of psychic despair. It served as the ironic space for the mushrooming of tens and thousands of Christian home circles. The underground homes virtually became rehabilitation centers for those

who have experienced a degree "homelessness" in the bewildering climate of the terror-filled politics of the time. Intriguingly enough, it even attracted those who defected from the communist camps either due to overall fatigue or disillusionment in the whole political enterprise.

7. Composition and singing of songs: The Pentecostals, who had previously succeeded in recruiting talented young men and women, effectively marshaled the intellectual and artistic resources of its member to combat Marxism and defend their faith. In most of their songs, they expressed their faithfulness and allegiance only to their God and not to any "system." There were many songs composed during the period of the revolution that were meant to uplift the sovereignty of God and to challenge the assumptions behind government sponsored political slogans. *Denke new lene geta* (He/God is awesome to me) by *Tamirat Haile, El Shaddie* (God is Almighty) by Derege, and *Keber Yegebahal* (Glory be unto you), author unknown, *Semay zufanu new* (The Heaven is his Throne), Geja choir, can be cited as few examples.[66] Tesfaye Gabiso' s songs, which used biblical narratives and allusion, highlighting refusal to submit before a man-made object, conveyed the message of triumphing through trials, even if it meant passing through fires, are good examples of acts of defiance.[67] Tamirat Welba's song *Bewengel alafrem* (I am not ashamed of the Gospel), was also sung to reassure Christians that the Bible contained the power of God. The song *Getachen new kehulum belay* (Our Lord is above all things), was written in 1978 in response to the slogan "the revolution is above everything." *Zingero aydelehum* (I am not an ape) by Derege Kebede, openly countered the theory of evolution. *Endet denq amlak new* (how Great Thou are) by Derge, was a popular song during the revolution.[68] Derge's songs, in most cases, were sung to counter the materialist philosophy the government was advancing.[69]

Sharing the same universe with the rest of the Ethiopians, who were subjected to a brutal regime, their discursive form of resistance through songs subverted the *Derg*'s ideological discourse. Commenting on the paradoxical situation, a prominent church elder noted, "the mouth opened more when it was stifled more, the more the voice was muted, the more the spirit shouted."[70] The story of the Pentecostals was one of the varied articulations of dissent expressed by Ethiopians, and hence, was part and parcel of the larger story of suffering, repression and collective protest. The songs composed during the revolution may not have an internationality to sound political, but according to Dunway, "...music may be said to be political when its lyrics or melody evoke or reflect a political judgment by the listener." [71] Most of the songs composed during the days of the revolution were generated by the political climate of the time they spoke about politics and evoke political judgments.

CONCLUSION

This chapter has outlined the contested grounds between Ethiopian Pentecostals and student radicals prior to the Revolution of 1974 and afterwards. I have argued that Pentecostalism in Ethiopia should not merely be viewed as a religious movement but must also be seen as a movement encapsulating diverse socio-cultural and political phenomena as its several trajectories indicated in the 1970's particularly so during the times of the Ethiopian Revolution. It is a potent social force attracting a cross section of the Ethiopian society that stood the test of time countering formidable challenges. The movement's survival in the midst of a hostile military state that mobilized its power to stifle it is part of the story of human saga, the indefatigable spirit of human freedom. By telling the story of Pentecostals and their fight for religious freedom the chapter firmly places Pentecostalism in the discourse of the Ethiopian revolution. In closing, I want to cite a famous quote of Abraham Lincoln. "Nothing is politically correct which is morally wrong." That explains the position of the Pentecostals towards those radicals who sought to achieve ambitious change in Ethiopia by valorizing violence without demonstrating the moral credibility that squared with their crusade, albeit a failed one.

6

FROM THE FRINGES TO THE CENTRE: PENTECOSTAL CHRISTIANITY IN THE PUBLIC SPHERE IN KENYA (1970-2009)

Damaris S. Parsitau

As mentioned in the introduction to this volume there has been tremendous upsurge and resurgence of religious revival and revitalization in Africa, signaling a shift of Christianity from the Northern to the Southern Hemisphere. Scholars of religion have noted the growing importance of Pentecostal and Charismatic religious expressions in the countries of the Global South with a "shift of the Centre of Christianity from the Northern Hemisphere to the Southern Hemisphere"[1] and that "Pentecostal Christianity is the fastest growing stream of Christianity in the world today and that the movement is reshaping religion in the twenty-first century."[2] This global Pentecostalism, described as "one of the most significant developments within Christianity in the twentieth century and [its] re-mapping of the demographic distribution of World Christianity and the reshaping of Christianity in these areas,"[3] has not only transformed the face of Christianity in the world but has changed the religious, social, and political landscapes of many countries in Latin America, Asia, and Africa forever.

In 2002, religious statisticians David Barrett and Todd Johnston estimated that there were roughly over 533 million Pentecostals and Charismatics in the world and that almost half of them are in the Global South: Latin America, Africa and Asia.[4] Further statistics from the same Database point out that Pentecostals now represent 12% or about 107 million of Africa's population of nearly 890 million people. This includes individuals who belong to classical Pentecostal denominations such as the Assemblies of God or the Apostolic Faith Mission that were founded in the early 20th century, as well as those who belong to Pentecostal denominations or churches that have been formed recently.[5] Charismatic members of non-Pentecostal denominations who are drawn mainly from Catholic and Protestant churches and African Instituted Churches number an additional 40 million or approximately 5% of the population.[6] Although some may question these statistics, even conservative estimates see the Pentecostal and Charismatic movement as having at least 250 million adherents worldwide,[7] and all agree that its most explosive growth has occurred in the Southern Hemisphere.[8] The impact of Pentecostalism goes beyond demographic figures as its presence is powerfully felt in almost all areas of public life. Pentecostalism has become an increasingly prominent feature of Africa's religious and political landscape.[9]

The civic and public roles and impact of Pentecostal Christianity in Africa has been the subject of much scholarly investigations (Anderson 2004; Asamoah-Gyadu (2004); Gifford (1998; 2004; 2009); Millar & Yamamori (2006); Meyer & Moors (2006); Adogame (2008); Kalu (2008); Ukah 2007; Parsitau (2009). These studies have argued that the recent democratic transition in a number of African countries seemingly go together with an increased influence of religion in the public sphere. Gifford (1998, 2004 2009) argues that these new churches have a rather unique agenda, one element of which is to walk the corridors of power but also censors them for not having a conscious social agenda. Indeed, in his identification and analysis of the three areas of the public sphere–the political, the economic, and cultural–in which churches could contribute to strengthening civil society, Gifford is highly dismissive of the roles of Pentecostal Christianity but approving of the roles of mainline Christianity as custodians of democracy and as leading social providers. An alternative assessment of the interaction of contemporary Christianity and the civil society reveals the social relevance of the new churches (Adogame 2008). Larbi (1999), for example, aptly demonstrates, with concrete examples, the dynamics of political involvement by Ghanaian Pentecostal churches. He shows that a church's attitude or response to government policies are not static or fixed but depends on a number of complex factors that may often not be visible to the public or even researchers. He demonstrates that Pentecostals are not aloof from society but rather advocate a constructive engagement, a radiant pursuit of abundant life in the here and now, through discipline, hard work, and proper ritual behavior. A proper grasp and analysis of the churches public and civic role will no doubt entail a broader contextualization of the political economy as well as taking cognizance of social and cultural realities. The mood and stance of the church is largely influenced and shaped by socio-economic currents and political wind of change much more than any said ideology of neither political involvement nor political ideology.

Similarly, Ogbu Kalu (2003) has written extensively on the role of African Christianity in the public sphere and from an African/insiders' perspective. Kalu's (2008) volume on African Pentecostalism focuses on the role Christianity is playing in Africa's socio-political and economic life and especially noting that Pentecostal political practice has become more socially engaged in many parts of Africa. He contends that these churches are not only engaging in politics today but are also attacking social political structures using non-political activities such as prayer and prophesy while also embracing a multi-faceted and holistic response to the human predicament using the resources of the gospel. Elsewhere, Kalu (2003) documents the political activities of Nigerian Pentecostals particularly those of the PEN of Nigerian and notes that they have evolved a Pentecostal theology of engagement.

Kalu's views are shared by African Pentecostal scholars such as Mathews Ojo (2004), Asamoah-Gyadu (2004), and Adogame (2005b) who have propagated a Pentecostal theology of engagement in which prayer and prophesy are used as political praxis. Afe Adogame (2005b) writes about the politicization of religion and religionization of politics in Nigeria, while Asamoah-Gyadu (2004) writes about the theology of transformation of Pentecostals in Ghana in which they have elasticized and transformed their engagement with public space in a conscious attempt at coping with the country's socio-economic and political realities.

Mathew Ojo (2004) was among the first African scholars to attribute a public role to African Pentecostalism and has always insisted that Pentecostals contribute to public life even through such activities as prayer and intercession. In an article on "Pentecostals and Public Accountability in Nigeria," Ojo argues that as major elements within civil society, Pentecostals have become active actors when it comes to the interplay between religion and politics (Ojo 2004). He argues that Pentecostals in Nigerian are civically engaged in the Nigerian public sphere and that the church has produced a huge Christian constituency that can influence socio-political issues in the country. Ojo has argued that rather than truncate Christian missionaries' social role and influence in public life such as in the establishment of schools and hospitals, the mainline churches and the Pentecostal/Charismatic churches have maintained these traditional roles in more or lesser degrees.

Ellis and Haar (2004) argue that we need to enlarge African political practice to include none political practice especially its ideological significance. They note that much academic work on religion and politics in Africa focuses on institutions and not on religious ideology or religious ideas. They suggest that greater attention needs to be paid to understanding religious thought in Africa, and the way it shapes and explains political action. Popular stories about witches, prophets, miracles, or the use of witchcraft, spirit mediums or diviners, are part of the political vernacular in different parts of Africa. They suggest a definition of religion as the belief "in an invisible worlds of spirits" spirits that have the power to make changes in the visible world is enacted or understood. These scholars used examples from across the continent to illustrate their case concerning the way religious thought is intertwined with political practice and notions of political power are embedded in religious ideas. Ogbu Kalu (2008) has argued along the same line of thought.

The importance of understanding Pentecostal Political practice is demonstrated in Harri Englund's (2000) study of Malawian Pentecostalism. He argues that while some Malawian Pentecostals are apolitical, this does not represent the reversal of democratic achievements. Rather, he suggests that the ideas of spiritual and corporeal unity contain their own tools for an effective critique of power. This helps to point to the complexity of interpreting Pentecostal understandings of democracy and forms of engagement. At the same time, scholars have engaged in discourses about these churches as key elements within Civil Society which, to borrow Maxwell's (2006) words, are "the domain of organized social life between the family and the state, concerned with public or collective goals and needs." In fact recent Pentecostal historiography has focused on the contributions of these churches in public space as groups within civil society. This is because religious groupings are widely accepted to be the strongest form of associational life in contemporary Africa and yet the precise working especially that of the Neo-Pentecostal Churches, are largely unknown (Gifford 1999). Another strand of scholarship keen on examining the role of Pentecostalism in the democratization process emerged in the late 1990s. Much of this literature has focused on the contribution of these churches to democratization (Martin 1990; Dodson 1997; Gifford 1998; Freston 1998; Ojo; 2004). These works were, however, dismissive of the role of Pentecostalism in democratization and tended to privilege Mainline Churches at the expense of the Pentecostal types. Scholars like Gill (2004) who have done the most far-reaching empirical studies in this field prefer to adopt a neutral stance on the question of the contribution of Pentecostalism to democratization.

In much of Sub-Saharan Africa today, "evidence of religious revival and renewal are visibly and conspicuously notable in different shades and forms across the landscapes of these countries." For instance, statistical estimates for 2000 according to Ogbu Kalu indicate that about 20 percent of the population in Zimbabwe, Tanzania, and Malawi were Pentecostals; 14 percent in Kenya; 11 percent in Nigeria; 10 percent in Ghana and Zambia; 8 percent in Democratic Republic of Congo and South Africa; and 4 percent in Uganda (2008, 5). Indeed, as Maxwell notes in Ghana, Kenya, South Africa, Uganda, Zambia and Zimbabwe, "Born agains" are so numerous and their leaders so influential that they are just as "mainstream," "mainline" and "established" as Anglicans."[10]

In Kenya evidence from the 2002 elections, 2005 constitutional debates and politics and the 2007 general election all point to increased involvement and contributions of Pentecostal Christianity in the public sphere. These developments that have expanded since the turn of the millennium seem to challenge a previous strand of scholarship that has always insisted that Pentecostal Christianity has nothing to contribute to socio-political developments of the nation states especially in modern democracies. This trend is not peculiar to Kenya alone as the trend is also noticeable in many other African nations such as Nigeria and Ghana where Pentecostal Christianity has become the single most important religious factor and one that is exerting increased socio-political and moral influence on these societies. I argue in this chapter that the resurgence of Neo-Pentecostalism and other social movements in the public sphere in Kenya has increased the social space they occupy and as a result nurtured a culture of civic engagement and fostered an active citizenry too. Despite this public presence of Pentecostalism the effects of religious ideas on politics have been little studied, mainly because many academics and journalists are firm believers in the idea of a further decline of the public role of religion and therefore points to signs of the contrary. I here examine the varied and significant ways in which Pentecostal Christianity has become a socio-political force in Kenya, providing further insights into the complex interaction between Pentecostal Christianity, civic engagement, and the public sphere in Kenya.

THE PENTECOSTAL AND CHARISMATIC LANDSCAPE IN KENYA

In the last three decades (since the 1980s), Kenya has experienced a phenomenal growth of Pentecostal and Charismatic church movements that cut across various social classes of the country from urban to rural areas (Parsitau, 2007). Although Kenyan Pentecostalism is essentially an urban phenomenon, the movement has recently begun establishing itself in rural areas. At present, Kenyan Pentecostalism represents the most powerful and visible evidence of religious renewal and influence in the country. It also constitutes the fastest growing group of churches within Kenya's different forms of Christianity, with all types including, Classical, Indigenous/Independent, and the Neo-Pentecostal and Charismatic, represented.

A 2006 survey conducted by the Pew Forum on Religion and Public Life, indicates that the Pentecostal and Charismatic movement account for more than half of Kenya's population. The survey also found that approximately seven in ten Protestants in Kenya are either Pentecostal or Charismatic, and about a third of Kenyan Catholics surveyed can be classified as Charismatic. Further, Ndegwa (2007) reports that increasing demands on registering such churches overwhelmed the Registrar General's office in Nairobi. While speaking at a workshop for church leaders Kenya's Attorney General Amos Wako revealed that the office is overwhelmed by increasing demand for registration of churches and that the facility is facing difficulties in processing 6,740 pending applications by various religious organizations. Wako also stated that there are about 8,520 registered churches and that about 60 applications are filed every month (Ndegwa, 2007). Although not all of these churches seeking registration are Pentecostal, the majority of them are of Pentecostal and charismatic inclinations. Thousands of these newer churches have sprung up and sprouted in all major urban centres some within less than three to five kilometers of each other. Some are huge mega churches while others are too small to be called churches but still add to the numbers.

The Attorney Generals' figures are further buttressed and comple-mented by Colin Smith's (2007) study of the plethora of Pentecostal churches in the Gatwikera informal settlement in Nairobi. In this study Smith (2007, 68) points out that in this small but densely populated settlement, he identified more that 60 churches some within a space of fifty meters of each other. In a preliminary observation I made as I drove daily through Kikuyu town to Dagoreti corner (in the outskirts of Nairobi) for about one month, I counted about 40 churches in a stretch of less than one hour's drive. Such is the tremendous growth of these churches, a trend that while more visible in urban centres, is increasingly in rural areas too.

This explosive growth and powerful visible presence of churches does not necessarily point to a tremendous spiritual reformation and transformation in the country nor does it signify high levels of church attendance. For as Smith (2007) points out, many of these churches have less than twenty attendees. This raises serious questions about the growth of the movement: is it really growing exponentially or it is just laundering and rotating among the same groups of people? There is also a lot of spiritual normadism within these churches where converts keep moving from one church to another. This tendency has been referred to as the "circulation of the saints." Despite these challenges, Pentecostal-ism at the moment represents the most dynamic, powerful, overtly and publicly visible form of religious renewal and influence in Kenya. An examination of its growth and developments equally leaves no doubt about its qualitative influence and impact on theological reformation and impact on religious renewal in East Africa. Its impact in the public sphere has also grown tremendously. It is to this that I now turn.

THE INFILTRATION OF PENTECOSTAL CHRISTIANITY IN THE PUBLIC SPACES

Churches have generally also taken over many open public spaces in towns and cities, including public parks, bus stations, markets, and any other places where people congregate. Any individuals occupying these spaces during the day are targeted for evangelistic crusades, lunch hour meetings, revival meetings, prayer meetings or bible study. Coupled with this development is the explosion of worship services at all times and spaces particularly in urban centres. In Nairobi's Central Business District (CBD), for instance, there are breakfast, lunchtime, and evening prayer meetings in cinema halls, hotel conference rooms, and other buildings.

Preachers who cannot afford the rates charged for use of the buildings conduct their business in open public spaces such as Uhuru Park and Jevanjee Gardens in Nairobi, Nyayo gardens in Nakuru and Tononoka grounds in Mombasa. In fact some of today's well-known televangelists such as Bishop Pius Muiru of Maximum Miracle Ministries (MMM) and Bishop Margaret Wanjiru of Jesus is Alive Ministries (JIAM) cut their teeth at these parks as street preachers. Most aspiring preachers hone their public speaking skills and preaching in open spaces. All these practices have produced a visible explosion in the Neo-Pentecostal and Charismatic movement that is increasingly gaining recognition in many African cities (Anderson 2005).

According to David Maxwell, this type of African Christianity has seized hold of popular culture and worship stores have sprung up in many urban cities selling a host of Christian literature.[11] Christian tracts and magazines are sold on the streets as gospel music tunes are played loudly in towns and gospel music shops and kiosks. The Christian consumer can now buy audiotapes, CDs, DVDs, and recorded sermons from bookstores, on the streets, and church tape booths. Born again graffiti, stickers and handbills pervade the public places such as institutions of learning, and streetlight poles. Vehicles have Christian slogan painted across the front or the rear:[12] "In case of rapture, this car will be unmanned"; "I am covered by the blood of the Lamb"; "heading the wrong direction, God allows U-turns." Shops and business enterprises are christened "Victory boutique," "Ebenezer hair Salon," "Kings Motors," "Faith furnishers and interior décor," and "Psalms 123 Hardwares and Electrical," to name just a few. In short this type of African Christianity is powerfully visible and pervades all sectors of public life. It is this overtly visible public prominence of this type of Kenyan Christianity that has led to a pentecostalization of public spaces almost as if to force its way into the public way of living.

PENTECOSTALIZING THE PUBLIC SPHERE

The tremendous growth of this type of African Christianity has led not only to the Pentecostalization of mainline Christianity (as Ross Acheson shows in this volume when discussing Catholicism in Ghana) but has equally led to the pentecostalization of the public sphere where Pentecostal manners and styles have infiltrated into the manners and styles of others. The Pentecostalization of mainline Christianity suggests an on-going process where mainline Churches are increasingly appropriating Pentecostal and Charismatic spirituality, ethos, practices, styles and manners in a bid to survive its impact as well as curtail the exodus of the youth to newer Pentecostal and Charismatic churches (Parsitau 2007). The pentecostalization of the public sphere also refers to the infiltration of Pentecostal manners and styles on others who are not necessarily Pentecostal or charismatic.

In Kenya this trend of the pentecostalization of the public sphere has been going on for over a decade or so now.[13] In this pentecostalization of the public sphere, the Pentecostals are not only using the mass media to propagate their religious messages but also to consolidate their own influence and pervade the public sphere with a force like never witnessed before. This pentecostalization of public sphere has invaded the airwave "as its media-savvy pastors-cum-superstars regularly fill the airwaves with their preaching and gospel music that has radically changed the many country's airwaves" and mediascapes.[14] But the pentecostalization of the public sphere goes beyond the appropriation of mass media technologies or increased presence of the Pentecostals in the public spaces. The Pentecostalization of the public sphere as Harri Englund has argued "does not simply refer to the increased presence of Pentecostals in public life, but also to their influence on the style and manners of others, many of whom can be resolutely anti-Pentecostal."[15] In Kenya for example, this is evident in the way mainline churches, even some Muslim organizations are heavily appropriating the style of Pentecostals in their preaching and sermons and the mode in which they relay their religious messages. These styles include adapting a rhetoric of spiritual warfare that continually requires deliverance, the common practice of loud and syncopated music, the public verbal expression of spiritual experience and the unrestricted church service that is usually "guided by the spirit."

To counteract the Pentecostal onslaught on their religion particularly the rhetoric of spiritual warfare, Muslims now organize public rallies and crusades at crowded bus stops, market places, parks, and children playgrounds or any other places where there are large crowds. Through the use of loud speakers (like Pentecostals), they preach and recite the Koran. Their preaching often appears to engage Pentecostals with philosophical debates about apparent contradiction in the Bible such as the Godhead or the trinity.[16] But this influence is not only visible within Islamic and mainline church circles but is also visible with the general public. At the same time, Pentecostal manners such as their style of greetings by hugging and kissing punctuated by words such as "*bwana asifiwe*" loosely translated as "praise the lord" has become a common way of Christians exchanging pleasantries or greeting each, a trend that has also infiltrated many mainline churches. This way of exchanging pleasantries has become the norm in the country's social life.

The Pentecostals have been able to infiltrate public space and bring about the pentecostalization of the public sphere for a number of reasons. For one Ilesanmi argues that the ability of the newer Pentecostal movements "to transform gender relations and bring about generational change and its willingness to provide infrastructure that the collapsed institutions of the state have neglected or abandoned have made Pentecostalism an attractive force to millions who have converted to this type of African Christianity."[17] Similarly Peter Berger suggests that, "conversion to this brand of religiosity brings about a cultural transformation, new attitudes towards work and consumption, a new educational ethos, and a violent rejection of traditional machismo.[18]

But these movements are not only bringing about a cultural reformation, they are increasingly having significant effects on politics, economics, and providing social services and other amenities. In Kenya for example, the Pentecostal clergy are influencing politics through the issuance of public statements and pronouncements, press conferences and contributing to public debates such as constitution making, human rights, and corruption. The recent growth and explosion of Pentecostal Christianity in Kenya's public sphere has developed into considerable socio-political significance and influence. In the last few years, the place and role of Pentecostal and Charismatic Christianity in Kenya's public sphere has changed drastically and become much more conspicuous. In fact, the growth and impact of this type of African Christianity in the public sphere may be one of the most important and significant developments within civil societal associations in Africa. This has several implications for social change in the country's socio-political history and has ushered a paradigm shift in the study of religion and politics in Kenya.

The separation of the spheres of politics and Pentecostal and Charismatic churches in Kenya ceased in 2003 following a February 2002 church leaders meeting, from about 40 Pentecostal Churches gathered at Lake Bogoria Lodge (West of Nairobi) to do some soul searching and seek divine guidance concerning their prophetic voice and calling (Samita, 2003, 116). Through prayer and fasting, participants realized and repented for their complacence in socio-political issues affecting the nation. These issues include the HIV/AIDS pandemic, poverty, corruption, nepotism, and bad governance. They repented for the loss of their prophetic voice and for not being involved in national issues and general development of the nation and sought God's guidance in their involvement (Parsitau 2009). The church leaders agreed to adopt a policy of full engagement in national issues, subsequently creating a paradigm shift from non-engagement to full engagement in socio-political and other national issues affecting the country. Since then, Pentecostal churches have developed a sort of theology of engagement in which they have been actively involved in pubic life (Parsitau 2008). Despite this welcome gesture towards a more public engagement with socio-political issues in Kenya, Pentecostal church leaders seem to have come to this realization only to protect their interests. Why do I say this?

The entry of Pentecostals into the public sphere coincided with the search for a new constitution. One of the provisions of the proposed constitution—the proposal to allow Muslims to have Kadhi courts, known elsewhere as Islamic courts—did not sit well with Pentecostals who were vehemently opposed to it. Kadhi courts are intended to decide on private issues of marriage, divorce, and inheritance as they affect Muslims but Pentecostals argued that the provision seemed to elevate Islam as a religion and yet it is a minority religion in Kenya. The debate on whether or not to entrench Kadhi (Islamic) courts within the proposed new constitution has occupied the minds of many scholars, lawyers, clerics, even the general public. It has generated huge public debates and discourses ever since the clamor for a new constitution begun in earnest in the 1990s.

The Kadhi courts controversy also featured highly during the referendum politics in 2005 and the highly contested 2007 general elections. More recently, the debate resurfaced again in 2010 and attracted a lot of media attention, evoking unnecessarily emotions and controversy and generating some level of religious tension, that if not checked may soon explode. This time round, the debate was driven by a section of Christian clergy notably leaders of the newer Pentecostal, Charismatic, and Evangelical churches that had fiercely opposed the inclusion of these courts in the proposed constitution. Many of the concerns raised by these Christian clergy are bereft of intellectual clarity and substance and borders on a sort of Islamophobia, ignorance and a tendency to spiritualize serious issues. All too often, the newer Pentecostal/Charismatic types tend to spiritualize serious issues of national importance hampering constructive dialogue and pragmatic engagement with non-Christian faiths or religious practices. In an interview on K24 television in Kenya in May 2010, Reverend Dr. Tomothy Njoya argued that the evangelicals that were opposed to the new constitution in Kenya had shown signs of ignorance because "many of them go to theological schools where they do not learn sociology or political science but only how to say hallelujah." He then went on to say that many leaders of evangelical churches went to theology because they could not qualify to be admitted to university to pursue architecture, medicine, or law.[19] While I know there are many evangelical clergy who went into theology as a way to pursue their passion, one cannot but question the sincerity and critical analysis among many of those opposed to the new constitution.

While some have debated the very constitutionality of the Kadhi courts' Act, located in Chapter 11 of the Laws of Kenya, some clergy spiritualize the issues by fronting unfounded fears. Lets consider some of the issues fronted by Christian clergy: that the inclusion of the Kadhi courts in the proposed constitution elevates and favors Islam, a minority faith comprising between 10-30% of the population against Christianity, a majority faith comprising about (70-80%) of the population. The fact that Christianity is the faith of the majority seems to give some

Christian clergy and laity a sense of entitlement as if Christianity is the de facto state religion.

Other issues cited by Christian clergy are an unfounded fear of a well organized, orchestrated plan (on the part of Islam) of transforming Kenya into an Islamic state, ruled by sharia law, and which will abolish Christianity and stop the immediate spread of the gospel as soon as Kenya becomes an Islamic state. These unfounded fears and issues are hardly convincing given that Kadhi courts have been in operation in the country for almost four decades now and have not constituted any national or religious threat in the country's history. It has not hampered the growth and spread of Christianity which has continued to explode over the last four decades now. More importantly, Kadhi courts only affect issues of concerns for Muslims such as marriage, divorce and inheritance. They have no jurisdiction over non-Muslims whatsoever. Despite these realities, however, Pentecostal, Charismatic, and Evangelical views may intensify and fuel animosity towards Islam. Although both religions are reflective of negative attitudes toward each other and their relationship has been marked by continuous competition for public space, the issue of the kadhi courts points to increased animosity and suspicion.

Conversely the Muslim agenda aims at defending their religious and cultural values against increased secularization and westernization. These values that receive the support of all Muslims in Kenya and elsewhere constitutes a common religious denominator of Muslim identity: the need to allow Muslims to be governed by Islamic Law, respect for Islamic dress code, provision of food in government institutions in accordance with required Islamic norms, and public regard for facilities for Muslims (for worship and the celebration of feasts) equal to those accorded to Christians. These are the grievances that these groups have had to grapple with and in my view these are the issues that have thrashed both faiths into the public sphere in Kenya.

Frustrated by this fierce opposition to the inclusion of Kadhi courts in the proposed new constitution, the Supreme Council of Kenyan Muslims (SUPKEM) announced that it was launching nationwide campaigns to educate Christians about Kadhi (Islamic) Courts. From the Muslim point of view, constructive dialogue, debate, and understanding are the only pragmatic ways to go about this issue. This to me is commendable as the Muslim community has shown that education is the way to resolve religious conflicts in an increasingly multi-ethnic, multi-religious, and multi-cultural society like Kenya. The Kadhi court controversy has a number of implications in Kenya's public sphere: it has propelled both Islam and Pentecostal Christianity into the public sphere. In fact over the last few years, there has been an increasingly growing contest for public space between Pentecostal Christianity and Islam in Kenya. This contest appears to have increased suspicion and mistrust between the two faiths.

Pentecostals' response to the proposal by Muslims to educate Christians on the Kadhi courts was to first condemn it and then engage in a series of nightlong prayer vigils. In these prayer vigils, the Pentecostals engaged in spiritual warfare and employed the use of militaristic language or what is called the rhetoric of spiritual warfare to pray against the demonic influence and spread of Islam. The rhetoric of spiritual warfare is used by Pentecostals as a non violent weapon against their perceived enemies and as Englund (2008) has argued, human rights activists could gain from an appreciation of this spiritual orientation that can diffuse physical violence. Nevertheless, while Pentecostals may not engage in physical warfare, their utterances, discourses and texts that associate Islam with demons, Satanism, and witchcraft equally inculcate a culture of intolerance and a lack of respect for other cultures and religions and is equally as dangerous and unacceptable as physical violence.

Pentecostals' relationship with their Muslim counterparts has been characterized by misunderstanding and name-calling on the one hand. Pentecostals associate Muslims with terrorists and sometimes as people who are possessed by demons and in dire need of salvation. On the other hand Muslims accuse Pentecostals of being fanatical and dismiss them as loud noisemakers who do not even understand the bible critically. They accuse them of taking scripture literally and as a people that cannot defend their faith intelligently and philosophically. These direct wrangles between Muslims and Pentecostals in Kenya may have been symptoms of a concerted effort on the part of Pentecostals to fully become public in their participation in the political process in the country. The period between 2002 and 2006, for instance, saw the civic and public roles of Pentecostal Christianity become ever more visible with many actively participating in the electoral process of 2007 as I show here below.

FROM FISHERS OF MEN AND WOMEN
TO FISHERS OF VOTES

Propelled by a heavy appropriation of mass media technologies, an obsession with public image, the fear of Islam, and the need to countercheck Islam's influence, Pentecostals in Kenya have pervaded the public sphere but especially political space. During the 2007 general elections, for instance, Pentecostals fielded presidential, parliamentary, and civic candidates and asked their congregations to strongly support those candidates. In fact, an unprecedented high number of men and women of the cloth from Pentecostal and Charismatic Churches fielded civic, parliamentary, even presidential candidates during the highly contested and largely discredited 2007 General Election that plunged the country into a series of violence and bloodshed.

The men and women of cloth that contested for civic, parliamentary and presidential elections are Bishops Margaret Wanjiru of Jesus Is Alive Ministries International (JIAM) who successfully contested for the Starehe Constituency on an Orange Democratic Movement (ODM) ticket, Pius Muiru of Maximum Miracle Ministries (MMM) who contested for the Kamkunji constituency and who was also a presidential candidate, Pastor Mike Brawan Lumbasio of Metro Church International (MCI) Nakuru who put up a spirited fight for the Nakuru Municipality Constituency and garnered 17,000 votes against his rival Lee Kinyanjui's 23,000 amidst claims of massive rigging, Pastor Paul Kamlesh Pattni of Hope International Ministries (HIM) and leaders of Kenya Democratic Alliance (KENDA) Party and the Rev Moses Ole Sakuda, formerly a US-based preacher who contested for Kajiado North Constituency seat.

Others include Bishop Walter Owade of Migori International Gospel Ministries, Rev Peter Arunga Indalo and Rev David Mairo of Maranatha Church in Kuria District, Bishop Titus Khamala of the Cornerstone Ministries for the Lurambi seat, former head of Pentecostal Assemblies of God (PAG), Rev Dr. Michael Otanga and Pastor Evole Asienga of Nairobi Pentecostal Church who both tried to challenge Emuhaya MP and now speaker of the National Assembly Kenneth Marende, Rev Marksen Wafula Masinde of Kenya Christian Reformed Church, Bishop Joseph Kimani of Subukia, Zakaria Muritu of Bible Way Installation Ministries in Nakuru town and Pastor Dan Amakobe from the Christian Community Life Church Nakuru. From the mainline churches, the Rev Mutava Musyimi formerly head of National Council of Churches of Kenya (NCCK) successfully contested for the Gachoka constituency.

In Nakuru District alone, six Pentecostal Church clergy were all political aspirants in 2007. These are Pastors Mike Brawan Lumbasio of Metro Church International, George Mwaura of the Nakuru Happy Church, Daniel Amakobe of Christian Community Church, Zipporah Kimani of Faith Harvest International, Bishop Joseph Kimani of a small Pentecostal church ministry, and Zakaria Murito of Bibleway Installation Ministries. At least 23 members of the clergy from Pentecostal and Charismatic churches were in the race to the August House in the 2007 general elections. These developments signalled a radical departure from their initial stance before the advent of the new millennium, where Pentecostals were initially preoccupied with evangelization, soul winning, and getting institutionally established. Pentecostal political practice has been characterized by an endeavor to replace mainline churches in the corridors of power, by addressing issues of national significance and by participating in the electoral process. I shall expound on these dimensions so as to build a composite image of Pentecostal political thought and praxis. Pentecostalism is not monolithic and neither are Pentecostals politically uniform. There are a number of factors that have shaped the style and extent of Pentecostal political participation in Kenya. One area in which this is increasingly visible is through what is now called the National Prayer Breakfast and the National Day of Prayer which I briefly discuss in the next section.

NATIONAL PRAYER BREAKFAST

A classic example that illustrates ways in which Pentecostals have infiltrated the bedrock of Kenyan politics to enter the public sphere is through what has come to be known as the National Prayer Breakfast meetings. This prayer meeting which dates back to the early 1990s but which gained prominence at the turn of the 21st century, involves "born again" Christian legislators, administrators, cabinet ministers, the clergy, civil society and other senior civil servants in a very public gathering to focus on corporate political and socio-economic issues deemed crucial for all Kenyans. Once a year, politicians and the clergy, cabinet ministers and other powerful civil servants, and members of the business community come together for a prayer service over breakfast normally held in a posh city hotel and sometimes attended by the president and some powerful Pentecostal preachers usually from America who are asked to give the sermon.

Over the years the event has steadily grown from a small event to a large and high powered meeting normally aired live by most media houses and one that discusses issues of national importance such as corruption in government, ethnicity, human rights, and other social and political issues. The National Prayer Breakfast meetings provide born again leaders, especially legislators, with a forum to discuss issues of governance while also serving as a mobilizing platform where they can strategise about the future of national politics. The National Prayer Breakfast offers a vivid illustration of the growing presence and increasing political influence of the Pentecostals in the public sphere and is significant in a tripartite sense: firstly, it puts the Pentecostal clergy at the centre of national politics as the born again legislators can now form a significant political voice on parliamentary bills and national debates. Secondly, Pentecostal Christianity becomes clearly present in the public sphere as such meetings often receive wide media coverage all the time they are held. Thirdly, the activity strongly projects prayer as a political praxis and that the social, political and economic fortunes of the country as Kalu (2003, 10) observes, can be changed and reshaped through prayer. Prayer therefore becomes a powerful and effective means of influencing national politics and can be mobilized just as much as the use the ballot box to vote out those perceived to be delivering poor or no services to their constituencies. Moreover Pentecostal Christians demonstrate through prayer breakfasts that they are good citizens who pray for the nation and seek peace all the time.

THE NATIONAL PRAYER DAY

Another event similar to the National Prayer Breakfast is the National Prayer Day. This event that is held annually equally brings together clergy particularly Evangelical, Pentecostal, and Charismatic leaders who are normally the main organizers. Together with politicians, civil servants, members of civil society, the business communities and the general citizenry the organizers pray for the nation. On this national prayer day, Kenyans of all walks of life throng churches, mosques, and temples throughout the country to pray for the nation. This is particularly so during hard times or when the country is faced by national tragedies such as air crashes, road accidents, earthquakes and others. For example, in April 21, 2006 a plane crashed in North-Eastern Kenya, near Marsabit town killing 14 Kenyans, 6 of who were legislators who had traveled to the region on a peace-finding mission. A national day of prayer was held. The tragedy that deeply shook and shocked the nation was one in a series of calamities and misfortunes that seemed to rock the country since 2003. Among these calamities were drought, famine, collapsed buildings, accidents, untimely deaths of a sizeable number of Legislators and massive corruption in government.

The clergy who have always given spiritual explanations to natural or man made calamities convinced the president to declare a national prayer and repentance day. The supposed need for prayer and repentance culminated in the national prayer day, an event attended by President Mwai Kibaki and his wife Lucy, Cabinet Ministers, Members of Parliament, the Official Leader of the Opposition, leaders from different political parties, the Clergy (Christian and non-Christian alike) and Kenyans of all works of life. The event was broadcast live from Uhuru Park, Nairobi and received extensive media coverage. For many Kenyans, it seemed like God was angry with the leaders because of corruption, tribalism, and many other evils. An often quoted verse, "if my people shall pray, and seek my face and turn away from their wicked ways: then will I forgive their sins and will heal their land (2 Chroniches 7: 14), was the focus of the prayer breakfast. This passage has also become one of the most potent symbols sustaining the commitment to renewal and to solving the problems in the country within a religious context.

In 2008 one of the chief speakers was President Paul Kagame of Rwanda who asked Kenyans to shun negative ethnicity. He drew a lot from the Rwandan Genocide experience and narrated how he pulled out his country from tremendous challenges. The 2010 May 28th National Prayer Breakfast was held at the Safari Park Hotel and attended by President Kibaki, Prime Minister Raila Odinga and Vice President Kalonzo Musyoka, Members of Parliament, Cabinet Ministers and Civil Society. The sermon was delivered by Bishop Cornelius Korir of Eldoret Catholic Diocese who urged leaders to forge unity and shun hatred. Bishop Korir was very instrumental in peace building initiatives and humanitarianism during the post election violence of 2007-08. He narrated how he personally escaped death as he attempted to shield and shelter the victims of the violence.

Even though National Prayer Days are basically a religious affair, they are significant in a number of ways and could be analyzed as part of an "emergent political theology of engagement" (Kalu 2003). First, they strengthen the fact that in Kenya, religion and politics symbiotically influence each other and that the political realm is sacrilized or enchanted and politics is a religious matter precisely because it is a moral performance (Kalu 2003, 10). Second, they bring out the perception of prayer as a political praxis and that the social, political, and economic fortunes of a nation can be changed and reshaped through the power of prayer. Third, national and individual misfortunes occur through internal sources such as sin, pollution and acts of disobedience that offend God and attract punishment or the withholding of benefits (blessings). Fourth, repentance becomes the key weapon against such misfortunes and Kenyans demonstrate this through the National Prayer Day. National prayer days are now a common occurrence all over Africa and are symptomatic of the quick resort to the sphere of religion in search for solutions to life's difficulties. In a sense this helps bring together Christianity and traditional African worldviews especially the source and/or causality of evil.

What are the implications of this development for social transformation? Firstly, the entrance of the Pentecostals into the public arena creates a shift in mainline Churches' monopolistic role in civic and public life. It equally challenges our thinking about the roles of mainline churches in social and political activism. This is because, while social political activism has characterized mainline churches for a long time now, they are no longer the main players in Kenya's public space. The entrance of Pentecostal and Charismatic churches into the public sphere since the turn of the 21st century has seriously challenged the role and place of mainline churches in the country. In fact, the Pentecostals have not only forced mainline churches to adopt Pentecostal and Charismatic spirituality in order to survive the latter's onslaught, they have also constituted a real challenge to their long standing history of political involvement and created a shift in the country's social-religious history. It has also challenged the monopolistic position of being the "voice of the people," the "conscience of society," "custodians of democracy" that the mainline churches have held in Kenyan history since independence. In fact this has created a paradigmatic shift that "explodes the myth that mainline Christianity is liberal, politically astute and has sound social vision while Pentecostal and Charismatic Christianity is conservative, politically naïve and pietistic" (Kenneth Ross 2006).

ANALYZING PENTECOSTALISM'S CIVIC AND PUBLIC ROLES IN KENYA

The increasing influence of Pentecostal Christianity in Kenya's public life since the dawn of the millennium can be analyzed variously. First, Pentecostalism's role in the public sphere has grown significantly and in fundamental ways. This is because while in the past these churches have not had any socio-political ideology, it has recently emerged as a lot that is socially, politically, and economically engaged. As Ojo (2004) observes of the Nigerian context, while these churches would not normally support any political ideology or party but have rather sought to support individual born again political leaders as a way of strengthening and expanding Christian influence in the country,[20] today things have changed and these churches have resolved to get directly and actively involved in politics as evidenced by the registration of their own Christian party and the fact that many Christian church leaders have shown interest in active politics. But why did this otherwise political neutral clergy suddenly shift to politics? And if politics is a dirty game, as it is often regarded, why would they want to soil their clean souls? This is very important in mapping out the reasons why some of these Pentecostal leaders are increasingly getting interested in politics. What are the implications of this development for social transformation? For one, the entrance of the Pentecostals into the public sphere has created a shift in mainline Churches' monopolistic role in civic and public life. It equally challenges received wisdom about the roles of mainline churches in social and political activism. This is because, while social political activism has characterized mainline churches for a long time now, they are no longer the main players in Kenya's public sphere.

Churches, as Silk (2002) points out, are possessed of available meeting places, recognized leadership, fund raising capacities and connection to many parts of the communities in which they exist. Above all, churches as Silk (2002) further notes are groups of people already connected by social networks and used to cooperative activity. It is therefore easy to tap into large congregations to mobilize them to support a particular candidate. In short they have a large and powerful Christian constituency. Ogbu Kalu (2003) correctly observes that the Pentecostal constituency constitutes a critical election mass that cannot be ignored anymore. This large Christian constituency can easily be mobilized and can have significant impact and influence on national politics. It can equally change or shape the electoral landscape in the country. This was evident and came out very strongly during the national constitutional referendum in 2005/6. The Pentecostals mobilized their followers into a critical constituency and rallied it to reject the proposed constitution draft in 2006 to the embarrassment of the government. This role critical as it is does not however answer the question why the Pentecostal clergy are keen to make it to the August House.

David Maxwell (2006) argues that it is not so difficult to understand why Pentecostals are contesting politics now because Pentecostal leaders wield their enormous followings to influence governments to re-moralize politics. Moreover, while some Pentecostals have formally entered the political arena standing in presidential as well as parliamentary elections, African Pentecostalism has ambitions that transcend the nation state. Maxwell maintains that Pentecostal church leaders have been cold-shouldered and have engaged with secular leaders for respectability and public recognition as well as access to the state media and that politicians desperate for new sources of legitimacy have sought to secure a born-again mandate and to make use of the growing born again constituency.

Other scholars have shown that struggles for political power in Africa have in fact entailed the manipulation of religious symbols and beliefs of both Islam and Christianity. Actors seeking political influence have used religion to gain legitimacy (Falola 1998). The relevance of this point for contemporary African states is important, for when the "elite believe that their positions are threatened they fall back on the religious element, emphasizing religious differences in an attempt to draw sympathy from those of their original faith (Nzeh 2002). Meanwhile, one of the most interesting features of the 2007 general elections in Kenya was the fact that it saw new ways in which the religious authorities shifted the approach to issues of social justice. The clergy argued that the politicians had failed the country by engaging in corruption, immorality, selfishness and ignoring the parliamentary motto of "the welfare of society, and just government of men." In this regard Pentecostals were interested in taking over the political sphere in order to offer an alternative leadership that was grounded in a faith-based morality that would counter the failed political leadership marked by corruption that had come to characterize the Kenyan government. One may also see the need for Pentecostals to be keen to get involved in politics as a way of defending Christianity against such threats as those posed by the inclusion of Kadhi Courts in the constitution.

Interestingly, Kenyan politicians continue to court church leaders, often looking a little suspect. In May 2009, for instance, Prime Minister Raila Odinga was baptized in a highly politicized crusade in Nairobi by self-proclaimed prophet David Owour even though he had earlier visited the Legio Maria shrine fully clad in the sect's regalia. Similarly, the Speaker of Parliament Kenneth Marende was baptized at the Nairobi Pentecostal Church Valley Road in September 2009. Bishop Margaret Wanjiru held a church service for Maina Njenga of the out-lawed Mungiki sect, in October 2009, a few hours after his release from prison. In the service, hundreds of Mungiki sect members thronged her church for prayer. Since then, she has received numerous death threats and even recorded a statement with the police.

While the marriage between the clergy and politicians is some-times suspect, it appears like there seems to be some who genuinely appear to want to reform civic culture and sanitize Kenyan politics. Peter Wambugu (2005), a born-again Christian and an advocate of the High Court of Kenya argues that Christians who are men and women of integrity should be in charge of the government and should contest for both civic and parliamentary positions in order to sanitize Kenyan politics and bring some morals back to political life. He explains that it is the obligation of every Christian to be at the centre of the country's destiny politically, socially, and economically. He further points out that Christians are supposed to be leading the way forward as people of light because they lay claim to God's authority.

There is a belief among Pentecostals of the divine right of their religious leaders to govern in the cause of building a Christian nation. But while preachers in the past have plugged into politics out of their own volition, today there seem to exist a conscious effort and deliber-ate attempt by a section of Pentecostal and charismatic Christianity to strategically position preachers from these churches for elective parliamentary and civic leadership. This is even supported by the fact that many Pentecostal clergy who are not aspiring for elective politics are now encouraging their members to vote and get directly involved in politics in order to influence their political destiny and the course of Kenyan politics. To many Pentecostal Christians, God fearing Christians would serve the nation better and help fight corruption in public offices. The Nairobi Pentecostal Churches, the Nakuru Happy Churches, and the Deliverance Churches encourage their members to campaign as parliamentary and Civic candidates. Many of these churches often line up political candidates in front of their congregations on Sunday and pray for them publicly.

CONCLUSION

The resurgence of religion in the public sphere not only in Kenya but globally indicates some emerging issues: first, religious organizations are not only major team players in national politics but are also critical for the successful governance of nation states particularly in Africa. Second, that the prominence of religion in the public sphere necessitates debates and discourses about the place and role of religion in modern and emerging pluralistic and democratic societies where the state is assumed to be inherently secular. And lastly mass media has emerged not only as new sites for contestation but as significant and popular locations to propel religion into the public sphere. Religion is no longer in the private sphere but has assumed an increased presence and dimension in the country's public sphere.

The role that Pentecostals have played in Kenya's public life has been varied, complex, and ambivalent but nonetheless significant. There has been a sharp increase in political participation. Pentecostals argue that the pauperization of individuals and communities often manifests itself in the physical (health), psychological (emotional) and material ways as people struggle to eke out a living while inflation reduces their purchasing power. Political instability and the militarization of the society combine to create vulnerability, insecurity, and hopelessness. In Kenya today it seems a public presence of Pentecostals, including in the halls of power, is one sure way of bringing about spiritual renewal. As for its actual ability to bring about tangible political and economic changes, only time will tell.

7

THE CATHOLIC CHURCH AND CIVIC EDUCATION IN THE SLUMS OF NAIROBI*

Christine M. Bodewes

INTRODUCTION

In Africa, where the most common form of associational life is in religious bodies, it is often assumed that faith-based organizations play a leading role in promoting democracy. However, there are virtually no detailed studies of the public role of faith-based organizations. This chapter is intended as a contribution to the civil society debate examining efforts by one particular civil society organization, the human rights ministry of a Catholic parish located in Kibera slum in Nairobi, Kenya, to inculcate democratic values, behavior, and skills in parishioners through a four-year civic education program. I not only show how the parish ministry was able to inculcate new democratic values, behavior and skills in a small percentage of parishioners but also how it was not able to mobilize them to hold local government officials to account for their corruption and abuse of power.

---

*   Data in this chapter have also been used in the publication titled "Civil society and the consolidation of democracy in Kenya: an analysis of a Catholic parish's efforts in Kibera slum," published in *The Journal of Modern African Studies*, 48: 547-571.

I focus here on a time connected to the period often referred to as Africa's Second Liberation that climaxed in the 1990s, following a period when African nations began to lose their strategic political and military status in the post-Cold War era as foreign donors started requiring evidence of demonstrated progress toward good governance, multi-party elections, and market-centered economies before resuming aid and investment in Africa. In Kenya this was spearheaded by churches and civil society organizations, that have been regarded by some as key to democratic reform in Africa including the promotion of human rights and the rule of law.[1] Efforts to inculcate democratic values – such as tolerance for opposing views, trust in other political actors, willingness to compromise, civility in political discourse and respect for other views - are usually attempted through civic education and human rights training. Further, a civil society organization has the potential to mobilize its members to resist a tyrannical regime. By building an organization that can act independently and is willing to confront the state, a civil society organization has the power to hold the government to account and influence policy.

A growing number of scholars less sanguine in their views on civil society, identifying a broad scope of objections to treating civil society as the panacea for solving Africa's long-term political problems. The fundamental criticism of these scholars is that the advocates' "vision is based on a flawed conception of social realities."[2] Pluralists maintain that as economic and social interests diversify, more groups will be formed to represent these interests and as these groups compete with each other to influence public policy, the government will attain more information and thus will provide more efficient solutions. The issues raised in the civil society debate have been addressed in Kenya, but in a limited fashion. Apart from a few studies in the early 2000s, most of the research examines the role of civil society during the country's transition to multi-party elections, a period of optimism and euphoria; there has been little study of civil society's efforts to consolidate democracy. That scholarship also focuses primarily on the role played by non-governmental organizations (NGOs) and offers little insight into other sectors of civil society, especially religious bodies which are considered by many to be the most significant actors that promote grass-roots democracy and human rights in Africa.[3] This chapter fills this gap by focusing on the dynamics within the Kibera community and the parish, which its affected efforts and then assess whether the parishioners' new knowledge empowered them to confront local government officials over corruption and abuse of power.

KIBERA SLUM

The specific locus of this study is Kibera slum in Nairobi, Kenya. Composed of 12 contiguous villages, it is located seven kilometers southeast of the city center and covers approximately 500 acres. Kibera has the distinction of being the largest and most densely populated slum not only in Nairobi, but in all of sub-Saharan Africa.[4] In the early 2000s, the Nairobi City Council (NCC) estimated the resident population was 600,000 people.[5] With average densities around 90,000 persons per square kilometer, the settlement occupies less than 1% of the city's total area and accommodates over 20% of its population.[6] I focus on six villages located within Christ the King parish boundaries - Soweto, Line Saba, Shilanga, Lindi, Mashimoni and Kambi Muru - home to an estimated 340,000 people.

Most Kiberans live in structures made of mud and wattle; on average five to six persons stay in one room that typically measures 9.3 square meters. Since the residents do not possess title deeds for the land they occupy, the state considers them to be "illegal squatters" and has absolved city authorities from any obligation to provide them with urban infrastructure and services. As a result, the vast majority of Kiberans do not have adequate access to potable water, sanitation, drains, electricity, roads or primary schools, hospitals, clinics and recreational facilities. The authorities' policy of neglect has had far-reaching consequences. More than 50% of the primary school children living in Kibera do not attend school and the vast majority of children who are schooled attend one of the many informal schools that are privately administered and of inferior quality.[7] The lack of access to basic education is linked to low literacy and income levels. According to a 2004 study, Kibera reported the highest incidence of people living below the food poverty line in Nairobi; around 80% of the households lived on less than $40 per month.[8] Employment is usually found in the informal sector where wages are low and work is uncertain. Most people work as security guards, domestic maids, and food hawkers or as day laborers in factories and construction sites. In the absence of viable income activities, many resort to theft, prostitution, smuggling and illegal brewing of alcohol.

Kibera has a complex ethnic mix. Unlike most slums that gener-ally have one or two main ethnic groups, Kibera hosts over 40 ethnic communities and many more from other African countries.[9] Despite its melting pot culture, most Kiberans prefer to live among their shared ethnic group. Although there is no accurate census data, it is widely believed that Luo make up the majority of Kibera's residents.[10] To understand how 600,000 people live in the sub-human conditions found in Kibera, it is helpful to understand the local social, economic and political dynamics of the community. Below I briefly outline the key factors that influenced daily life in Kibera in the early to mid-2000s, a slum where conflict, instability, and violence were pervasive.

LAND OWNERSHIP

Kiberans lived in a chronic state of fear and instability because of an on-going conflict among five different groups over the ownership of Kibera. The primary claimant was the government who claimed it was the sole owner because the legal title of the land was vested in the Kenya Railways Corporation, a public corporation that has owner-ship rights over the Mombasa-Uganda railway which crosses through Kibera. As a result, the state contended that Kiberans were in illegal occupation and could be evicted at any time.

The Nubian community, a small ethnic and religious minority also asserted a legal claim to Kibera based on its historical relationship with the colonial government. Their claim goes back to 1912 when the British government first settled ex-Sudanese soldiers who had served with the King's African Rifles at a military reserve located in present-day Kibera.[11] Viewed as allies of the colonial regime, the ex-soldiers were encouraged to settle in Kibera, so they could act as an informal military reserve should the colonial government need their services at short notice. Although the colonial government denied the Nubians' request for formal title deeds,[12] the Nubians were given permission to construct rooms to rent to the growing influx of rural migrants, turning them into the dominant class of structure owners.[13]

Kikuyu structure owners who were allocated plots in the 1970s and 1980s by the local chief also laid claim to Kibera. After nearly 60 years of total domination over Kibera's commercial development, Nubian control was challenged in 1974 when the Nubians lost their seat in parliament to a Kikuyu politician and a new Kikuyu chief was appointed to administer Kibera. Protected by the Kenyatta administration, the new chief gave his associates an opportunity to build structures for rental incomes in exchange for unofficial bribes. Within five years, Kibera's population tripled and the Kikuyu structure owners emerged as rivals to the Nubians. Even though the Nubians were a small minority by the early 2000s, numbering around 10,000, they were a well-organized group that still possessed influence because of their commercial interests (they owned 15% of the rental houses) and political networks.[14] In 1999, Nubian leaders secured the assistance of the British government to negotiate for 350 acres of Kibera but the negotiations broke down due to internal conflicts within the Nubian leadership. Recognizing that they will be displaced if the Nubians are granted ownership, other Kenyans living in Kibera viewed the Nubian community with suspicion, mistrust and even hatred.

Following the lead of the area Member of Parliament (MP), the Luo tenants also asserted ownership rights because of their majority occupation. To further complicate matters, it is widely believed that most, if not all, Kibera was illegally allocated to undisclosed private interests during the Moi regime.[15] The ambiguity and conflict over the ownership of Kibera has pitted different ethnic communities against one another for decades, turning it into a slum infamous for ethnic clashes and violence. During the early 2000s, the most deadly clash occurred in December 2001 when 25 people were killed and over 30,000 people were rendered homeless as Luo and Nubian youth engaged in hand-to-hand combat for two weeks.

CORRUPT LOCAL GOVERNANCE STRUCTURES

Another contributing factor to the high level of unrest in Kibera was the pervasive corruption on the part of local government officials. Nairobi has a complicated and overlapping system of urban governance consisting of the Provincial Administration (the PA), an antiquated remnant of colonialism, as well as elected members of the NCC. The apex of the PA's authority in Kibera was the District Officer (DO), appointed by the Office of the President, who supervised several government-employed chiefs and their assistants. Even though the PA had limited authority to oversee minimal administrative duties, in Kibera it operated as a shadow government that was exploitive, rent-seeking, and frequently violent. Corrupt local officials routinely extracted bribes for ordinary activities such as repairing a leaky roof, selling vegetables on the road or walking along the railway at night; residents who resisted or were unable to pay the bribe risked being beaten, having their structures demolished or being thrown into a cell. Kiberans were also frequently arrested and incarcerated without cause as a way to extort payments of additional bribes. In addition, the chiefs acted as a self-appointed judiciary resolving a wide array of complaints such as landlord/tenant disputes, domestic arguments, robberies, and petty crimes. The chiefs typically rendered judgment in favor of the party who paid the highest bribe without regard to the merits of the case. Finally, members of the PA controlled who could hold meetings in the community, routinely disbanding gatherings where residents criticized government policies or advocated for a change in living conditions. Residents who tried to organize such meetings were frequently harassed, detained and even arrested.

POLITICAL VIOLENCE

Because Kibera constitutes a large voting block and is the political base of the area MP, Raila Odinga (commonly referred to as Raila); Kiberans experienced a greater degree of political interference in their day-to-day lives than most other slum areas. The son of the late Jaramogi Oginga Odinga, the nation's first vice-president under Jomo Kenyatta, Raila inherited the mantle of leadership of the Luo community after his father's death in 1994. As the most powerful Luo leader in the country, Raila dominated the community's political economy. First elected the area MP in 1992, Raila is well known for his ability to mobilize the grass-roots support of Kiberans, especially the Luo youth, sometimes using unorthodox tactics. During the 1997 election, Raila was criticized for manipulating youth wingers, young Luo men brought from his home area, to buy voter cards and threaten voters who did not support him. In the 2000s, youth wingers began to expand the scope of their activity regularly threatening and intimidating anyone in Kibera perceived to be interfering with Raila's or the Luo community's interests.

CIVIL SOCIETY

Given this history, political strife, and socio-economic challenges, what role do civil society groups play in Kibera? Because a full analysis of the functions of the different civil society actors in Kibera is beyond the scope of this chapter, I briefly identify the main sectors of civil society active during the early 2000s. The development NGOs, who numbered approximately 400, made up the largest sector.[16] The majority were small organizations staffed by local residents with limited resources and expertise that provided basic services including schools, clinics, water, latrines, drainage, and refuse collection. In the mid-1990s, some extended their services to micro-finance, economic development and community organizing. There were also a number of large international NGOs that addressed health issues, especially HIV and AIDS.

In addition to three mosques, there were over 300 churches; the vast majority was Pentecostal and African Independent Churches (AICs).[17] Most of the Pentecostal and AIC pastors came directly from Kibera and did not have formal theological training (see Josh Kuipers chapter in this volume for a specific example of such a church). Their memberships were small and usually numbered from 20 to 40 people; the largest churches had up to 200 members. The mainline Protestant churches and the Roman Catholic Church were also present,[18] but only the Catholic and Anglican churches had parishes inside Kibera— Christ the King (3,000 members) and St. Jerome's (120 members).[19] The others built churches on the periphery of the settlement to attract a mix of slum dwellers and middle-class people.

Christ the King Catholic Church, the parish which is the subject of this study, was administered by Guadalupe missionaries from Mexico. Organized into one main compound and four smaller, regional sub-parishes, the parish provided members with the regular cycle of mass, sacraments and religious instruction. Approximately 10% of the Catholics belonged to a small Christian community (SCC), groups of 15 to 35 Catholics organized by their specific locale that met on a weekly basis. At a typical meeting, members might recite the rosary, sing hymns, and read and discuss passages from the Bible. The parish also supported a number of social ministries including a primary school, health clinic and groups for women, youth and job seekers. There was also the Office of Human Rights (OHR), started by the parish priest in 2001 to supplement the efforts of the parish's justice and peace group. During 2002-2005, the author of this chapter, an American lawyer and Catholic lay missioner supported by Maryknoll Lay Missioners, coordinated the OHR with support from a parish-based team.

THE OHR'S CIVIC EDUCATION PROGRAM

Under its first two presidents in the post-colonial era, Jomo Kenyatta (1963-1978) and Daniel arap Moi (1978-2002), Kenya evolved into a neo-patrimonial state defined by personal rule, repressive authoritarianism, and clientelism. Poverty, ethnic clashes, large-scale corruption and human rights violations became Kenya's trademark characteristics. The repressive state also created a political culture of fear that turned many Kenyans into silent and passive spectators. Although pressure brought by a number of high-profile Christian clerics and activist lawyers led to the introduction of multi-party elections in 1992, the state and its structures, especially the constitution which had been amended over 30 times to give the president sweeping executive powers, remained authoritarian and repressive.[20]

In March 2002, following a 10-year struggle by pro-democracy groups to reform the constitution, the parliament unexpectedly empowered the Constitution of Kenya Review Commission (CKRC) to hold public hearings to listen to views of ordinary Kenyans and convert them into a new constitution. At the same time, the CKRC invited civil society organizations to provide civic education to raise awareness on constitutional issues and prepare citizens for the upcoming December election. This was the first time in Kenya's history that citizens were given such an opportunity. Taking advantage of the newly created political space, the OHR coordinator recruited a volunteer team of Kenyan lawyers to design and implement a civic education program for parishioners.[21] In order to reach a large number of people quickly, the OHR decided to train trainers from the existing parish groups who would then transmit the classes to their group members. The coordinator added a secondary target group, parishioners who were not members of the SCCs and were commonly known as the Sunday Christians because their only connection to the parish was attending weekly mass. The Sunday Christians would be taught the main points of the core curriculum during 10 to 15 minute inputs after Sunday mass.

From September through November 2002, a team of five volunteer lawyers, working in teams of two, facilitated classes on eight Saturdays. Approximately, 90 parishioners participated in the classes. Between 30 and 40 participants were the appointed representatives from the 16 SCCs and 10 parish groups while the other participants were youth members. The lawyers taught the national curriculum including classes on nation building, constitution making, democracy, and good governance. However, the course had a strong Catholic bias; each session started with prayers and a scripture reading that related to the topic followed by a short theological reflection led by one of the participants. In addition, the lawyers went beyond the abstract concepts and directly confronted the particular issues facing Kibera residents such as political violence, tribalism, and the corrupt practices of the chiefs and police. The lawyers also facilitated discussions on democracy and good leadership not just in the government, but also in their families, SCCs, the parish and the Catholic Church.

During the participants' evaluation of the course, discussions about the classes were positive, particularly about the class that addressed the election process. For many, the highlight was being provided with a sample ballot and then walked through the process of how to vote. Women felt especially empowered. According to one participant, "I learned that it is my right to participate in elections as a woman and I can't be denied the right to vote. I have to participate and I need to know the person I vote for is the right person and will help me."[22] A number of participants also commented about the impact of lawyers teaching the classes. The following comment is illustrative: "It was the first time for lawyers to come to us. There was a feeling that lawyers were rich people and could not come into Kibera especially when it was raining, but the lawyers were there all the time."

Despite the positive assessment and affirmation for the course, the overall impact of the civic education program was limited. The greatest challenge was the lack of interest by the Sunday Christians; fewer than 10 of approximately 800 were willing to stay after mass for a short civic education input. In response to this situation, the OHR arranged for the youth to enact several dramas during Sunday masses to convey the key concepts of the course. Although the dramas were well received, these occasions were limited in number because the youth, having spent considerable time to write, rehearse, and perform the dramas for the Saturday classes, wanted free time on Sundays to purse their regular activities. An evaluation of the Saturday classes showed that only six of the 16 SCCs were able to teach the lessons in their SCCs and, of those six, only three felt they had adequately communicated the lessons to their members. Only one of the 10 groups succeeded in adequately teaching the full curriculum. For those that received the inputs, the quality of the classes varied considerably; some trainers were given only 10 or 15 minutes while others were allowed a full hour to teach the class. Despite the sincere commitment of most trainers, there were a number of obstacles that prevented them from teaching their members.

LACK OF TIME

The number one challenge for the trainers was the lack of time, which was directly linked to parishioners' economic reality and their daily struggle to meet survival needs. During the evaluation, trainers repeated a common mantra that SCC members were "too busy looking for their daily bread" to spend time studying the constitution. Another common time constraint for parishioners was the constant need to return to their rural homes to assist relatives. Since many parishioners were the sole wage earners in their extended families, cultural norms dictated they assist family members struggling with financial matters especially illness and funerals. The growing number of HIV and AIDS cases was also a factor; three of the trainers were frequently unable to attend classes or SCC meetings because of reoccurring illness. There were also a number of trainers that admitted they were just "too tired and overwhelmed" at the end of the day to teach a class in their evening SCC meeting.

AUTHORITARIAN LEADERS

The nature of leadership in the parish was also an inhibiting factor for several SCCs and groups. Since many of the SCC leaders had been given limited training, many were capable of doing little more than reading the Bible or leading the group in prayer. Mirroring the top-down, paternalistic patterns characteristic of the Moi government, some ran their groups like a personal fiefdom, holding office year after year with little to no opposition, discussion or participation. This cadre of leaders viewed the trainers' attempts to teach about democracy and good governance as a direct threat to their power and they refused to give the trainers an opportunity to teach.

FINANCIAL MOTIVATIONS

Numerous trainers reported that some of their SCC members did not attend the classes because the OHR refused to pay allowances. According to one trainer, "People in my SCC didn't show up for the classes because they want to be paid. They think I'm crazy because I am doing this for free." Faced with a chronic impoverishment, many parishioners were not willing to participate in activities unless they provided a tangible benefit either in the form of money or a skill that could be parlayed directly into a job. In the experience of most parishioners, civic education provided neither and its possible long-term benefit of promoting greater democracy and accountability in the government was not perceived as a value. Expectations for payment were not unreasonable given that the payment of allowances was a widespread practice among NGOs that taught civic education. Indeed, it is almost the norm in the country for participants at any workshops or training activities to expect to be paid for participation. One of the civic education lawyers who worked full-time in a NGO explained:

> As NGOs we had to pay slum dwellers to attend our classes or we would not have had any programs to implement for our donors. We were outsiders with no point of access to the community so we established our credibility by paying sitting allowances. We enticed people to attend by putting them up in nice hotels, paid their transportation and gave them posh meals. For most of the participants, it was nothing more than a money-making venture.

Even though the OHR anticipated parishioners' expectation of allowances, they deliberately decided not to pay them. The OHR not only lacked the financial resources, it wanted to teach people who were willing to voluntarily share their learning, not people who attended only because they were waiting to be paid at the end of class.

APATHY

During the evaluation, the trainers also pointed out that many parishioners simply were not interested in civic education and many frequently referred to it as "a waste of time." Much of the community's ambivalence and apathy was directly related to Kibera's political reality. Decades of neglect by an authoritarian government that survived on ethnic patronage and violence had caused most Kiberans to turn away from the state. There was a sense among most parishioners that the government and politicians existed only to serve the interests of rich and they had no ability to influence the process. One parishioner noted,

"We only see politicians during the elections when they need votes. We don't know where their offices are or even how to reach them." Others pointed out that teaching civic education was a futile exercise because, regardless of what people learned, the chiefs still asked for bribes and parishioners still paid them.

FEAR OF POLITICS

Trainers from almost every SCC reported that some of their members resisted the classes because they objected to the parish talking about the government and the election; topics, which they felt were strictly off limits for the church. In addition, many SCC members felt that their meetings were the exclusive preserve of religious matters such as prayer and Bible reading, not issues of a secular, social or political nature. Like many Kenyans, some parishioners had a negative view about civic education because they associated it with corrupt politicians and vote buying. Some were also afraid to participate because they feared retribution by the chiefs and youth wingers.

CULTURAL BIASES

Cultural practices restricted the ability of some female trainers to teach. In keeping with cultural mores, women, particularly unmarried women with children commonly referred to as "single mothers," were usually given few opportunities to speak in their SCCs. As a result, the eight single mothers trained in civic education struggled with varying degrees of success for the chance to teach in their SCCs. In addition to gender obstacles, in at least one SCC the trainer was blocked because of age bias. The trainer, a woman aged 28, was prevented from teaching by her fellow SCC members on the grounds that she was too young. From the perspective of the elders, it was an insult for a young woman to hold herself out as knowing more than they did.

THE 2003 PROGRAM

The next phase of the civic education program started in the aftermath of the 2002 election, which witnessed the defeat of Moi's handpicked successor, Uhuru Kenyatta, by Mwai Kibaki. Despite an outpouring of national jubilation and high hopes that the new government would usher in a period of political reform including a people-based constitution, only 35 people regularly attended the Saturday classes in 2003. Many stopped participating because they felt civic education was relevant only during an election period; others were frustrated that they had not been paid at the end of the course. The 35 parishioners who stayed active in the Saturday group represented all but three of the SCCs and half the parish-based groups; the group was mixed with respect to ethnicity, age and gender with an almost equal ratio of men and women.

In 2003, the lawyers took turns facilitating 15 sessions on the following topics: the historical evolution of the constitution as well as the proposed changes and their impact, the rights of the accused, worker's rights and inheritance law. At the end of the year, the Saturday group also prepared a year-end mass and feast, which featured food and customs from their different ethnic communities, in order to celebrate their new knowledge as well as their ethnic diversity. During the mid-year evaluation, members of the Saturday group expressed a unified sentiment that learning about the law and human rights had improved their lives. They also said that more parishioners, especially the SCC members, should know their rights. In recognition of their limitations, the group members asked the OHR coordinator to hire a part-time team from their membership to teach the classes. The group identified a number of criteria that the members should satisfy to be considered; a degree or certificate from secondary school was not a qualification because the group did not want to exclude women. Following a formal interview process, the OHR coordinator hired four people, one woman and three men (referred to as the OHR Team), to teach in the SCCs. Prior to teaching the classes, the OHR Team was trained on the legal substance of the curriculum, participatory methodologies and Catholic social teaching that specifically addressed human rights and social justice issues.

Based on the feedback of the SCC members, the OHR Team and coordinator developed a new methodology that better suited the SCCs. Working in pairs, the OHR Team taught the classes through small group discussions and role-playing in order to facilitate greater participation and comprehension. They taught four topics: what is democracy, how does democracy work, the principles of good governance and nation building. After using several sessions to build consensus around the meaning of concepts such as equality, justice, the common good, and the rule of law in the context of their families and ethnic communities, the Team then facilitated discussions on these topics as they related to parishioners' SCCs, the parish, the Catholic Church and eventually Kibera and the country at a national level.

The response of the SCCs was unexpectedly positive evidenced by the amount of time the SCCs were willing to give to civic education. In contrast to the trainers who had struggled for 10 or 15 minutes, most SCCs allocated anywhere from 45 minutes to two hours for each class. A year-end evaluation as well as personal conversations between the OHR coordinator and the SCC members showed the OHR Team resolved a number of problems that had faced the trainers. As official representatives of the parish OHR who had been given substantial training, the Team had more credibility and skill than the trainers to teach the classes. Half the SCCs were so enthusiastic about civic education that they asked for the classes to be taught on a weekly basis. Although the participatory methodology slowed the pace of the classes, it was more effective. One Team member observed: "The level of participation was high. People spoke freely regardless of their age or tribe because everyone wanted to share their experiences in their families and what they saw happening in society."

THE 2004 PROGRAM

Based on positive year-end evaluations by the participants, the parish priest and OHR coordinator decided to continue the civic educa-tion program in 2004. The lawyers took turns teaching a total of 10 ses-sions that covered the following topics: rights of children, marriage and divorce, advocacy and lobbying and landlord/tenant rights. In addition, a university student studying African culture and Christianity taught sessions on poverty and African culture. The group also met for a plan-ning/evaluation session and a year-end mass and party celebrating cul-tural diversity. At the start of 2004, the core members of the Saturday group dropped from 35 to 20 with some classes attended by as few as 10 people. The cause of the decline reflected the reality of the Kibera environment. Five of the most active men in the group found jobs in other parts of Nairobi and moved to other slums. Two women suffered chronic illnesses and two others returned to their rural homes to care for sick relatives. A very active woman from the youth group started a hair salon and could not afford to close her shop on Saturday mornings. There were also a handful of middle-aged women who wanted to spend their Saturday mornings in their shops or houses taking care of their families and they felt they could learn the classes in their SCCs.

In an effort to attract more participants, the OHR invited all interested parishioners as well as a number of neighboring churches and youth groups to attend, but only a handful of people responded. The parishioners were either not interested in or available for the classes. The representatives from the churches and youth groups attended only once and did not return after they realized there were no allowances. The low attendance levels presented a dilemma to the OHR. Even though the Saturday group was small, the core members were very interested and they were the only parish group that consistently monitored human rights abuses as well as provided important information to the OHR. The lawyers resolved the issue by committing to teach classes if a minimum of 15 participants attended.

The OHR Team also continued to teach classes in the SCCs; the topics were good governance, nation building, forced evictions, rights of an arrested person, children's rights and inheritance. Attendance in the civic education classes remained high with an average of 15 to 20 people in each SCC attending the classes.[23] There were, however, some classes that were attended by more people because the particular topic related directly to practical problems in their daily lives. For example, the topic in greatest demand was inheritance due to the high prevalence of AIDS-related deaths. Not all SCCs, however, were interested in the classes. Leaders in two SCCs felt they had already been properly trained about their rights through other programs. In addition, most SCCs reduced their meeting times from three to four times a month to once or twice a month as a result of a conflict between the OHR and the parish's faith formation department. As the civic education classes became more popular, a power struggle ensued between the catechists and the OHR Team. The catechists felt the OHR Team was a threat to their status and influence because many SCC members preferred civic education classes over religious formation. A number of catechists urged SCC members not to attend civic education classes on the grounds that only the catechists could teach about the Bible and Catholic social teaching. Eventually, the OHR Team took the lead in resolving the dispute and it was agreed that each SCC should decide if it wanted civic education and, if the members did, they should choose one or two days a month that did not interfere with the catechists' schedule. Every SCC voted to continue with civic education classes.

THE 2005 PROGRAM

Although attendance in the Saturday group remained relatively stable in 2005, the number of classes was fewer due to declining interest. Between April and July 2005, one of the lawyers taught four classes on international debt, tribalism, political and economic rights and facilitated a planning and evaluation session. The university student facilitated additional sessions on culture and witchcraft. The group also met for its traditional year-end mass and cultural celebration. While interest had begun to wane in the Saturday group, enthusiasm for civic education in the SCCs peaked in 2005. During the assessment of the SCCs, which had grown to 28, all but two asked for the classes; the SCCs that declined were new and not yet organized. When the SCCs that had previously resisted civic education discovered that the other SCCs were learning about inheritance and property rights, the women in these groups insisted that the OHR Team teach civic education in their SCCs. From January through August 2005, the OHR Team taught classes on inheritance, marriage, divorce and slum upgrading. In September, the lawyers developed a curriculum to teach parishioners about the proposed constitutional changes after the president unexpectedly scheduled a nation-wide constitutional referendum in late November.[24]

In evaluating the 2005 course, the greatest amount of attendance and participation was in the classes taught to prepare parishioners for the constitutional referendum. All SCCs participated and the number of people attending the classes in the SCCs rose to an average of 35 or more. The OHR also taught the classes after mass in each of the four sub-parishes; attendance was high with 50 to 60 parishioners from each sub-parish participating on a weekly basis. Second to the constitution, topics related to day-to-day problems such as marriage and the rights of the arrested were the most popular and highly attended.

THE IMPACT OF CIVIC EDUCATION

Measuring the impact of the civic education program is complicated. Not only is it difficult to assess rising levels of knowledge and empowerment, the impact is also not always obvious or immediately visible. In some cases, the impact may evolve gradually and become manifest long after the lessons end. Despite these limitations, the annual evaluations and on-going conversations between the participants and the OHR revealed a number of findings about the impact of the civic education lessons on the Saturday group and SCC members.

INCREASED KNOWLEDGE

There were approximately 500 parishioners who enhanced their knowledge and awareness about the rights and duties of democratic citizenship, good governance, constitutionalism and a wide array of legal and human rights and over 1,000 parishioners were educated on the country's constitution during the referendum campaign. The classes helped demystify the law and equipped parishioners with information, both legal and non-legal that enhanced their ability to respond to socio-political and cultural issues that they considered important. Taught from a Christian perspective, the classes also helped parishioners begin to connect their faith to the responsibilities of democratic citizenship. Despite the increased levels of knowledge and awareness for the participants, the scope of the civic education program remained small; 85% of the parishioners chose not to participate. Learning about democracy and human rights was not a priority for most parishioners because of their preoccupation with survival needs. Civic education had also been politicized in Kenya. In an environment heavily influenced by ethnic politics, many parishioners were afraid to be associated with civic education because of its political overtones. Others lacked interest in learning about the government and political processes due to feelings of apathy, frustration and cynicism caused by decades of government corruption and mismanagement. Although the number of participants was negligible given the population in the parish and the Kibera community, the program led to an observable change in the participants' democratic behavior and practices in the SCCs and in the personal lives of the participants. The classes, however, did not empower most parishioners to hold local government officials to account for their corruption and abuse of power. Before analyzing why, I first describe the ways in which it enhanced democratic values, behavior, and skills.

IMPROVED LEADERSHIP

The most visible impact of the civic education classes was manifested during the SCC leadership elections in July 2004 when approximately 75% of the leaders were voted out of office. In the words of one Team member

> After we taught the classes on good governance, the idea that leadership in the SCCs was only for the elite changed. Many SCCs voted out old leaders who had education but no leadership qualities. People realized that it was more important for the leaders to be honest and fair than a graduate of secondary school.

Many parishioners also credited civic education with changing the approach and mindset of the leaders. The senior catechist noted, "Before civic education, parish leaders spent their time discussing small, petty issues. After they learned about governance and democracy, leaders started addressing bigger issues like violence and tribalism." In addition to removing the clique of ineffective leaders, the SCCs also voted for a two-year cap on all leadership positions, a practice they learned about during the classes on good governance.

ENHANCED PARTICIPATION

The civic education program also enhanced the level and depth of participation in the SCCs and the Saturday group. Many of the leaders in the SCCs adopted the methodology used by the OHR Team and started giving everyone in the SCC the opportunity to speak as a matter of routine. One Team member explained, "When the SCC leaders started to change their approach, for the first time, many people had the opportunity to talk and share out their feelings and ideas." Heightened participation was most notable among groups that were traditionally excluded, the illiterate and single women. Several women noted that before the civic education classes started, they did not feel free to pray in public in front of men because they feared being ridiculed. One woman explained, "In the SCC I now can say what I feel and I even disagree with men because I learned about my rights in civic education. I am no longer afraid that I will be laughed at." Parishioners' ability to discuss and debate difficult issues improved in an even more visible manner in the Saturday group. According to one lawyer

> The Saturday group started out with a lot of facilitation
> because they expected the lawyers or the church to have
> all the answers. Later there was much more listening by
> the lawyers and very little facilitation. We were able to tell
> them the law and they had the ability to question it and
> talk about what it meant in Kibera in their reality.

In both the SCCs and the Saturday group, civic education also enhanced the ability of parishioners to discuss sensitive issues related to tribalism, marriage and divorce and property rights for women, taboo topics that most parishioners had previously refused to discuss. In addition, parishioners grew in self-confidence and became less afraid to criticize the government or the parish. For example, in 2003 during classes on good governance, members of the OHR Team reported that the class was difficult to teach, "because people were not ready to criticize the government or ask questions." There were many people in the SCCs who felt the structure of the church was not following the structures of good governance, but were afraid to criticize the parish priest and leaders because they did not want to jeopardize their relationships especially if they were being given assistance with school fees or access to income-generating projects. The SCC attended by most of the parish workers refused to even discuss these topics out of fear that what they said might be repeated and they would lose their jobs for criticizing the parish. The situation was much different in 2005. After two years of openly discussing difficult topics, although a few SCC members still expressed reservations, most felt free to expose shortcomings in the parish including actions takes by the parish priest and other pastoral team members.

RESPECT FOR THE RULE OF LAW

Another visible change in attitude was the participants' increase in the respect for the rule of law evidenced by the number of cases that they referred to the OHR lawyers for assistance. In 2003, parishioners active in civic education referred around five cases per month to the OHR. By 2005, the average number of cases rose to 45 each month. The increase in referrals was attributed to parishioners' enhanced awareness of rights. Most cases related to landlord/tenant and domestic disputes, conflicts that had previously been resolved by paying a bribe to the local chief. In addition, there were numerous cases involving child abuse, rape and incest, illegal abortions and corruption on the part of the local officials. At the same time as the number of cases rose, the number of parishioners trained in civic education who visited the OHR for advice on personal legal problems gradually dropped. These parishioners started analyzing problems on their own and taking the initial steps to solve them; they came to the OHR only when they needed specific advice from a lawyer, not the basic information on the law. Parishioners' ability to resolve their own disputes was most visible in the area of landlord/tenant conflicts. In 2003, 20% of the cases related to landlord/tenant disputes. With the passage of each year, the percentage dropped. In 2004, these cases accounted for 15% of the cases and by 2007, rental issues numbered only 5% of the caseload.

BETTER CONFLICT RESOLUTION SKILLS

Civic education also equipped participants with better conflict resolution skills. Many parishioners who received civic education helped family and friends resolve personal conflicts and problems, especially those involving domestic matters, landlord/tenant disputes and demands for bribes by chiefs. As an example, one participant narrated

> My SCC had a lot of widows from AIDS and there was a
> woman whose in-laws tried to take her land. They burnt her
> house and were ready to chase her away. We told her what
> we had learned about inheritance laws in civic education so
> she went home and reported the actions of her in-laws to
> the chief and he stopped the in-laws from taking her plot.

Another parishioner, an elderly woman who was illiterate, was able to help numerous Kibera residents. She explained, "When one of my neighbors told me her rent was going up, I told her about her rights as a tenant so she refused to pay the rent. She explained the law to her structure owner and he stopped trying to raise the rent." It is not possible to measure with precision how many SCC members took personal actions to assist someone because many did not report their interventions to the OHR.

During this time, one sub-parish demonstrated how these enhanced conflict resolution skills were implemented at the parish level. In May 2002, the SCCs members from one of the sub-parishes decided to repair holes in the walls and roof of their chapel. When the local assistant chief demanded that the parishioner pay a bribe, they complied despite protests by the parish priest. Three years later, the same leaders were asked to pay a bribe to the youth wingers in connection with the parish's purchase of 10 structures near their chapel to build toilets and a kitchen for the nursery school. The youth wingers threatened to burn down the chapel if the leaders did not pay the tenants who had been living in the structures. The leaders from the sub-parish refused to pay a bribe or be swayed by the local community's call to use physical force in removing the tenants. Instead, relying on what they had learned during civic education, they organized the SCCs from the sub-parish and officially reported the matter to the local authorities. Following weeks of peaceful prayer meetings and negotiations, the tenants eventually moved.

GATHERING AND DISSEMINATING INFORMATION

The Saturday group members created an important communications network that gathered and disseminated information about human rights issues that arose in Kibera. At the end of each Saturday meeting, parishioners gave inputs on the emerging issues, problems and concerns in the community. They also regularly reported to the OHR any human rights incident they either observed or heard about from others. The OHR was able to document this information and disseminate it to outside interested parties from the church, government, the press, diplomatic community and other civil society organizations for use in lobbying efforts; no other organization in Kibera provided this kind of detailed information. Besides supplying information about how these issues were affecting the community, parishioners also disseminated information and advice to their SCCs, friends and neighbours about how to respond to these issues. This was important because the state's failure to provide the community with information had created an environment rife with rumors, lies and speculation.

In addition to improving the flow of information internally, the Saturday group played a key role in transmitting the viewpoints of the community to outside decision-makers. For example, there were numerous individuals, including academics, human rights lawyers, ambassadors and high-level international officials, whose interest in Kibera grew following UN-Habitat's decision to undertake an upgrade in one of Kibera's villages. The Saturday group was asked on a regular basis to participate in discussions with these constituencies about the issues arising in Kibera. The process of dialogue and exchange with high-profile decision makers enhanced the quality of information received by the visitors and raised the confidence and self-reliance of the parishioners involved in the discussions.

THE CREATION OF LEADERS

During a number of human rights crisis related to eviction threats and political violence, it was the OHR Team and the Saturday group members that provided leadership and guidance to other parishioners. They also regularly attended community meetings and spoke out for the interests of the parishioners. The Saturday group also produced several leaders in the broader Kibera community. As an example, one of the parishioners, an illiterate woman from Soweto, was elected as a representative for the structure owners in Soweto during a UN-Habitat slum upgrading project. Explaining her decision to stand for office she said

> I was willing to be the representative for the structure owners because I was not afraid. It was not easy for a woman to stand in public and speak but I got used to standing in front of men in civic education classes and I spoke out my own ideas so I wasn't afraid to get involved.

Two OHR Team members also assumed leadership roles. After four years of facilitating civic education, they learned skills in planning, participatory methodologies, documentation, and record keeping and organizing meetings. They also learned how to assist parishioners to resolve personal legal problems. As these two team members grew in confidence and skills, they became the primary liaison between the parish and the PA. For the first time, they started initiating meetings with the chiefs and DO to resolve problems in the community which was an important step in reversing a long-term pattern of obeisance and capitulation to the PA. In 2006, one of the OHR Team members joined the People Settlement Network, a grass-roots group representing all slum dwellers in Kenya and was elected the regional chairwoman to represent Kibera. In that capacity, she presented the People's Budget to more than 5,000 people including NGO personnel, diplomats and other slum dwellers gathered for a national forum to expose the shortfall of the country's national budget. Publicized on national television and in the daily newspapers, her analysis presented Kibera's economic reality to the whole country. In 2007 another team member was invited to establish a human rights ministry similar to the OHR in the neighboring Catholic parish.

INTERNAL DEMOCRATIC PRACTICES

The Saturday group also became more democratic in its internal practices. Unlike the early classes that were dominated by the educated men, by 2005 everyone in the group spoke freely and no one was excluded from the discussions. Moreover, the group on its own volition formed small committees to plan the curriculum and follow specific issues in Kibera. All decision making was by consensus, not dictated by a small clique. Accountability was also important. This was best exemplified in the group's insistence on following a merit-based interview process with the parish priest. Members of the OHR Team were the first people hired in the parish's history that followed such a process and it set a precedent that was subsequently followed for all parish employees. The group also insisted on regular evaluations of the program and the OHR, a practice that was eventually replicated in all parish ministries.

HEIGHTENED TOLERANCE, CIVILITY AND RESPECT

The program enhanced parishioners' tolerance and respect for other views. As a mixed ethnic group, the members of the Saturday group were keenly aware of the challenges of tribalism. But as the group discussed issues of tribe and ethnicity, the conversations became more open and respectful as the participants gained a deeper understanding of historical factors and their own role in perpetuating tribalism. Although few in number, their ability to meet as an ethnically mixed group and discuss deeply engrained prejudices and conflicts represented the potential of parishioners to address the multi-faceted issues related to ethnicity in the parish and Kibera. The group's diverse ethnicity was the center piece of their annual liturgy and feast to celebrate the successes and losses of the year.

RELUCTANCE TO PURSUE ADVOCACY

Notwithstanding the positive impacts of civic education, contrary to the expectations of civil society advocates, four years of civic education did not empower parishioners to proactively confront the myriad human rights abuses in Kibera perpetuated by corrupt local officials. Although some individuals in the OHR Team and Saturday group took small steps, the majority remained either uninvolved or dependent on the OHR to lead them. In evaluating the reasons why parishioners remained passive the OHR Team identified three key factors: (1) fear of retaliation, (2) restrictive church protocols and (3) lack of capacity and resources.

First and foremost, parishioners were keenly aware of the dangerous and hostile political environment in Kibera; the chiefs and youth wingers would not tolerate any activity that addressed human rights issues or challenged the status quo. One Team member explained, "Parishioners knew their rights were being violated but they couldn't publicly mobilize against the DO or chief by writing letters or holding meetings because they were afraid they would be 'spotted' and then targeted later for retaliation." The level of intimidation was high. The chiefs monitored the content of the classes and some members had already been questioned by one of the chiefs about what they were learning and what they were doing especially during the classes on landlord/tenant rights and the PA. Parishioners knew that if they confronted the chiefs they risked having their property destroyed and/or being flogged and thrown into a cell.

In addition to their fear of the PA, parishioners were afraid of the youth wingers who worked for Raila. One Team member explained

> As Catholics we were able to discuss sensitive political issues like corruption and bad governance by the PA, but we were not ready to take any action. If someone had tried to organize a meeting or protest an injustice, the youth wingers and politicians would have known about it; they have agents everywhere and they know everything. If someone is from their tribe, the youth will send people to warn that person off. But anyone who did not listen to them would be attacked at night or targeted for harassment later and even killed. So we knew our rights but we couldn't fight for them because the youth wingers were malicious and there was nothing we could do about it so we just didn't get involved.

In 2004, more than 40 bodies were found dismembered along the railway line; all people who had been involved on the wrong side of a political issue. Given the parishioners' fears and the real threat of danger, neither the Saturday group nor the SCCs wanted to become a strategic group within the parish that played a front-line role mobilizing for the parish's or community's interests. When parishioners shared their fears and concerns, the lawyers agreed that the threats were genuine and did not push members of the Saturday group or the SCCs in a direction that could risk their lives. In light of the political environment, parishioners preferred to take a less risky tactic of attending meetings and gathering information that could be used by the lawyers to facilitate greater dialogue with the DO, chiefs and youth wingers. Unlike the residents of Kibera, the lawyers had greater immunity; they did not live in the community and their families and homes could not be threatened. They also knew how to use the legal system to protect their rights.

The parishioners' desire to avoid lobbying activities also related to restrictive rules and practices in the parish and local Catholic Church that prevented parishioners from discussing human rights issues in their SCCs and organizing other parishioners to respond to the issues. According to one Team member

> A SCC member who raised any issue in his SCC that could be considered political like speaking out against corruption or the government would have been rebuked in front of everyone. Our Christians thought political problems needed to be solved by politicians and the church was there only for spiritual matters. If a SCC member raised a political issue it would have been seen as dividing people in the SCC because each person had his own political agenda.

In addition, the unspoken protocol in the parish dictated that a parishioner could not ask his or her fellow SCC members or the parish priest to take action on a socio-political issue unless the issue followed the chain of command. According to another Team member

> An individual Catholic was not able to call a meeting after getting information on something that happened in Kibera. If he or she wanted to address an issue in the community, they had to first tell the leader of their SCC

and ask him to address it and then the SCC chairman had
to pass it up to the sub-parish leaders who had to ask the
parish pastoral council and finally it was those leaders who
could pass the issue to the parish priest.

A parishioner who breached this practice and tried to take information
directly to the community or the priest without first passing through
the designated gatekeepers would have experienced retribution in
his SCC. Group members were also afraid to single themselves out
as knowing more than the others in their SCC. One active Saturday
group explained, "If you acted like you had new information for the
SCC, people would start saying you were pretending to know more and
wanted to be seen ahead of everyone else. No one wanted to be seen
that way because you would have been abandoned by your friends and
left on your own alone." In an environment where people rely heavily
on friends and neighbors as a safety net, parishioners in the Saturday
group, for the most part, chose to remain silent.

Parishioners' ability to take initiative on problems in the community was also inhibited by hierarchical practices endemic in the Catholic Church. Following a traditional Roman model, most parishioners,
similar to Catholics throughout Kenya, paid a high level of deference
to the bishops and felt they could not take a stand on a particular social
or political issue unless the archbishop first made a pronouncement
on the church's official position. The limitations of the church's hier-
archy were also felt at the parish level; there was a strong culture of
dependence on the parish priest to take the lead in all issues affecting the parish. One parishioner explained, "We waited for the priest
to do something first for us because we believed that was the proper
protocol. Any issue about justice and peace had to start up there with
bishops and priests and then move down to us." Although the parish
priest spoke about the need for the parish to pursue human rights
issues, his public statements were limited to generalized messages. As
a consequence, many members of the SCCs felt that they could not act
because the parish priest was not fully behind them.

Finally, the Saturday group and SCCs lacked the basic capacity
and resources necessary to lobby the government. According to Robert
Fatton, for a voluntary organization to participate effectively in advocacy, the members of the group require relatively high levels of education, access to financial resources and free time; all attributes of the

middle class (Fatton 1992). Parishioners had none of these traits. Most had low levels of education and even less knowledge of complex policy matters related to land, housing and corruption. They also did not possess adequate resources to undertake advocacy; they had no electricity, computers, printers, telephones and office supplies. People who participated in civic education were wholly dependent on the OHR coordinator to fundraise for basic materials such as pens and paper. They also had no formal leadership, organizational structure or access to decision makers. Parishioners in the SCCs and Saturday group also did not share the same goals and aspirations. Although four years of meeting together, praying and supporting one another on a personal level had created a new level of trust and friendship, parishioners were still divided along ethnic lines. Their willingness to expose the underlying tensions around the issue of ethnicity and share their customs and traditions did not translate into a broader sense of solidarity or a shared sense of Kiberan identity that trumped ethnic identities. As a result, even if they had overcome other inherent obstacles, parishioners were not in a position to mobilize a united front on the key issues that had political or ethnic overtones.

CONCLUSION

I have shown here that with organizational assistance and funds provided by an expatriate missionary combined with the professional expertise of a team of Kenyan lawyers, the civic education programme was able to inculcate a small percentage of parishioners with democratic values and principles in a modest, but significant way. The civic education programme not only raised awareness and enhanced the participants' communication and participation skills; it also improved their ability to resolve personal and local conflicts. However, only about 15% of the parishioners participated in the programme. The civil society advocates' hope that civic education can transform ordinary citizens into political actors is unrealistic in an environment like Kibera where people struggle with poverty, ignorance, violence and corruption on a daily basis. The majority of parishioners were either not interested or not available to learn about democracy and human rights; they preferred to use their time securing a daily wage or opting to maintain the status quo.

The advocates' belief that citizens trained in civic education will use their enhanced knowledge and skills to promote the community's common interests in the civic and political arena is also overstated in Kibera. After four years of consistent participation in civic education classes, apart from a handful of parishioners, the majority of people in the Saturday group and SCCs did not take initiative to hold local officials to account for a variety of injustices regularly meted out by the government functionaries. The key reason for avoiding the political sphere was related to fears of violent retaliation by corrupt government officials, politicians and youth wingers. Parish structures and practices, in addition to limited resources and capacities, also did not foster a supportive environment for active participation in social justice issues.

Given the repressive political environment in Kibera, the most important role of civic education was to break the culture of silence in parishioners' families, the SCCs and the broader parish. The main concern of the parishioners was spreading their new knowledge and responding to the personal legal problems of their families, neighbors and SCCs. As a result of decades of government-enforced silence and ignorance, holding the state to account was not as important as securing a place for open and honest dialogue where they felt their input was valued. Members of the Saturday group wanted to create a sense of community within the parish and discuss things together beyond issues related to their basic survival. Even though they lived almost on top of each other, they were not a unified group; they were too divided and too busy trying to cope to create a proper community. Dialogue and debate on social and political issues was a luxury, especially for the women. Through their Saturday discussions, the participants were able to see that they had common interests and they started to try to reconcile their differences and find a different way to respond. They wanted to find equal footing with other Kenyans in terms of their knowledge and understanding of the government, politics and the legal system. Although their dialogue did not empower them to immediate action, it was an important step in reclaiming their dignity and identity as Kenyans citizens.

8

REFLECTING ON CHURCH-STATE RELATIONSHIP IN KENYA

Njonjo Mue

"The need today is for Christians who are active and critical, who don't accept situations without analyzing them
inwardly and deeply. We no longer want masses of people
like those who have been trifled with for so long. We want
persons like fruitful fig trees, who can say yes to justice
and no to injustice and can make use of the precious gift
of life, regardless of the circumstances."

– Oscar Romero, Archbishop of San Salvador,
The Violence of Love

INTRODUCTION

This chapter is a reflection on the impact of Christianity on the
larger Kenyan society focusing on the role of Christianity in
shaping Kenya's political discourse. I also briefly highlight the role of
Christianity in ethnic and political crises in Kenya focusing specifically
on the violence that engulfed Kenya after the disputed presidential
election of December 2007. I do this knowing full well that this volume
is not just about Kenya, but Africa in general, but also having to admit
that although I have worked in three African countries and traveled
the length and breadth of our beautiful continent, it is Kenya that I am

most familiar with, and taking solace in the fact that Kenya does offer an example of some of the dynamics facing Christianity elsewhere on the continent. Finally, as a Kenyan human rights lawyer whose activism has been shaped very much by my Christian faith and inspired by the example of Christians elsewhere who have used their faith to push for social change, I will also share some of my personal experiences of speaking truth to power in an unpredictable and dangerous environment and the lessons I have learned on the difference individual Christians can make in Africa by taking personal responsibility not only to practice their faith privately and when it is safe, but also publicly and when it is risky.

CONTRIBUTION OF CHRISTIANITY IN SHAPING KENYA'S POLITICAL DISCOURSE

On 1st January 2008, as Kenya tittered on the brink of a full scale civil war following a disputed presidential election, I sat pensively at Ufungamano House in Nairobi amidst a hundred or so top church leaders from all denominations who had gathered at short notice to deliberate on a Christian response to the violence that was quickly engulfing the country. The city was in a 24- hour unofficial curfew as most people chose to remain indoors while the country collectively held its breath and prayed. They watched scenes on television that were reminiscent of what we had only come to associate with the worst of African civil wars with marauding youths marching bear-chested, menacingly brandishing machetes, and chanting *"haki yetu,* (we demand our right!)." In the Rift Valley, Central, Nyanza, and parts of Coast provinces, thousands of people trekked from their homes with their meager belongings on their backs and terrified children in tow to escape murderous gangs who were out to avenge what they considered to be a stolen election.

Incumbent President Mwai Kibaki had been declared winner of a highly flawed election and had rushed to have himself sworn in for a second term at dusk, but challenger Raila Odinga had rejected the result. By the time the brinkmanship between the two men and their respective parties was resolved through the intervention of the international community, over 1300 Kenyans would have met brutal and violent death while over 300,000 would be displaced from their homes and sheltered in camps for internally displaced persons (IDPs). The

emotional toll on countless others who were raped, forcibly circum-
cised, otherwise permanently injured and whose homes were razed to
the ground and crops burned in the field cannot be quantified.

My wife Katindi and I remember in the early days of the violence
watching on local TV a sad story of a Luo family facing the same predicament that faced others who had been caught at the wrong place at
the wrong time. The husband and father had been viciously attacked
and was admitted at ICU at the Kikuyu hospital while his young wife
who was eight months pregnant and her two year old boy sought
shelter out in the cold at the local Police Station as she and a hundred
or so migrant Luo workers ran to escape certain death at the hands of
Kikuyu youths out to eliminate them. We felt the need to help, and not
just because this was our Christian duty; we felt very deeply that the
very meaning of being a Kenyan was at stake and it was vital that we
go as the messengers of the Kenya that we were struggling to build; a
Kenya where the pain of anyone, regardless of the sound of their last
name, was the anguish of us all.

We therefore took great risk, set aside some of our own clothes and
gifts that we had received from our wedding guests barely three weeks
before, we shopped for some basic supplies, and headed off for Kikuyu,
about 20 miles North of Nairobi, in search of this family. We found the
young mother outside Kikuyu Mission Hospital with her toddler as
they waited for visiting hours to see her husband. We introduced ourselves and our purpose and struck up an immediate friendship. Soon,
it was visiting time and without missing a beat, she asked if we minded
looking after her baby as she went in to see her husband. The fact that
a Luo woman, whose husband had almost been killed by Kikuyu men,
would leave her child under the care of a Kikuyu and Kamba couple
whom she had not known ten minutes before was a sign from heaven
that, despite the dark clouds that had descended upon our skies, Kenya
would survive, and our generation would yet become the eyewitnesses
of the miracle of our rebirth.

But back to Ufungamano House. I had been urgently summoned
this New Year's Day by a friend who worked with a Christian organization to work with the church leaders in thinking through an
appropriate response to the unfolding tragedy. After struggling with
accusations and counter-accusations as to which tribe was to blame
for the catastrophe, the church had set up three committees to address

the immediate needs – a humanitarian committee to mobilize succor for the IDPs, many of whom were seeking shelter in church sanctuaries across the land; a political committee to try and broker dialogue between the two protagonists; and a spiritual committee to mobilize prayer and deal with the spiritual dimension of the crisis. This was supported by a media liaison committee to help the church communicate with the nation about the emergency efforts being undertaken. As a member of the media committee, I had a front row seat and was able to witness the division of the church leadership as it was usually near-impossible for them to agree even on the wording of a simple press statement without degenerating to finger-pointing across ethnic divides. As we wrestled with the various issues to be considered, news came in that a church in Eldoret, in which villagers fleeing the violence had taken shelter, had been burned down and that 35 people, mainly women, children, and the disabled had been burned to death. This was the most extreme but by no means the only case of a church being burned down during the crisis.

News of church burnings and Christians turning on other Christians from different ethnic groups added a whole new dimension to the unfolding tragedy. Kenyans are generally a religious people who revere their places of worship. That churches could now be torched seemingly with so much ease as a result of political conflict begged the question as to how seriously one could take the oft-quoted statistic of Kenya being a Christian country where 80% of the people claim to be Christians. Was this a classic case of Christianity in Africa being "a mile wide but less than an inch deep" as noted earlier in the introduction to this volume? As I contemplated the unfolding tragedy and as I listened to the church leaders who seemed unable to speak coherently, let alone prophetically, to the unfolding situation without themselves retreating to tribal loyalties, I could not help but wonder to myself what the role of the Church was in Kenya's volatile and polarized politics. I wondered how the Church had come full cycle from being considered the voice of reason in its consistent and courageous stand against dictatorship and oppression in Kenya during the one party days - a voice which even the most diehard Moi supporters dared not ignore- to the sad place where it now found itself on this New Year's Day. No one seemed to take it seriously when it attempted to express itself on matters political.

To understand the role the Kenyan Church played in the lead up to the 2007 General Election and how it was left struggling to find its voice during Kenya's darkest hour, it is necessary to go back in time and examine the way the Kenyan church has faced the challenges of each new political dispensation. But before we do this, let's get some figures out of the way that will help us have a feel of the now. There is no doubt that Africa "is now Christianity's most ebullient frontier [and] Kenya is no exception to the African rule of energetic Christianity."[1] An estimated 80 percent of the Kenyan population claim to be Christians. Of Kenya's religious groups, Christianity represents three quarters of the population and is characterized by a mix of Catholic, mainline Protestant, evangelical, and Pentecostal churches. It should be noted that a fairly recent survey of African Pentecostal and charismatic Christians revealed Kenya had the highest percentage (83%) of respondents saying religious groups should express views on social and political questions (Pew Forum 2006).[2]

CHURCH AND STATE IN KENYA: A BRIEF HISTORY

The Kenyan church as we know it today owes its roots to the missionary church, which made a huge contribution to Kenyan society, especially in the areas of education and health. I for one am a result of a missionary education having attended The Alliance High School, which was the first high school founded to educate African boys in 1926 and the brainchild of the Alliance of Protestant Missions. But if the Church did well in helping to lift the living standards of the colonial populations, it is also an inescapable fact that it did little to openly challenge the social injustices of the colonial era, preferring instead to engage in quiet diplomacy with the colonial powers rather than seeming to rock the imperial boat. As a result the church acquired the image of a collaborator in the evils of colonialism. This image of the Church in the colonial era can be gleaned from an article I stumbled upon in the *Daily Telegraph* of Friday, 9th May 2008. Reacting to calls for disestablishment of the Church of England, George Pitcher wrote, "The Christendom paradigm withered with the British Empire. The idea that the Church and the State co-extend is long gone, a dim historical memory of missionaries converting the noble savage, Bible in one hand, Union flag in the other. Furthermore, the Church should never have got itself into its unholy alliance with the State; the Church's ministry is at its most authentic when it is not at the State's heart, but a thorn in its side, a national conscience rather than a national Church."[3] There are a number of instructive points in this critique of the relationship between church and state in England. As a former British colony, Kenya did inherit many of the qualities being critiqued here. As Parsitau shows (this volume) there is no clear separation between church and state in Kenya and many of the challenges I mention here have to do with the church's close relationship with the state. This relationship makes it very hard for church leaders to hold politicians to account especially when ethnic identities and affiliations come into play as they often do. The same politicians who were fueling the post election violence were the same ones being prayed for and anointed in their various churches in the run up to elections. This precarious relationship, however, is not sporadic but rater has a history.

From Colonialism to Kenyatta

During the colonial era, the Protestant denominations and missionary societies were "politically quiescent."[4] They resisted the Mau Mau rebellion, which had been cast as anti-Christian especially its oathing ceremonies. This gave the impression that these Christians lacked nationalistic desires. After Independence, the National Christian Council of Kenya became actively involved in reconstruction efforts and its members were also theologically more liberal and dedicated as much to a social gospel as they were to the message of individual salvation.[5] This new focus on social issues led to a cordial relationship with the new Kenyatta government. After independence, the fact that the leadership of the mainline churches was primarily Kikuyu also led to amicable relations with the Kikuyu-led government of Jomo Kenyatta. "When you have religious and political elite controlled by the largest ethnicity, one would expect relative amicable relations, and when this balance is upset, a decline in conviviality."[6]

From Kenyatta to Moi

During the Moi regime, a sustained Christian critique of authoritarian one-party rule that was condemning ever more Kenyans to poverty and misery was a key factor in the success of Kenya's second liberation in the 1990s.[7] However not all churches participated in playing this role. The mainstream churches, Catholic, Presbyterian and Anglican "who used a standard incarnational theology, which holds that while the realms of God and Caesar may be autonomous, and while secular authority can be said... to be divinely authorized, nonetheless there are Biblical and Christian justifications for insisting on consultative government, on the protection of the human rights of God's children, and the more abundant life such as Christ said he had come to bring requiring more personal moral responsibility than an authoritarian state would permit."[8]

As Bishops from mainstream churches such as Henry Okullu, David Gitari, and Kipsang Muge of the Anglican Church, and Reverend Timothy Njoya of the Presbyterian Church, as well as the National Council of Churches of Kenya (NCCK) and later the Catholic Episcopal Conference, were taking on the Moi dictatorship, Moi himself closely aligned himself to the evangelical churches and was a staunch member of the African Inland Church (AIC) and never skipped Sunday service even as his repressive regime assassinated rival politicians, detained others without trial and tortured those who threatened his power base. As Lonsdale points out, "Kenya's evangelical churches, with a conservative theology, were more preoccupied with a call for the personal brokenness of being born again to a salvation that did not depend on political activism but upon faith."[9] The AIC in particular went so far as to formally disassociate itself from the NCCK, primarily over the issue of political involvement.[10] In addition to critiquing the Moi state, the mainstream church also engaged in civic education, especially in preparation for the first multi-party elections in 1992 and was at the forefront of domestic efforts to monitor and observe the landmark multiparty elections. The church was also instrumental in pushing for constitutional reform in the late 1990's. The church remained engaged until the 2002 General Election during which the KANU party, which had ruled the country for a straight 39 years since independence in 1963, was defeated.

From Moi to Kibaki

Following the defeat of KANU, the church, which had been vocal against the excesses of the Moi regime, was suddenly conspicuous by its silence on political issues. Observers noted the church's reluctance to criticize the Kibaki government even as the new ruling coalition crumbled under the weight of a pre-election memorandum of understanding that the President refused to honor following the 2002 General Election, allegations of grand corruption and other signs that the new government was not really committed to a new way of managing the country. In the run-up to the referendum on the new draft constitution for the country in November 2005, the Church seemed to find its political voice once again, though its agenda was narrowly focused on resisting the inclusion of Islamic courts in the new constitution. This was hardly the prophetic voice that the Church had come to be associated with during the Moi years. The referendum became the new frontline for forces aligned to President Kibaki and those coalescing around his former ally turned political foe, Raila Odinga, who was then leading a group of renegade ministers in opposing the draft. The campaign for and against the new constitution assumed the character of a campaign for and against the status quo with opponents of the draft arguing that it was meant to consolidate power in the hands of a few (read Kikuyu) elite.

At the beginning of the referendum campaigns, a vocal segment of the Church mobilized to reject the draft and publicly and forcefully stated their positions. However, with time, many key Kikuyu church leaders backtracked and counseled their followers to "vote with their conscience." This was interpreted by the "No" camp to indicate that the Kikuyu church leaders' change of heart was ethnically motivated. The church was thus seen as divided and serving narrow political interests depending on the ethnic group to which its leaders belonged. The prophetic voice of the Church to act as the conscience of society was lost, and the Church did nothing to evaluate its own role even after the people voted to soundly reject the draft constitution.

Approaching the 2007 General Election

In the run up to the 2007 General Election, the Church was seen as being openly partisan, along ethnic lines. Christian believers were clearly confused by conflicting "prophesies" of prominent Christian leaders, which predicted victory for various candidates and prayed and anointed them as God's choice for President. The uncertainty generated by these conflicting views fuelled the divisions within the Church. Reports from the Rift Valley indicate the church leaders used civic education, prayer meetings and other occasions to openly campaign for their preferred parties and candidates. It is no wonder that at the height of the violence in January 2008, when asked to comment on the role of the Church, a political analyst famously quipped, "During this crisis, we have seen the Church of PNU and we have seen the Church of ODM but, pray tell, where is the Church of Jesus Christ?"[11] PNU (Party of National Unity) was led by Mwai Kibaki, from the Kikuyu ethnic group and ODM (Orange Democratic Party) led by Raila Odinga from the Luo ethnic group. It was no surprise that political opposition and the ensuing violence was quickly seen as one of Kikuyus against Luos, as the rest of the country's ethnic groups were left to choose which of the two sides to support.

Against this backdrop, it is unsurprising that when the political crisis erupted leading to widespread violence in the wake of the disputed presidential election results, the Church struggled to find its voice. Church leaders could not rise above their partisanship and give the country a clear moral direction. Instead the church was reduced to a helpless spectator to the emerging tragic drama. The burning of over 400 churches during the violence was a sad reminder that many had come to regard churches not as sacred and neutral places of worship and sanctuary, but as part of the contested terrain of partisan and ethnic politics. In the immediate aftermath of the elections, the overwhelming impression was that Christians had been betrayed by their own brothers and sisters and their own leaders. Since the election, the Church has struggled to rebuild its credibility. The NCCK began by apologizing for "...sins of among others taking partisan positions on national issues [and] elevating our ethnic identities above our Christian identities..."[12] and is frequently in the news issuing statements critical of the excesses and failures of the Grand Coalition Government.

Challenges facing Kenyan Christianity in its relationship with the state

Given this roller coaster ride in the relationship between church and the state in Kenya I would like to offer the following examples of the challenges facing Christians in Kenya today:

1. Lack of spiritual formation and genuine discipleship among Kenyan Christians. This becomes easily evident when there is a crisis as happened in 2008 that so easily brought out the worst in us causing John L. Allen Jr. to write during the

violence that, "Kenya's slide into ethnic violence... ought to arouse the conscience of global Christianity, and not just for the usual humanitarian and geostrategic reasons. Nothing less than the shape of Christianity in the 21st Century is at stake."[13]

2. Ethnicity has historically complicated and restricted the Kenyan church's ability to critique the state. Lonsdale reminds us that many of Kenya's churches bear an ethnic rather than national character in the popular mind. "This segmentation makes it easy for politicians to scorn clerical critics as representatives of ethnic self-interest rather than of the common good."[14] Allen adds, "For Africa Christianity to fulfill its potential, however, it will have to come to terms with the contagion of tribalism."[15]

3. There is little or no biblical basis for socio-political engagement and not enough reflection on righteousness in the public square. Kenyan Christianity has not taken the time to develop the resources to engage meaningfully and prophetically with the powers. While writers like Okullu, Njoya, Gitari, Kinoti, and Kobia have written on the subject, they are not only the exception to the rule, most of them wrote for a different time. Today, Christian bookstores are filled with prosperity gospel and self help books and there are few resources to help Christians to engage the state. It is no wonder that Christianity has become inward looking with Christians hanging around Christian circles and rarely venturing out to engage the society in which they live. In this regard Kenya Christians are no different from US Christians who according to James Hunter, have been misguided to assume they can change the world by, among other things, changing individual hearts and minds.[16] Indeed, when Rev. Mutava Musyimi—former NCCK leader—decided to go into politics, many Kenyans, especially Christians, saw him as an important change agent in the political realm that has become "corrupt and misguided." After a year and a half in parliament Kenya's leading daily newspaper --the *Daily Nation*-- interviewed Rev. Musyimi on his role in

parliament especially because, unlike the days when he was vocal against the political establishment when he was with the NCCK, he had be conspicuously quiet in parliament. In response to this reality Rev. Musyimi said that he had learned that "the country is in the hands of the ruling elites and their gatekeepers [and] these people wield power and set the agenda."[17]

4. All this leads to a distinct disconnect between faith and practice as faith faces the structural and systemic realities of power and how it shapes everyday practices. Moreover many of the same 80% of Kenyans who profess Christianity as shaping their lives are the same ones who contribute to Kenya featuring regularly among the ranks of the most corrupt nations in the world. Sunday is sacred to most of them and they faithfully troop into churches all over the country only to go back to the market place on Monday through Saturday and do whatever it takes to get by.

5. Lack of balance between charity and justice. Kenyan Christians and the church in general have tended to focus on works of charity and shied away from questioning the structural and systemic causes that make charity necessary in the first place. Rev. Timothy Njoya made a scathing attack on this tendency when he wrote regarding the church's behavior during the Moi dictatorship of the 1990s:

> Rather than stand eyeball to eyeball with the dictators, as Jesus and the prophets did, churches waited for the crisis to pass with conflict avoiding prayer, looking for the opportunity to do reconciliation. [18]

THE ROLE OF INDIVIDUAL CHRISTIANS

As we reflect on church state relationship and the social impact of Christianity in Africa, our critique should not just be focused on the institutional church but on individual Christians as well. In an excellent review of African Christianity at the beginning of the New Millennium, the late Kwame Bediako captured it well when he wrote:

> If the 'Christ paradigm' has any significance in the public sphere, therefore, however essential it may be that transformation should find expression in socio-political institutions and structures, it needs also to find incarnation in personal lives. In this regard, Africa's most important resource for its needed transformation may well reside in its current Christian spiritual vitality, whilst the churches' greatest challenge lies with their ability to 'conscientize' their Christian communities in the direction of the 'social' meaning of their religion.[19]

Njongonkulu Ndungane, retired Archbishop of Cape Town, quoting Archbishop William Temple, also reminds us that "when it comes to political life, the church is bound to 'interfere' because it is by vocation the agent of God's purpose outside the scope of which no human interest or activity can fall, 'nine-tenths' of this would not be done by the church formally, but by individual Christians in their capacity as engaged citizens." This brings me to my own story as a Christian involved in engaging state power in the realm of human rights.

Though I am a lawyer by profession, I regard my human rights work as an intricate part of my Christian calling. My early inclination to stand up with the weak and speak with the voiceless would seem to have manifested itself early in life as I watched my mother, a worker and trade unionist at the multinational Del Monte factory in my home town of Thika, articulating workers grievances to management and motivating workers on strike. Despite her modest education and relatively low rank as a factory floor cleaner, my mother engaged in this risky activity because she said that all God's children should be treated fairly and should be able to get reasonable working conditions and a fair return for their honest work. When the time came to make my own career choices, though at the time I did not consider myself a practicing Christian, I naturally gravitated towards a career that would enable me to help people to access justice. My thinking on the Christian justification for doing what I do has been much clarified by my own coming to faith while at Law School and my study of the theology of social change as I read for my MA at the Nairobi School of Theology.

My reading of Scripture tells me that by refusing to leave their comfort zones and remaining silent in the face of oppression and injustice, individual Christians in Kenya and Africa have not been faithful to their calling. I do not judge them, but I do what I do because I have a passionate dislike of injustice. As I stated earlier, I have run into trouble countless times with the authorities for taking a stand against injustice. I do not go looking for trouble. Many times trouble finds me as the following two examples illustrate:

> As a believer and following the teachings and example of our Lord Jesus Christ, I have a strong belief in creative nonviolent action to bring about sustainable social change as well as to highlight injustice. On 31st May 1997, during a rally called by pro-reform activists to press for a new constitution, I led a group of activists in forming a human shield by kneeling before a fully armed contingent of riot police and GSU personnel to protect our civil society colleagues and members of the public as they attempted to hold a peaceful rally. While the rest of my fellow activists developed cold feet, I was left alone, unarmed, kneeling to face the police. The following morning, the local paper carried a picture of me on my knees against the backdrop of menacing riot police and paramilitary personnel under the caption, 'Praying for the Nation.'

In November 2004, as most Kenyans were grumbling and complaining about a new government had stopped the gravy train just long enough to get on and continued the culture of corruption, impunity and abuse of office, I undertook a one-man nonviolent act of defiance in order to dramatize the outrage most people were feeling at the time but did not quite know how to express. I drafted a 10-point memorandum of protest addressed to Parliament making the case why they had lost the moral authority to govern and pasted it on the main entrance of the National Assembly. A few days later, on 30th November 2004, after having done a reconnaissance tour, I scaled the wall of Parliament and took away a pennant flag off a cabinet minister's limousine (a pennant flag in Kenya is the symbol of a cabinet minister's dignity and authority, and only the country's president and members of his cabinet are allowed to fly it on their limousines). I did so to symbolically demonstrate the government's loss of moral authority to govern.

I was promptly arrested and charged in court with creating a disturbance. When the charge was read out to me, I sang the national anthem (whose words are a prayer of supplication to God to bless our land and nation) to remind Kenyans in court and the millions watching on TV how far our country had departed from the values that had inspired the founding mothers and fathers of our nation to struggle for freedom from British colonial rule. I then proceeded not only to plead guilty, but to beseech the judge to hand down the harshest sentence provided for by the law. The incident caused quite a stir around the country. Commenting on what became one of the most daring nonviolent action in Kenya's recent history, one commentator wrote:

> "There is something terribly wrong in this country. There is a devastating and looming crisis in our midst, and direction out of this needs to be established fast. Government and local authority functions have crumbled to the detriment of an entire nation. It is this sheer frustration that drove an exasperated Njonjo Mue to confronting two government ministers on the grounds of parliament on 30th November 2004. Njonjo Mue's bold and courageous act of confrontation will one day rank alongside that of the Boston Tea Party of 1773, the storming of the Bastille in Paris on July 14th 1789, the beginning of the modern civil rights movement in the United States on December 1, 1955, when Rosa Parks refused to give up her bus seat to a white passenger in Montgomery, Alabama and the brave, bold and courageous manner in which civil rights activist James Chaney met his death at the hands of white captors in June 1964 by telling them to their faces, "I aint running."[20]

On January 17 2008, at the height of Kenya's post election violence during which police gunned down unarmed protestors, playwright, civil society and human rights activist Omtatah brought activities at the Kenya Police Headquarters to a standstill after he chained himself to the gates of police headquarters in what he called the "protest of justice" to end the merciless killings of innocent people by security agents. Omtatah, a Catholic, was protesting a widely condemned TV footage that captured a police officer shooting two unarmed civilians in Kisumu.[21] During his "protest of justice", Omtatah yelled: "Action and inaction of a police officer on duty are not supposed to be motivated by any other interest other than public interest. This was not the case in the Kisumu murder." Omtatah, who had a statement addressed to the police commissioner waved a catholic rosary as he protested the loss of innocent lives at the hands of Kenya Police. It took 5 police officers about two hours to unchain him and another 50 paramilitary GSU officers to frog-march him to a nearby police station. Like me following my protest in Parliament in 2004, Omtata was charged with creating a disturbance in a manner likely to cause a breach of the peace. The question that arises from this then is, to what extend are Christians willing to create a disturbance to point out to the state when it has gone off course?

CONCLUSION

The Church in Kenya has had a checkered history in engaging the state. While some sections of the church have at times risen to the defense of the people against authoritarianism, others have tended to focus exclusively on personal salvation and shy away from political engagement which they have seen as too earthly. However, as one of the voices crying in the wild during the Moi regime poignantly reminds us

> There are some sections of the Church, which have stressed the utter hopelessness of this world and called upon the individual to concentrate solely on preparing his soul for the world to come. By ignoring the need for social reform, religion is divorced from the mainstream of human life. Christianity is not meant just for the soul; it is for the whole person... The Church must seek to transform both individual lives and the social situation that bring to many people anguish of spirit and cruel bondage.[22]

As if church leaders did not learn from the 2007 tensions and rifts, 2010 saw another protracted tug-of-war pitting the church and many politicians as they opposed the new constitution on grounds of the inclusion of the Kadhi courts and a clause on abortion. Only time will tell us the role the Kenyan church is going to play in shaping the political future of the country because the new constitution was passed as many ignored the call by church leaders to oppose it.

9

LITERACY, TEACHING, AND LEARNING IN SIERRA LEONE

Johanna Kuyvenhoven[1]

INTRODUCTION

From September until June, I am a Calvin College professor, preparing new teachers of reading and graduate students for a reading specialist Master's Degree. For the rest of the year, I work in Sierra Leone (SL) West Africa, to support the teaching of reading in primary schools. I've done this for nine consecutive years. I'm learning about learning to read in circumstances that are very different from Grand Rapids, Michigan. My learning emphases have necessarily shifted over the years. Pedagogy for effective teaching of reading demands understanding its complexity of discrete but interdependent factors. These include Sierra Leonean children's entry language skills and knowledge about print; primary school teacher classroom practices; teacher trainers' knowledge and practices; national syllabi, curricular directives and texts. To that end, I work with parents, teachers and children; with the SL Ministry of Education directors and colleagues from SL teacher training colleges. Over the years I have garnered financial support for research, workshops, conferences through Redeemer University College; Calvin College's Kuyer's Institute for Christian Teaching and Learning; The Canadian International Development Agency (CIDA), from USAID, and UNICEF.

The urgency for developing literacy abilities in SL is strong. The national rate is less than 40%. That statistic shows no sign of rising; today children are failing their national school exit exams in ever increasing numbers. The situation suggests that the potential for Sierra Leoneans to participate effectively in their own development, as it depends on abilities to read and write, is very low. I am responding to these conditions for reasons of friendship and my Christian understanding about peace, forgiveness, and responsibility. In this chapter I offer a model of how a Christian educator might respond to such a need. At the same time, the long story of (White) Christian educators in West Africa demands my being thoughtful and careful about a "response." The Christian missionary history of building and running schools in a country like SL, is strongly criticized by many scholars. When Kingsly Banya reviewed Sierra Leonean institutional education from 1700 until as late as 1960, he showed that missionary schools accounted for the vast majority (about 98%) of formal and institutionalized education. Into the present day, most schools in SL remain affiliated with a church. Banya wonders why such a long history of western-supported education has not culminated in a population readied to meet pressing current demands and blames the colonial legacy. He charges the church with playing a strong role in separating communities from their children's education and people's civic interests from education. He describes schools as church nurseries, established to create church membership. Missionaries developed curricular materials, which did not prepare students for civic leadership but rather for church participation. He accuses Christians of advancing social alienation on a community level; and denominationalism nationally. He makes a compelling case for missionaries' responsibility for a situation today in which schools have little relevance to the real needs of graduating students.[2] Overall schools did not nourish literacy abilities for economic, political or intellectual engagements on civic and social levels. Banya's point is not new or singular. Post-colonialist work demonstrates that missionary and other colonial interests failed to empower students for fully democratic and equal participation with those who established the institution of formal education.

These facts of the past gnaw at me, a White Christian of European descent. They tempt me to renounce the task; but faith in forgiveness and belief that we are called to be agents of justice in this broken creation urge me forward. I am discovering that my admittance of the pain and wrongs wrought under the name of Christ, lodge like a splinter under my skin, pressing against the repetition of past mistakes and warning against new ones. I am reminded to make prayer for peace and forgiveness real; to be humbly careful; remembering to submit my support to the real lives and needs of people I'm pledged to work with. Additionally, my commitment to literacy teaching and learning in SL is long term; working friendships are not projects or missions: they are human relationships that span place, time and experiences in genuine mutuality.

A SHORT HISTORY

My relationship began in 1981, when I lived with my young family in a northern village of SL. I learned to speak one of the indigenous languages at that time, while developing an adult literacy program. That experience did much to help me appreciate another way of living and traditionally oral ways of interacting. Since then, years and events have intervened, but my friendships and heart-connection with the Sierra Leonean people remained fast. In 2001, near the end of the brutal war (1991-2002) I returned to consider doctoral research for means to complement literacy instruction with traditionally oral narratives. I went back "home" and spent six weeks in the ruined landscape with old friends. Every village, town and city was scarred with burnt and bombed homes. Every home in the North could name lost family members and friends. Every person carried inner wounds of grief, horror, and loss. When I asked if there was anything, anything I could do to help, my friends said, "Yes, we need a school. If our children were educated, this wouldn't have happened." I experienced their request as a Call; to participate in healing for Shalom (true peace) in the world.

Dennis took the story of my SL friends' invitation for restitution to his community when they planned to build an addition to his Canadian Secondary School. He told them about a small town in SL that needed a school. His school community decided to share out of their abundance for the development of a school where there was no abundance. They believed that a Christian community is not local. The needs in Kabala, SL are also the needs in Vancouver, Canada. Both communities had wealth that the other needs. Canadian High School students would work for a genuine understanding about what it means to live in a "global community," shaped by economic, corporate, spiritual and educational interdependence. In Dennis' words, it was also an action for restorative justice, given the long colonial history that can still be read in events like SL's civil war. Christian communities take responsibility for one another's well being.

In short, by September 2007, a small Christian school of 180 students opened in the rural north of SL. While supported financially by the Canadian high school in Canada, it is completely directed and run by a school board made up of parents, local leaders, and the indigenous church. The school is providing education for the children of parents and grandparents I'd met after the war. The school is also a place of learning about the teaching of reading *in* Sierra Leone. In 2007, I was able to apply six years of research and studies conducted with my colleagues in SL teacher training colleges, and develop strategies and materials for more effective teaching of reading at primary levels. The new Christian school became a pilot study site where we could work with staff, parents, and children to explore the efficacy of new pedagogy for the teaching of reading. After the first year, I conducted the first tests to compare children's performance with peers at other schools. The results (which I outline later) show that small changes carried out using key variables may yield large effects. Before examining those results, I take some time to discuss the importance of literacy in SL and the too many other places, which share similar circumstances.

LITERACY EDUCATION: THE PANACEA?

Both secular-humanitarian and Christian donor agencies focus on education as a key component of International Development work. There are good reasons for this:

> Literacy for all is at the heart of basic education for all...
> Literate societies [are] essential for achieving the goals of eradicating poverty, reducing child mortality, curbing population growth, achieving gender equality and ensuring sustainable development, peace and democracy (UN Resolution 56/116. January 18, 2002).

As the UN resolution suggests, there is a common idea about a link between national wellbeing and literacy abilities. That link is born out in the United Nations Human Development Program (UNHDP)

Index[3] where low level literacy consistently aligns with nations who show the highest levels of poverty. The idea is that national capacities for literacy increase a people's business and commercial potentials. Literacy increases abilities for transparent accounting and international economic memberships. A population that can read has a higher facility for democratic participation through more equalized access. They can find and get information about practices and products that are critically needed. Readers have more choices for their independent development. As research demonstrates, when female heads of homes are literate, there is a higher likelihood of a healthy household.[4] In short strong national literacy abilities affect well being in every aspect of life. Thus, in SL and similar locations, donor supported development and post-war reconstruction efforts target primary school education.

The role of literacy instruction in education is prior; it crosses all educational contents and critically facilitates all school learning. Thus, educational, social and economic development, depend on reading abilities. For this reason, the Millennium Development Goal (MDG) of universal primary education is richly supported internationally. Primary education promises to prepare the ground for people's improved future. Children who can read can, later, use their abilities to participate in civic and national governance, commerce, self development, resource access, health prevention, agriculture and so on. These are extraordinarily high hopes placed on the development of a single "ability." The idea is succinctly summed up by Suso, "[there is] an undisputed connection between literacy and poverty ... literacy is a crucial socio-economic factor in poverty."[5] This reaility seems to be born out in SL, ranked within the "bottom three" of 179 nations for the last 10 years of the UNHDP listings. Concurrently, its literacy statistics are at 38.1%. For this and other reasons, a large portion of post-war reconstruction donor monies are allocated to education. However, the vast expenditures in programming are not yielding expected change. Suso's "undisputed connection" is not supported by the realities.

As development agencies act and spend for improvement, the paradigm of the literacy "cause-and-effect" is cast in doubt. The example of Sierra Leone, is just one among others,[6] to challenge the paradigm. Money and resources have been poured into support for educational enhancement but the results are worse than disappointing. From 2003-6, approximately 1.22 billion dollars (USD) have been taken in by

SL to support post war reconstruction.[7] It is difficult to know exactly how much of this money was allocated to education; but extraordinary efforts have gone into the construction of new school facilities; the (re)publishing of teaching and learning materials; distribution of text books; and increased teacher training and hiring.[8] During that period, while enrollment supports and school facilities went up, achievement fell. Today, SL students' performance scores are dropping while resources increase. From 2000-2005 the pass rates for primary school children dropped from 90 to 72%.[9] The Junior Secondary School exam results dropped from 50 to 40% (p. 81-83).[10] Similarly, during the same time span, the Senior (final) Secondary School exam results showed average pass rates dropped from 22% to 9%.[11] The trend continues. In 2008 the declining performance on national standardized performance tests was catastrophically realized when just 150 students, or 1.2% of all secondary school candidates, passed the exam. Examiners judged the main reason for mass failure to be students' weak reading abilities.[12]

In spite of the long passage of time during which literacy has been considered the panacea for development, we actually do not know "how" or "if" literacy activities and engagements really do spur development. Two decades ago Graff wrote:

> Perhaps the most striking feature of UNESCO discussions on literacy since 1965, when a campaign to wipe out world illiteracy got going, is that it is remarkably little based on either experiment or historical precedents. [A]ction seems as much based on self-evident axioms and hope as on anything else. UNESCO assumes that literacy is a good thing –more latterly, *functional literacy*. Furthermore, in no clearly defined or understood way are progress, health, and economic well being connected with literacy (1986:77-78. Italics mine).

The problem is at the root: understanding exactly "what" literacy is. A problematic paradigm directs practice today. The paradigm or framework of current expectations and literacy instruction needs to be challenged and re-developed. Literacy is a comprehensive social practice, an extension of participants' own language and daily interactions that depend on communication.[13] The constituent community of the school cannot be separated from teaching and learning in the classroom.

Without authentic linkages and shared practice across classrooms and homes, literacy is an empty activity; learning to read has no foreseeable practical use beyond classroom practice. Secondly, current teaching methods need to develop concurrently with social practices for including print communication. SL educators need to design effective and locally apt pedagogies, which merge localities with understandings about how children learn to read – in SL classrooms. These two ideas direct my work in Sierra Leone: the importance of linking authentic reasons for reading and writing with teaching; higher level participation in learning and developing more effective literacy teaching with those who carry national responsibility for programming.

FUNCTIONAL LITERACY AND SOCIAL PRACTICE

Current, common approaches consider literacy a skill, like driving a car, tailoring, or playing an instrument. It suggests literacy is a kind of task that entails special materials and tools; it can be employed for certain needs and then put to the side. This is nourished by a literacy "cause and effect" paradigm. Literacy is the skill to open access to resources, receipting practices, record keeping, participation in governance that demands reportage and reading, or to health practices of prevention. If they can read and write, they can do these things. Ultimately, this view of literacy is part of a deficit model in which the introduction of literacy yields abilities, practices and outcomes that are currently "missing." In Pierre Walter's "Defining Literacy and its Consequences in the Developing World," he suggests such ideas are at the root of ineffective literacy programming in development work. Walter writes, (considering adult literacy programming):

> The idea that functional literacy – literacy as tasks – will necessarily enable adults in the developing world to function more effectively in their encounter with the process of change and modernization can (also) be seen as a value judgment largely unsupported by empirical research (45).

Such functional approaches serve the need of the powerful stakeholders working for the development of a "work force" for its own benefit. They do not serve the political, social or personal lives of the target population. They perpetuate oppressive structures and deny genuine development.[14] Teaching for functional literacy, skills designed to fulfill roles delineated by outsiders, diminishes and misses the scope of an authentic literacy practice. It limits potentials for the empowerment of a people to develop its own path towards wellbeing. This understanding is also applicable to the non-print literate populations in Europe or the USA. The "literacy myth" as Gee calls it (1991:268) serves to perpetuate social inequalities. Nancy Hornberger writes:

> The often ignored language and literacy skills of non-mainstream people and the ways in which mainstream, school based literacy often serves to perpetuate social inequality ...[are part of a] long dominant assumptions that literacy is a technical skill, neutral, universal and key to both individual and societal development.[15]

In such a view, literacy is a skill that can be taken up, something like sewing or bicycling. This paradigm traditionally served development agencies as well as economic and political structures that depend on work forces that do not challenge hegemonic practices. Current scholarship is working to apply what is known about literacy as a social-cultural life practice; an extension or enhancement of a people's own communication activity.[16] Genuine literacy practice is inextricable from daily and ordinary social life.[17] Developed from Freirian principles, literacy is a social activity wherein participants enlarge their thoughts, interests and abilities through print interactions. Literacy becomes part of the complex of communication modalities, which enhance existing cultural and personal practices into new possibilities. It expands social capacity and networks of interaction, nourishing cultural understandings of identity, history, hope and experience. As Paulo Freire writes, reading is a practice that makes it possible to "create new human relationships and a new style of life radically opposed to the previous one" (1985: 31). Education for genuine and sustainable social change, creates possibilities for readers to be "concomitantly engaged in a critical analysis of the social framework in which men (sic) exist" (57). Literacy facilitates self knowledge and thus the shared "conscientization of learners" (57).

Authentic literacy develops with and out of indigenous needs for communication. It grows in a context that genuinely reaches for print as a best cultural practice. Uses of print direct the development of apt materials, relationships, applications, contexts for print.[18] When literacy instruction comes out of an intention to serve "economic development" programmers cut practice from its nourishing life force: social engagement or usual life practices. This has ramifications not only for the potential of literacy to enhance and extend the power of communication; it cuts literacy practice from deeper meaning making. Freire describes the functional approach to literacy teaching as one that educates subjects to "renounce(s) critical thinking" (Freire 1985, 117). True social cultural development depends on the capacity for the constituents to actively engage their practice and rooting literacy instructional planning and development beyond the classroom. If the goal is a fully inclusive and empowering literacy practice, constituent lives must be genuinely enlarged and deepened by a communication practice.

A utilitarian use of literacy does not unleash the generating and satisfying engagement reading and writing offers personal and social life. Rather, expectations for "basic" literacy teaching and learning:

> remains concerned with "effectiveness" often measured through statistics on skill outcomes, attendance, etc... and justified through correlations with important development indices such as health, agricultural production and economic take off (Street 2001, 1-2)

By my thinking, an immoral gap of standards is opened between the North and South for literacy. Southern "programmers" perpetuate the very condition it is dedicated to change by not yielding development to its constituency; denying true participation in knowledge and skill growing. As long as practice is not part of socio-cultural life, it will always need high level support for its development.

It seems to me that such a paradigm has made the low level hiring standards conscionable for primary school teachers. Since 2000 a massive hiring of volunteers and poorly trained teachers, has been conducted in SL, nearly doubling the number of teachers.[19] In Koinadugu District, for example, 89% of primary school teachers (2007) were untrained. These teachers take up positions in classroom that are extraordinarily challenged for success, as I will outline shortly. At the same time, children will need a level of literacy skills, which offer high levels of facility with print. SL children will be confronted with situations of extreme poverty related to complex factors. They abilities, which include the use of communication technologies to firmly keep

or establish peace, maintain good governance and fend off the vora-
cious appetites of non-indigenous entrepreneurs. Thus, their teachers
need expert skills, knowledge, and professional creativity to support
their preparation of children who must learn to read words to enlarge
and engage their world, which includes players who are out of sight.

LITERACY TEACHING FOR FULLNESS, NOT FUNCTION

Perhaps for those who come from settings like mine, a place where
schools are well endowed, enjoy sturdy facilitating infrastructures, and
are in the midst of a print-culture setting, there is a tendency to take for
granted the fullness of literacy as a way of life. In SL, schools are characterized by a rarity of textbooks, few paper, writing supplies or visual aids;
a predominance of overcrowded classrooms; and poorly or fully unfur-
nished rooms. These absolutely affect teaching and learning. These problems are currently targeted by aid agencies with the Government of SL.
School buildings are being raised across the country through SABABU,
Catholic Relief Services, UNICEF, PLAN and many other agencies. Furniture supports, and book distribution is underway. Teacher hiring is at
an all time high. Yet performance scores decrease or remain static.

The lack of success is due to more than material support. It may
well be because children and parents know that education promises
no authentic or useful application. Learning to read offers very little,
or no meaningful and interesting engagements beyond work in the
classroom. Literacy ability cannot be demonstrably linked to social
transformative power for the learner. Especially in a northern, rural
town like Kabala, models of literate citizens are rare. They hold jobs
with NGOs or visiting government personnel. They are few and they
are outsiders to the community.

Effective literacy instruction is challenging even under well-
endowed conditions. At Calvin College, Michigan, I teach for my
student teachers' abilities to "balance instruction." This means that I
work for my students' abilities to merge understandings of literacy as a
set of skills and knowledge with understanding its activity as a socially
constructed praxis. Literacy is an interdependent ecology of parts in a
complex, interdependent relationship. Children must be led through
these "parts;" using practices that are recursive, overlapping, balancing and connecting. They learn how the alphabet works while learning
how valuable it is to engage print. They learn how to read and recog-

nize a word while paying attention to their contexts which are on and off the page. Decoding skills and word-learning are meaningful when situated within authentic applications; comprehension depends on the learner's immediate circumstances, history of experiences and intentions. Teachers help children develop senses of usefulness as well as pleasure during print learning. Thus, the teaching of reading demands orchestrating personal and social practices with technical, visual and conceptual abilities. The discussion that follows shortly will show that in all of these aspects, instruction that meets the reader's need for social relevance to support skill development is not only challenged in Sierra Leone but unlikely.

In Kabala Christian primary school in northern Sierra Leone, we seek to grow children's abilities for a literacy that is such a social praxis; grown into complexity from foundational classes onwards. This means we work for developing understandings about social participation, critique, and discernment as part of learning to read in Sierra Leone. We want to support children's development for service, participation and leadership in their own local and national struggle against tough social realities.

AN INHERITANCE THAT CHALLENGES DEVELOPMENT

SL schools are challenged by an educational system not designed to respond to local and national needs for their children. Institutionalized education was established by the British government and missionary groups as early as 1824. Since then, other European and North American missionaries have also established schools across the country. As discussed by Banya and other post-colonialist writers,[20] curricula were designed to facilitate local non-indigenous governance structures and prepare students for church participation. Teaching was modeled on English as Second Language instruction; much characterized by pronunciation drills. Teacher-student relationships were characterized as rigidly separated; authoritarianism was characteristic. Because early education was conducted by non-indigenous persons, that distance between the teacher and student was developed through a history of difference. These and other aspects persist in affecting present day conceptions of education practice and relationships. Similarly, understandings about what should be learned was presented in timetables, to which teachers rigidly adhered.

In spite of independence and the ubiquitous, dynamic vehicular language of Krio, English remains the language of governance and education from the beginning. After independence in 1961, the educational model that was developed over the century and a half, was maintained for over thirty years. By the time the Government of Sierra Leone (GOSL) took up responsibilities for all national schools in 1994, patterns and curricula were well established. Although some structural and content emphases were changed, instructional delivery and its framework remain similar to what was done in the decades before this. It was not reformed to meet the learners' interests and national realities as these might guide teaching.

European or Western models are inadequate to children's educational needs in SL. Their environment is profoundly unlike that in Britain or the USA. The difference tempts many to consider Sierra Leonean children as handicapped by surroundings in which they are "missing print." This is emphatically not true. For children in a rural town like Kabala, life is rich and complete. Surrounded by family, friends and neighbors, children develop linguistically into the full capacity necessary to engage their world. Children tell stories, describe what they've seen or done, and ask for what they need. They demonstrate a rich repertoire of games and songs and ritual word routines. A large proportion of children have linguistic ability in two or more languages. They know histories, develop understandings about relationships and are actively apprenticed into household tasks. Under the guidance of adults and older children, they learn everything they need in order to be part of the social culture. They do not "miss" having print. Such a deficit view obscures the path towards developing literacy as a necessarily indigenous and genuinely useful practice. It denigrates the rich and existent language practices of the community and the complete readiness children have for learning.

The circumstances from which children come to school, must direct best instruction. That axiom means that lesson planning begins with the student's entry-level skills, their print abilities and understandings because these contextualize and animate learning. In Britain or the USA, this means that teachers expect that their children have learned that letters communicate information, give directions, name ingredients, tell stories and guide activities before they come to school. By means of environmental encounters and engagements, children have learned about the uses of print. They have developed schema, or mind-held categories for print that support further learning about print use. Children have understood that if they learn how to use letters they can know what is on a menu, find the bathroom, play video games, and drive a car when they grow up. These motivate the new readers who come to school. Teachers expect that their entry-level children have begun to understand a little of how the alphabet works; the alphabetic concept of sign for sounds of words is in development.

Such expectations contradict the reality of most Sierra Leonean children who come to their first classroom. As noted earlier, it must be emphasized that children and their parents live very well without using paper, books, or other notes. The problem lies in curricula that do not meet the circumstances of social experiences and environments from which these children enter the classroom. Instruction is poorly designed to meet children's abilities and knowledges when they come to school. Examination of national syllabi and texts, and my extensive classroom observations bear this out. Rather than scaffolding with children's genuine starting points for learning about print, they take up material, activities, social relationships, and communication work to purposes, which elude their capacity for meaning making or application. They engage with learning that has weak relevance to their lives outside the classroom wall. This disconnection has ramifications beyond literacy, teaching, and learning. Additionally, neither is education directed by current economic, social, political, cultural realities.

MEETING THE CHALLENGES TO TEACHING READING

I have been learning about the teaching of reading in SL since 2001. With colleagues from all the national teacher training colleges in the area of language arts, we have conducted research, focus group studies and conferences at which we studied the complexity of contributing components to effective instruction. In the Kabala Christian school, I had the opportunity to take this learning and develop practices to respond with an intervention. Together with the headmaster we integrated several emphases and changes with the current national curriculum and directives of the SL Education Act 2004. I was careful in this. It was important to choose key strategies, a few emphases that promised significant variation. They had to be compatible with existing practices; be possible for locally certified teachers to take up; be in congruence with the classroom and its locale.

The Alphabetic Concept

Sierra Leonean children's print understandings are in their very earliest stages. Most children have had no opportunity to learn about how print works. They know that writing can be used to communicate through personal letters. This is one of the most common uses of print. However, children that I have interviewed do not easily distinguish print from design on products or fabric. The great majority of children I have observed and worked with in more rural villages, do not have experience handling paper, pencils, or books. When they go to school, they simply know this is important and their parents want them to go there.

There is one strong example of reading and writing for most young learners: Q'uranic learning. Although nearly all children have experienced this literacy practice, it is fundamentally dissimilar with alphabet based reading and writing in concept, materials and practice. Q'uranic learning entails rote memorization of copied, Arabic scripted text. It is usually written with ink or charcoal on hand held boards from right to left. As it compares with alphabet-based literacy, there is, importantly, a difference in directionality and material use. Text is read from right to left. Boards and ink are used for writing. Writing activity is copying. The instructional interaction is also at variance. Students repeatedly recite the text until it is memorized during regular sessions on the Imam's[21] veranda. By practice and application, the goal is memorization of Arabic language text, not decoding abilities. The text serves to remind. Reading is action relevant only to religious and legal practice (Sharia) or related discussions. Q'uranic texts and Arabic script are rarely used beyond these applications. For example, I have never seen it used to write any of the Sierra Leonean languages.

Q'uranic reading is vital to its spiritual and religious application. However, as a model for literacy practice, it does not offer an exemplar for the teaching of reading with the alphabet. It involves significantly different cognitive engagements. Memorization of letters and words creates memories of precise sections of Q'uranic verse to be accessible and deployable from mind to heart or to mouth. Script instigates remembrance of scripture. As we think about children's learning about literacy, it is important to realize that reading the Q'uran entails materials, approaches, skill developments, teaching and learning relationships and applications that vary entirely with alphabetic abilities. Using the alphabet to read and write depends on first understanding that language is made of sounds and that those sounds can be represented by letters that help a reader recall "talk." Letters do not make words, they make sounds. Letters together and sounds together make words. These can "talk" in any language. I've expressed this as simply as possible; however this understanding is a profoundly complex and abstract idea.

It is fair to say this relationship between words and sounds is an understanding that develops over extensive time and experience; perhaps 2-3 years. Consider then, that children begin learning this concept in another language (English) and without supporting experiences. The concept is completely disconnected from any meaningful or real situation. Additionally, they learn this abstract idea in crowded rooms with only a chalkboard before them. They need to learn how to make and use those letters-that-make-sounds well enough to automatically decode letters, words, and whole texts. They must learn that texts are dynamic; that is, word choices and their order vary with subjects of reading, which in turn differ by genre, usage, and applications; that reading and writing are actions for planned outcomes subject to intentions and needs. There is no text to be memorized. This difference between two kinds of literacy teaching and learning, Q'uranic scripture and alphabet literacy abilities is critical. It must be realized by professional educators that children experience both literacies in the same location of low-level print. This has far more significance to the discussion of "literacy learning" in similar circumstances than I have been able to find.

For now, I point out that in the classrooms I observed, and in my conversations with over three hundred (300) primary school teachers at workshops, the current approach for teaching the alphabet is wholly inadequate. Instruction needs to support children's development of a sound-letter relationship while using real contexts for thinking about it. In the first place, not enough time or emphasis is given to learning correlations between signs and sounds to an automatic ability. Secondly, teachers do not successfully teach how the alphabet *works*. Teaching is guided by a whole language approach, or whole word memorization strategy. While this approach works within a more balanced approach, or where there is an abundance of material, the prognosis for its success here is minimal if not doubtful.

This situation may also be noted in children's writing. Writing letters critically supports alphabet learning. For example, if I say to my listener, "Write 'bligshterisk." Not knowing the meaning of this "word"

I made up, the writer repeats in her mind: "blig- shhhh- ter- isk" while matching sounds to letters on the paper. This develops phonemic awareness, fluency, syllable pattern recognition, spelling abilities, and letter-sound automaticity. Children need much work with writing in early instruction. The paucity of writing materials, that is just paper and pencils, is especially extreme at the earliest school levels. However, it is critically needed at that time.

My studies of children's visual and motor skills through their drawings showed good, even high levels of fine motor skills and control. Given paper and crayons or charcoal, and some encouragement, they draw lorries, houses, people, common foods, and so on. They demonstrate proportion, relationship, and good understandings of two-dimensional drawings as representations of reality. To me, that was especially astonishing given the amount of practice children had. But it is uncommon to find what is usual among children who live in print cultures. Such children regularly provide "text" in the form of small markings alongside their drawings. Often called "scribbling," children distinguish these additional markings from the other more figurative or representational parts of the drawing. Print-culture children distinguish one kind of representation from another. In this, they develop the concept of "talk on paper;" they develop habits of directionality and letter concepts. In all the drawings I have collected from children in Sierra Leone, such markings are rare.

The previous short descriptions suggest several key points for instructional planning. Teachers need to include their school community when they work for authentic applications of print. They must link homes and schools to support and share literacy teaching work. Early classroom instruction must include high levels of print engagements to learn about how print works. For example, product labels, names of children and towns, maps, lists should be commonly brought into the room. Materials can include children's songs and games on chart paper, storybooks, announcements, and information texts. Reading aloud should happen very often, to link talk with print. A knowledgeable teacher realizes that children need many and varied print engagements before they begin to develop understandings of print and alphabetic concepts. Alphabet-concept learning is a matter of experience that gradually becomes knowledge. And finally, developing automatic relationships between letters and their sounds entails extensively repeated practice in an environment of unfamiliarity with print. At this time, none of this is common.

My work in the pilot study with the Kabala Christian School shows that if such emphasis is applied, it is possible for children to grow such understandings over the course of a year. The Kabala Christian School hosts regular meetings with parents where they talk about how they together support their children learning to read. Parents are taught to give attention for print on products and other local uses of print. In the classroom, teachers bring products to classes to show and make meaningful examples and applications of letter use. They bring name cards, labels, personal letters, notes, maps of the school area and so on. All the classes in Kabala have an alphabet strip above the board; their teachers have a set of flash cards we made together. Every day, teachers in the first 3 classes (grades 1-3) play one of the 12 games and activities we learned together. The games begin with simple alphabet letter recognition and move on to letter-sound associations. As recognition and automatic associations develop, teachers move to using letters for initial sounds and then to naming items with "that sound" at the beginning or end. These games demand only 10-15 minutes per day. It is a lively time, full of the sounds of play and laughter. However, the results are plain. After the first year, my tests showed that the children in this school outperformed the two other primary schools in the same area by significant margins. In the letter recognition test, at the end of their first year of instruction, Class I children in the pilot study scored 95%; their counterparts scored 47% and 36%. More significantly, children in the pilot study scored 80% on the test for phonemic awareness; both comparison classrooms from two other schools scored 0%. Class II scored 72% on the phonemic awareness tests (sign = sound) and the comparison classes scored 2% and 0% respectively after two years of instruction.

These results show that intentional, sustained teaching of sign and sound relationships can be successful in a SL classroom where teachers had support for such an emphasis. The results also show that change is possible with very minimal materials and instructional time. Children at the model school and all the other schools have strong language abilities, access to many songs, games and ritual oral interactions. If this uncommonly strong set of resources were joined with literacy teaching and learning, so much can happen.

Learners need reading materials

As the chief in Yiriah commented, "Without tools we cannot farm; without books, how will children learn to read?" He summarized well an established body of research without having read it. Predictors for the successful acquisition of independent reading abilities are directly related to the amount of reading done in the early years. In such print cultures as in the USA, successful readers in grade three minimally experienced 1000 hours of read-aloud time with caregivers before they reached Kindergarten. The more a child reads in grade one and two, the more successful that child is in the middle and secondary years of schooling. Often called the "Matthew Principle" of reading, it summarizes the situation to say that, "to those who read much, more success will be given." There are reasons for this, beyond the motivation of pleasant experiences of reading with a beloved caregiver. Repeated textual engagements develop key print concept understandings such as directionality of writing; conventions of print such as punctuation, letter clusters, word groupings, and such book concepts as titles, page numbers and captions. Children who read a lot, develop a repertoire of sight words, clusters of letters read as one sign. Only frequent reading develops fluency in the same way that lots of swimming develops a good swimmer.

In this case children in all SL schools from the lowest to highest levels are nearly prevented from growing fluency. In the early years, there are many children who do not hold or read a book or even work with paper at all. I have met many college students who say they never held a book in their hands until they were in Class IV or V (Grade 4-5). There were students who told me that they used a slate until Class VI. Travels and extensive classroom visits have proven that in the great majority of cases, SL children's learning to read depends on a single book held at the front of the class; or more commonly, on a section of text printed on the blackboard.

The paucity of reading materials in Sierra Leone is well documented.[22] From Class I to Form VI (grade 1-grade 12), many learners' print resource-access is only what they have copied from the blackboard. Only in the older classes that children begin using notebooks for copying. In Class I-III, most children have spent most of their time chanting word lists; copying text fragments on slates; repeating content after a teacher's dictation. Most classrooms have no more than one or two readers for the school year. These may be as long as 14-18 pages.

A few copies of one or two storybooks are a common circumstance. Within two readings of a text, such as *Ola and the Red Ball*,[23] children have completely memorized the text. I have checked with a good many children who recited the book to me in the absence of the text, guided by pictures. In another example, I worked with children in Class IV to learn about teaching vocabulary. I distributed a single page on which a fable was typed in large print. I read it; then we read it together. When we began talking about the story, children quoted whole sections of text in their answers. The capacity for attention to (new) words is as astonishing as their abilities for remembering. However, memorizing is not reading. The lack of possibility for reading practice prevents the development of reading skills.

The paucity of material leads teachers to reading aloud, parsing the passage into small section; leading with these and having the class repeat the words. Children are not learning to decode. They are memorizing and repeating. Script is static. And without personal engagements with a variety of texts the likelihood of developing more fluent decoding skills is almost nonexistent. This leads to what I notice at the highest levels of learning. College students approach their reading of new texts, working through print word by word; then pausing at the end of phrases or sentences to piece the meaning together. This is not a "poor reading ability," it is simply the lack of enough practice to develop fluency with syllable patterns; low levels of sight words and lack of familiarity with syntactic patterns and genre. More experience would provide fluency. However, as we'll see shortly, this is unlikely. The lack of text materials significantly affect learning possibilities.

While the "remedy" for material paucity is far off, at least three immediate actions could be taken. We have taken the following three strategies at the pilot school. First, all children have regular classroom use of the national curriculum mandated textbooks. These are just 4 soft cover texts (Language Arts, Science, Math and Social Studies). Children's regular handling and use of the books engages them with a variety of print genres. They have the means to develop print concepts, content literacies and reading skill growth. It is surprising that of all the current efforts to support better literacy instruction, a higher level of priority isn't given to this efficacious response. However, simply giving out books is not enough. Teachers will need training to best use these texts for cross content or discipline specific literacies. They will need support for their teaching children to use shared books with care. Additionally, the situation at this time would also demand good storage for the books to prevent damage from weather, insects, and other factors.

Secondly, all schools should have a modest library of teacher read-aloud materials. In the pilot study school, we developed a small library of African content and context materials, used by six classes. Although fewer than 100 items are on the shelves, this is a most effective strategy. Materials include magazines, storybooks, information books, and charts. These are used for the mandated reading and talking aloud time of 20 minutes daily at *every* class level. Teachers must check out an item from the headmaster on a weekly basis and return it at the end of the week with a brief oral report on its use. During reading aloud and talking-about-it time, vocabulary is developed; expression and (English) syntactic patterns are modeled in authentic contexts. Children grow print concepts that include directionality, pages, titles, illustration use, genre, and so on. Children are learning about text as a social engagement and meaning-making activity in discussions surrounding text. They engage with a widening variety of contents and topics. This develops topic specific vocabularies. For example, a story about fishing will bring in a wide variety of associated vocabulary; names of fish, fresh water, current, still water, bait, net, line, hook, sinker, and so on. In the hands of a knowledgeable teacher, instructional work with reading aloud is richly educative. This site also provides a significant way to help learners become participants in reading. They make meanings and connections; they add ideas and critique the reading. A reading-aloud text about fishing can lead to discussions about environmental issues of pollution, over-fishing, gender roles, or nutrition.

Finally, teachers can be given materials to create classroom print materials. Chart paper is moderately easy to procure; ironed cement bags or cheap white fabric are commonly and cheaply available. While good permanent markers are difficult to obtain, the uses of ink could be developed for this. Teachers can make a poster every week. These might present short stories, riddles, a word family list (foods, bicycle parts, farm tools), songs, greetings, proverbs, and other texts. This engages and empowers teachers as text-makers. It supports the development of self efficacy in teaching; participation in material production and the development of locally apt reading materials. It is one of the most cost effective and immediate ways of getting more print into classrooms. However, again I offer a caution grown out of experience. It is not possible to simply tell teachers to do this. Teachers need guidance for their choices of topics and words, support for making good use of materials. Before beginning, some presentation skill development is helpful. Teachers need abilities to develop abilities to develop an instructional unit around a poster presentation.

Although we have not implemented this yet, I look forward to a time when primary school teachers could go to a local center where they engage with a supported writing process that culminates in publishing their stories and other texts for classroom use. The ease of desktop publishing would serve the urgent need for locally relevant materials at low cost acquisition. There are other factors that affect instruction that I cannot take up in this section including overcrowded classrooms. In combination with the paucity of materials, collaborative and peer teaching would support some of the needs developed by these problems. The lack of furniture is another factor that constrains performance. Students don't have a good writing surface or privacy for learning to decode. Another significant factor concerns classroom language use. Instruction is in English but students rarely share any other language. Without a common language, instruction is much challenged.

LEARNING TO READ DEPENDS ON THE TEACHER

The most significant factor for successful literacy learning is the teacher. The teacher transforms a space into a classroom and orchestrates material, activities and persons into a learning event. A teacher carries responsibility for developing educative experiences to grow new readers. While the teacher's responsibility is a social contract and includes supporting obligations from their community and governing structures, a teacher ultimately carries the community's trust to meet their shared hope. In Sierra Leone, primary school teachers are weakly prepared to create effective instruction.

As the scores on national standardized test suggest, teachers' successful instruction is uncertain. The reasons go beyond material paucity, uncomfortable facilities, and overcrowded classrooms. Particularly at the lower level classes, teachers have minimal or no pedagogical or advanced content training. In Kabala, for example, where 89% of primary school teachers are uncertified, over 90% have not completed secondary school. The least educated are assigned Class I and II. Although they offer high levels of commitment and care for children, they do not have the knowledge or abilities for effective instruction. Their preparation is their own prior classroom experience. The adage that teachers teach as they were taught might be considered worrisome in this case especially. It is my thought that without urgent attention to this state of instructional affairs, current literacy teaching outcomes will repeat themselves for a long time. The weak instruction for the relationships between sounds and letters, the rote memorization of words, copy work, and the lack of meaningful social and environmental connections to print learning will continue to prevent the growth of deeper and more socially authentic literacy abilities.

Our work in the Kabala Christian Primary School shows that change is possible. We are working in an area of least print support and with indigenously trained, local teachers. Our staff is made up of teachers with two levels of certification. In the first year, two teachers were hired with a higher level teaching certification (HTC); and two with lower level Teaching Certificates (TC). The first had 3-4 years of teacher education beyond secondary school; the others had 2 years. Readers should note that the completion of secondary school does not mean teachers passed their subject exams. We also determined to choose teachers who spoke children's local language and were familiar with the constituency. This supported the need for instruction that includes children's social cultural identity. In contrast to common practice nationally, we encourage teachers' use of local languages to explain scientific, agricultural or other concepts.

After hiring the staff I worked with them. We read and talked together, I demonstrated and then we practiced certain strategies. As noted earlier, I worked to develop abilities for key instructional variables, which promised the highest potentials for success. In all cases, I tried to choose change or extensions, which demanded the least amount of materials and strategies that connected with familiar experiences. I worked for a relationship close to that of a collaborative action research. Teachers participated in the design of practices and in the testing of children and, later, the results. (They acted on our findings afterwards). Such collaborative approaches promise possibilities for their own extensions of what we are learning.

In my work with the UNICEF project for teacher trainers in the summer of 2010, this last point took much emphasis. In an environment of material paucity and a lack of access to professional development, it is especially important to empower educators to ask questions and find answers. If schools can become educational sites for collaborative action research to improve practice, much is possible. In the next year we are working to support the staff to work with other primary school teachers in the town to develop more successful practices. Our work with Kabala Christian School demonstrates that professionally guided educational development that are also based on valuing students' abilities and practices promises success. The most vivid example of this happened with a Class I teacher and children in the class. When it was time to assign classes to the teaching staff, it took considerable discussion to convince the board that the strongest, the best teacher should take Class I. At the end of the year, the results were most eloquent. The assigned teacher successfully taught alphabet letter recognition and made automatic connections between letters and sounds (phonemic awareness). At the end of June, this group of children read 51% of our Sierra Leonean revised Dolche (common) word list while the comparison sample scored 7% and 5% respectively. In the onset and rime test, a test for decoding abilities, his children scored 63%. The comparison sample scored 21% and 14%. This example promises possibility.

It is hoped that schools will be increasingly staffed by certified teachers. However, we find that tertiary teacher educators work under similar constraints and conditions. In 2009, supported by a grant from the Higher Education for Development (HED) with USAID, Aske Gbla and I conducted research to learn about support and preparation for the teaching of reading. With a team we interviewed 75% of all Sierra Leone language and language arts college instructors, their students and administration. We observed classrooms, reviewed course materials and visited libraries. Our findings form a grim prognosis. In the first place, like the primary schools, more than half of college classrooms have inadequate furniture, lighting and space. We found that instructors teach 26% of their courses supported only by personal notes. Libraries are very small and significantly outdated. For the most, instructors work from their remembered post-secondary schooling, notes and grammar handbooks. Teaching consists of blackboard use and lectures. Although the Internet might supply materials and access, only 27% of all instructors have used the Internet at all.

It was in the area of language arts teaching methodology that we found the greatest paucity. There is no one in all of Sierra Leone who has a degree in the teaching of reading or education and language arts teaching. Faculty members use their studies in linguistics and English grammar to guide their teaching. Although most are very willing to engage professional development, there is no access to conferences, current journals or texts. We found no LA Methodology text books at any of the colleges. Surprisingly, we also found that no teachers used the more commonly available primary school standard texts to prepare their student teachers. No college instructor used any children's literature. Student teachers do not learn how to work with texts, decoding, or other literacy development skills in these conditions.

More troubling, we found teacher educators do not have, what are considered to be fundamental understandings for the teaching of reading. Almost all, or 97% of instructors do not think of reading abilities as a development that depends on stages (from print and alphabetic concepts, through decoding skill development to fluency). Almost one third (32.7%) could not explain the term "phonemic awareness." The majority of teacher educators (55%) indicated that words should be taught before letters. Two thirds (66%) thought children could learn the alphabet and how "it works" in less than six months. And almost as many (64%) do not teach or discuss the use of syllable patterns in the teaching of reading abilities. There are many reasons for my colleagues' professional knowledge gaps. They do *not* include commitment, love for their students, and professional interest. My colleagues teach very large classes in the most challenging possible conditions. They inspire courageous teachers who will teach in spite of the little and irregular salaries they can expect along with the hardships to which I've alluded. If more effective reading instruction and raising the literacy level in Sierra Leone is important, our task begins in higher education.

CONCLUSION

Literacy, authentic capacities to enlarge personal and social communication interaction, promises much for a developing nation like SL. Of all the possibilities for inclusion at the world's table, literacy has the greatest potential. However, such capacity is not developed in a "project," or in a hurry. It entails the diligent effort and knowledgeable vision of teachers who trust learners' abundant lives to nourish it. It demands the time it takes to grow culture. In this chapter I dwelt on the instructional needs for children's literacy learning. Missing from this chapter is the richness of the work that draws me across the distance year after year. Often I challenge my motivation; searching my heart and plumbing the reasons that drive me. On one hand my impetus is a kind of leaning of the heart. Inexplicably, it is weighted towards my colleagues, friends and the shining faces of young students doing their best in Kabala. It is drawn by the plight of clever and lively children whose parents look at them with sudden thoughtfulness. They know the future looms with foreboding. My heart is drawn by my company, friends in long evenings of discussion after the generator grinds to a halt. Stars crowd the night sky, children sing and clap nearby. The same moon that will be over Grand Rapids in a few hours shines over us. We talk about our work, of keeping hope, about our families and uncertain futures. My heart overflows, tips with gratitude and the privilege of this gift, drawing close across the great gulf of geography, culture, and economies.

Sometimes, my heart accuses me. Such a great gulf gapes between us. The disparity between the material wealth and resources is so immense. If *I* taste the injustice, how terribly bitter it must be for my colleagues. They have no access to journals, conferences, textbooks, or professional library. They have no personal offices, supplies of unlimited and available paper and a photocopier to use. No one has a computer and using one is costly. No sales representatives call, email, or drop in to ask if they would like complimentary desk copies of the newest texts. These are just surface details of differences that penetrate to the bones of our lives. When I consider this, it overwhelms me. I cannot repair or make expiation for the abandonment and indifference that has replaced colonialism; nor for the corruption and self service that increasingly characterize international and politically delivered Aid. But I can take the words spoken by Micah to help me understand my felt responsibility to "act justly and to love mercy and to walk humbly with your God" (Micah 6:8). Supporting education in Sierra Leone is not an act of compassion or "help." It is about doing what is Right.

Notes

INTRODUCTION: AFRICAN CHRISTIANITY AFRICA, POLITICS, AND SOCIOECONOMIC REALITIES

1. See, for instance, Paul Gifford, 1998, *African Christianity: Its Public Role*, Indiana University Press; Terrence Ranger, 2008, *Evangelical Christianity and Democracy in Africa*, Oxford University Press ; Timothy Longman ,2009, *Christianity and Genocide in Rwanda*, Cambridge University Press, Amy Patterson *The Church and AIDS in Africa: The Politics of Ambiguity*; forthcoming 2011. Boulder, CO: First Forum Press, among many others.

2. We read Kwame Bediako, 1995, *Christianity in Africa: The Renewal of a Non-Western Religion*, Orbis Books; Erica Bornstein, 2005, *The Sprit of Development: Protestant NGOs, Morality and Economics in Zimbabwe* Stanford University Press; Barbara Cooper, 2006, *Evangelical Christians in the Muslim Sahel* Indiana University Press; Paul Gifford, 1998 *African Christianity: Its Public Role*, Indiana University Press; Dorothy Hodgson, 2005, *The Church of Women: Gendered Encounters Between Maasai and Missionaries* Chicago: University of Chicago Press; Ogbu Kalu, 2008, *African Pentecostalism: An Introduction* Oxford University Press; Diane Stinton, 2004, *Jesus of Africa: Voices of Contemporary African Christology* Orbis Books; and Terence Ranger ed., 2008, *Evangelical Christianity and Democracy in Africa* Oxford University Press.

3. Paul Gifford, 1998, *African Christianity: Its Public Role*, Bloomington: Indiana University Press, pp. 348.

4. Katherine Marshall, 2005, "Africa: How and Why is Faith Important and Relevant for Development," available at http://www.vanderbilt.edu/csrc/marshall-africa.pdf accessed July 12, 2009.

5. Philip Jenkins, 2002, *The Next Christendom: The Coming of Global Christianity*, Oxford University Press, pp. 2.

6. Anthropologist James Ferguson has argued that conversations about globalization have not been conducted with Africa as a player because of the inconvenience of fitting Africa in the "global convergence narratives" (2006:28).

7. Robert WuthWuthnow, R. 2009. *Boundless Faith: The Global Outreach of American Churches*. Berkeley, CA: University of California Press, pp. 62.

8. Ibid, pp. 61.

9. Lamin Sanneh, 2003, *Whose Religion is Christianity?: The Gospel Beyond the West*. Eerdmans Publishing Company, pp. 22.

10. Lamin Sanneh, 2003, *Whose Religion is Christianity? The Gospel Beyond the West*, Grand Rapids, MI: Eerdmans, pp. 15.

11. Adrian Hastings, "Christianity in Africa," in Ursula King (ed.) *Turning Points in Religious Studies*, Edinburgh: T. and T. Clark, 1990, 208.

12. Jonathan Bonk, 2007, "Africa Unbound," *Christianity Today*, available at http://www.christianitytoday.com/ct/2007/november/38.46.html accessed January 12, 2009.

13. In *Spirit and Power: A 10-Country Survey of Pentecostals* available at www.calvin.edu/nagel/resources/pentecostals-08.pdf, accessed April 4, 2008.

14. David Kasali, "Kenya: Plagued by Superficiality" *Christianity Today*, Vol. 42(13): 56-58.

15. Saskia Van Hoyweghen, 1996, "The Disintegration of the Catholic Church of Rwanda: A Study of the Fragmentation of Political Religious Authority," *African Affairs*, (95):380, pp. 379–402.

16. Paul Gifford, *African Christianity: Its Public Role*, Bloomington: Indiana University Press, 1998, (especially chapter 2). See also, John Lonsdale, "Religion and Politics in Kenya" The Henry Martyn Lectures 2005 presented on Wednesday February 9, 2005 at the Henry Martyn Center, Trinity College, Cambridge, UK, available at http://www.martynmission.cam.ac.uk/CJLonsdale3.html accessed 12th May, 2008; and David Gitari, 1996, *In Season and Out of Season: Sermons to a Nation*, Carlisle, UK: Regnum.

17. Jeff Haynes, 1996, *Religion and Politics in Africa*, London: Zed Books, pp. 123-25.

18. Paul Gifford, 2002, *Christianity and Politics in Doe's Liberia*, Cambridge: Cambridge University Press.

19. Timothy Longman, 2009, *Christianity and Genocide in Rwanda*, pp. 10, Cambridge University Press.

20. Ibid.

21. See statement on the "National Pastors Conference-Covenant" of August 20-23, 2008 found at http://www.ncck.org/info_center/items-view.asp?secid=1&itemid=127 accessed December 23, 2008.

22. See, Tristan Anne Borer, 1998, *Challenging the State: Churches as Political Actors in South Africa, 1980-1994*. Notre Dame: Notre Dame University Press for those opposing apartheid and Tracy Kuperus, 1999, *Civil Society and Apartheid in South Africa: An Examination of Dutch Reformed Church-State Relations*. Palgrave MacMillan, for those supporting apartheid.

23. "David Livingstone," *Dictionary of African Christian Biography*, available at http://www.dacb.org/stories/southafrica/livingstone1_david.html accessed on July 7, 2010.

24. Raymond Hopkins, 1966, "Christianity and Sociopolitical Change in Sub-Saharan Africa," Social Forces, 44: 555-562.

25. T.O. Ranger, 1999, *Voices from the Rocks: Nature, Culture, and History in the Matopos Hills*, p.45. Bloomington: Indiana University Press.

26. See, for instance, Jean Comaroff and John Comaroff, 1993, "Introduction." In *Modernity and Its Malcontents: ritual and Power in Postcolonial Africa*, J. Comaroff and J. Comaroff, eds. Pp. xi-xxxvii. Chicago: University of Chicago Press.

27. Erica Bornstein, 2005, *The Spirit of Development: Protestant NGOs, Morality, and Economics in Zimbabwe*. Stanford: Stanford University Press, pp. 46.

28. As cited in Paul Gifford, 1998, *African Christianity: Its Public Role*, Indiana University Press, p. 240.

29. See, for instance, Ashforth (2005); Ellis and Harr (1998); Moore and Sanders (2001); van Djik (2001).

30. John Mbiti, 1990, *African Religions and Philosophy*, Nairobi: Heinemann Publishers, pp: 106.

31. Terrence Ranger, 1999, *Voices from the Rocks: Nature, Culture, and History in the Matopos Hills of Zimbabwe*. Bloomington: Indian University Press.

32. Birgit Meyer, 1999, Translating the Devil: Religion and Modernity Among the Ewe in Ghana. Edinburgh: Edinburgh University Press.

33. As recorded in Erica Bornstein, 2005, *The Spirit of Development: Protestant NGOs, Morality, and Economics in Zimbabwe*. Stanford: Stanford University Press, pp.86-87.

34. You can read more about Max Weber's writing on Capitalism and the Christian ethic here http://xroads.virginia.edu/~HYPER/WEBER/toc.html.

35. See Harri Englund, 1996, "Witchcraft, Modernity, and the Person: The Morality of Accumulation in Central Malawi," *Critique of Anthropology*, Vol. 16 (3): 257-279.

36. Adam Ashforth, 2005, *Witchcraft, Violence, and Democracy in South Africa*. Chicago: University of Chicago Press.; Henrietta Moore and Todd Sanders 2001, Magical Interpretations and Material Realities: An Introduction." In *Magical Interpretations, Material Realities: Modernity, Witchcraft, and the Occult in Postcolonial Africa*. Moore, H. and Sanders, T., eds. Pp. 1-27. London and New York: Routledge.

37. See the work of Erica Bornstein (2005), for further discussion of this mindset among World Vision workers in Zimbabwe.

38. See, Andrew Walls, 1982. "The Gospel as the Prisoner and Liberator of Culture," *Missionalia* 10: 93-105 and Kwame Bediako, 1996, *African Christianity: The Renewal of Non-Western Religion*, Orbis Books.

39. Personal conversation with Richard Ssewakiryanga, Ministry of Finance Poverty Eradication Action Plan, Government of Uganda, June 24, 2008, Kampala, Uganda.

40. See Charles Banda's story on a documentary by Amy Hart titled Water First, Hart Productions, 2008 and further information at http://water-doc.org/data/content/view/31/62/ accessed January 12, 2009.

41. See http://www.timesonline.co.uk/tol/comment/columnists/matthew_parris/article5400568.ece accessed January 12, 2009.

1. FAITH AND FREEDOM IN POST-COLONIAL AFRICAN POLITICS

1. Between June 2-16, 2009, The Nagel Institute at Calvin College brought together nine African and American scholars in a faculty development seminar on Christian political thought held in South Africa. Participants focused on a number of important issues pertaining to Christianity and public theology, including the need for just public health policies; immigration, refugees and the crises in bordering states (Zimbabwe); democracy, political parties and governmental accountability; and constitution, the courts and executive power. Such activities point to an important role Christians can play in bridging the gap between fait and politics. For more information on this seminar go to http://www.calvin.edu/nagel/gospel-culture/south-africa/.

2.   There are numerous theories and explanations of why and how Africa's current socioeconomic challenges are tied to colonial history and readers are invited to look at some of these explanations available in such texts as Todd J. Moss's *African Development: Making Sense of the Issues and Actors* (2009, Reinner); Walter Rodney's How Europe Underdeveloped Africa (1973, Bogle-L'Ouverture); and William Moseley's *Taking Sides: Clashing Views on African Issues* (2007, McGraw Hill), among many others.

3.   It is quite evident that compared to its neighbors (especially Uganda and Kenya) there is no recorded interethnic animosity in Tanzania despite it having more ethnic groups than both Uganda and Kenya combined.

3. CHARISMATIC RENEWAL IN THE CATHOLIC CHURCH IN GHANA

1.   Cephas Omenyo, *Pentecost Outside Pentecostalism: A study of the Development of Charismatic Renewal in the Mainline Churches in Ghana* (The Netherlands: Boekencentrum Publishing House, 2006), p. 87. This book is one of my principle sources for this paper.

2.   Ogbu Kalu, *African Pentecostalism* (New York: Oxford University Press, 2008), back cover.

3.   Answers.com. "Charismatic." http://www.answers.com/charismatic.

4.   This quotation is taken from the definition of charismatic in the Encarta Dictionary: English (North America) accessed through Microsoft Word. The words in brackets are my additions to the definition.

5.   Bruce Metzger, *Lexical Aids for Students of New Testament Greek*, 3rd ed. (Grand Rapids, MI: Baker Publishing Group, 1969), p. 29.

6.   Cephas Omenyo, *Pentecost Outside Pentecostalism: A study of the Development of Charismatic Renewal in the Mainline Churches in Ghana*, p. 91.

7.   Ibid, p. 36.

8.   Kwame Bediako, *Christianity in Africa: The Renewal of a Non-Western Religion* (Maryknoll: Orbis, 1995), p. 69.

9.   Cf. 1 Cor. 2.4: "and my speech and my message were not in plausible words of wisdom, but in the demonstration of the Spirit and of power."

10. Cephas Omenyo, *Pentecost Outside Pentecostalism: A study of the Development of Charismatic Renewal in the Mainline Churches in Ghana*, pp. 65-75.

11. Ibid, pp. 88-90.

12. Information on Peter Kwesi Sarpong was gathered from watching James Ault's documentary on African christainity available at http://vimeo. com/channels/57182/page:3 accessed December 2, 2010.

13. Michael personal interview, 11/23/08. Michael is the leader of the Shepherding Ministry of the Legon Catholic Charismatic Renewal.

14. Cephas Omenyo, *Pentecost Outside Pentecostalism: A study of the Development of Charismatic Renewal in the Mainline Churches in Ghana*, pp. 248.

15. John 15.5.

16. Ebenezer Akesseh, personal interview, 11/20/08.

17. Constancia Atachie, personal interview, 11/23/08.

18. Ebenezer Akesseh, personal interview, 11/20/08.

19. Constancia Atachie, personal interview, 11/23/08.

20. Ibid.

21. Cephas Omenyo, *Pentecost Outside Pentecostalism: A study of the Development of Charismatic Renewal in the Mainline Churches in Ghana*, p. 108.

22. Ebenezer Akesseh, personal interview, 11/20/08.

23. Cephas Omenyo, *Pentecost Outside Pentecostalism: A study of the Development of Charismatic Renewal in the Mainline Churches in Ghana*, p. 294.

24. Ibid, p. 296.

4. CHARISMATIC RENEWAL: LESSONS IN MISSIONS FROM THE KENYA CHURCH

1. Joel Carpenter, "World Christianity and the Ministry of Expatriate Churches," Presentation to the Strategic Planning Meeting of the American & Foreign Christian Union Calvin College, 26 August 2005, available at http://www.americanandforeignchristianunion.org/Newsletter%20 Downloads/Provost%20Speech%20at%20AFCU%20Retreat.pdf.

2. www.adventures.org/about/about.asp.

3. www.adventures.org/a/trips/trips.asp?locationID=191.

4. As listed in the CIA-The World Factbook, available at https://www.cia. gov/library/publications/the-world-factbook/geos/rw.html (for Rwanda) and https://www.cia.gov/library/publications/the-world-factbook/geos/ sf.html (for South Africa), accessed July 7, 2010.

5. David Kasali, "Kenya: Plagued by Superficiality" *Christianity Today*, Vol. 42(13): 56-58.

6. Barbara Cooper, 2006, *Evangelical Christians in the Muslim Sahel*, Bloomington: Indiana University Press, p. 365.

5. THE GOSPEL FOR ETHIOPIA BY ETHIOPIANS: MAPPING THE CONTESTED TERRAINS BETWEEN PENTECOSTALS AND MARXIST RADICALS

1. Informants: Evelin Brant Thompson and Dr. Howard Brant.

2. According to an American missionary who was in charge of the center in the early 60's, the radical students not only disrupted programs but were also engaged in verbal attacks and character assassinations. The missionary was sarcastically called "General Manzke" of the CIA, and Christian students associated with the center were labeled as disciples of "General Manzke." Informants: Albert and Marian/ Manzke.

3. Informants: Manzke, Philipos Kemere and Kebebew Daka. The Crocodiles were small radical groups, characterized by their contemporaries as "communists" who have strongly influenced the student movement and set the tone for its future direction.

4. Harold Fuller, *Run While the Son is Hot (Eynesbury: Hazel Watson, and Viney, 1967)*, p. 208. *Lij* Kassa received his education in Canada mainly with the help of SIM missionaries and later became a prominent figure through his marriage connections to a member of the royal family.

5. Informant: Evelyn Thompson. This is also attested by several Ethiopian informants: Tiruwork Mesfin, Tenagne Lemma, Tekeste Teklu, and others.

6. Dr. Alemu Biftu, a graduate, and a former faculty member of the Faculty of Education at Michigan State University, is an itinerant evangelist with an international outreach program based in Denver. Mulatu became the African Director of Compassion International based in Kenya. Yohannes Yigzaw became a university professors in England and others ended up in working for international NGOs.

7. Informants: Mulatu Belachew, Berhanu Negash, and Shiferaw Wolde Michael.

8. On a brief history of the Youth Hostel, see Emmanuel Abraham, *Reminiscence of My Life.*(Lund: Lunde Forlag, 1995), pp. 252-255.

9. Informant: Kebebew and Tekeste.

10. Informant: Tekeste.

11. According to some informants, Sven Rubenson, the ex-Swedish Luther missionary, who later joined the HSIU as a History professor, initiated the beginning of university Christian fellowship. Informants also mention students like Fasil Nahom (now a prominent law professor), Wolde Ab (who became President of Asmara University after its independence), Asrat Gebre, were active in the early days of the Christian youth movement in the university. Informants: Professor Seyum Gebre Sellassie, Asrat Gebre, Solomon, Tenagne, and others.

12. Informants: Shiferaw Wolde Michael, Berhanu , Kebebew, and Solomon.

13. Later, the name changed to EvaSU, Evangelical Student Union. For more see, *Hebron*, 1, 1 (1993), pp.11-14.

14. According to Hege, the list of those joining the Pentecostal movement include; Bedru Hussein, a student from a Moslem background, Teka Gabru, Girma Tessema, a distinction student who later became one of the finest soil experts of the nation, Asnake Erque, Tilahun Adera, currently a professor in Pharmacy (US), Tekeste Teklu, formerly a university professor in US called Chaltu Geffawossen(now deceased), Tenagne Lemma, currently Country Director of World Vision Int/Ethiopia, Yenagu Dessie, and Tiruwork Mesfin, now assistant pastor of an Ethiopian church in California. Nathan Hege. *Beyond our Prayers* (Scottdale, Pa., Herald, 1998) p. 151. Informants: Tekeste, Tiruwork, Solomon, and others.

15. The tension between the Pentecostals and radical elements of HSIU students, definitely requires a separate study. At the moment of their history, the Pentecostal students, small as they were, keenly understood the danger of Marxism, perhaps more than any other group in the university or even outside of it, and combated it on all fronts, be it in dormitory discussions, public meetings, Ethiopian University Students (EUS) service stations.

16. For more see, M. Lundgren, *Proclaiming Christ to His World. The Experience of Radio Voice of the Gospel* (Geneva: 1983). One of the main reasons for establishing RVOG was the belief that the Ethiopian society, illiterate by and large, could be effectively reached with the Gospel through the air.

17. John Cumbers, *Living with Red Terror* (Charlotte: Morris Pub.1996), p.120.

18. It is also reported that the prayer sessions led to intimate relations, which finally led the Emperor to promise the missionary that they would be welcomed to start missionary work in his country. Seleshi Kebede," The History of Genet Church", BA thesis, Mekane Yesus Seminary, 1990, p.2; Bekele Wolde Kidan, *Revaival: Itiopia ena Yemechereshaw Revival* (Addis Ababa: Mulu Wengel, 2001/2), p.131. The Emperor had several

contacts with church leaders and leading evangelical figures, who prayed for him and assured him that he would be restored to his country and to his throne. For further, see, Doris M. Rouse, *The Intercession of Rees Howells* (Cambridge: Luterwoth Press, 1983), pp. 22-23.

19. Karl Ramstrand, the first missionary from the SPM, reported that he came to Ethiopia after encountering a vision, while he was in Liberia as a missionary, in which he saw a powerful light originating from Liberia stretching across the map of Ethiopia. He interpreted the vision to be a new call from God to serve the nation of Ethiopia as a missionary. Bekele, *revival*, p, 67; Heywet Berhan: *Ye Awasa Bete Krestian Arbagna Amet Misereta, Liyu Etem*. Awasa: Nehase 1992/ 2000, p. 3.

20. Ibid, p. 9.

21. Informants: Pastor Ashenafi Zemat, Dr. Berhanu Habte , Abere Darge, Evangelist Fasil Kebede, and Abera Tilahun. The issue of personal salvation, which the Pentecostal share with other evangelicals in Ethiopia, is the most contentious and the one that strikes a sensitive chord amongst members of the Orthodox Christians.

22. Informants: Kebede and Dr. Betta Mengistu.

23. Some of the young evangelists from the Pentecostal background actively involved in its expansion in outlying areas were: Endalkachew, Rev. Itefa, Tsadiqu, a Moslem convert, Merid Lemma, evangelist Taddese Negewo, Mekuria Mulugeta, Pastor Tekle Medhin, Pastor Taye Takele, Pastor Tehsome Worku Dr. Betta and Sewhit.

24. Informants: Asefa Zeleke, Melese Wegu, Ashenafi, Ferne Miller and Eearlin Scottman.

25. On the concept of " geographical peel off" see, Luther P. Gerlach, *People, Power, Change: Movements of Social Transformation* (New York: The Bobbs-Merrill Company, 1970), p. 46.

26. This is based on information obtained from those who were then in the leadership position. Informants: Zeleke, Betta, Assefa, and Melese.

27. Informant: Dr. Tilahun Mamo. This is also a view shared by Philipos. Philipos, in fact, gives a theological twist to it by stating that, "the Almighty God raised a new generation of Christians to counter the challenge of atheism that was already there and that was to come." Informant: Philipos.

28. Informant: Afework Kebede.

29. From the point of view of the Pentecostals, the student radicals were not only anti-God, but also of low moral standards, who could not be emulated as examples. R. Ronning Balsvik, *Haile Sellassie's Students* (East

Lansing: Michigan State University Press, 1985). p. 242. Informants: Ayalew Bale, Solomon Kebede and Solomon Lulu.

30. Messay Kebede, *Radicalism and Cultural Dislocation in Ethiopia, 1960-1974,* (Rochester Studies in African History and the Diaspora, 2008 p. 134.

31. Informant: Solomon Lulu.

32. Balsvik, pp. 240-241.

33. Ibid.

34. Sandra Rickard, "The Ethiopian Student and Ethiopia's Transition into the Twentieth Century," a paper submitted in partial requirement of the Students for Amity among Nations (SPAN), University of Wisconsin, May 1, 1967, p. 56.

35. Though Pentecostalism has succeeded in embracing fine intellectuals of the country (from the filed of social as well natural sciences, including many university professors at home and abroad), political voice is missing from their discourse. This is unlike many countries in Africa, Ghana for instance, which has produced Pentecostal like Mensa Anamuah Otabil, whose political articulation approached an African version of liberation theology. See, Emmanuel Kingsley Larbi, *Pentecostalism: The Eddies of the Ghanaian Christianity* (Accra: SAPC Series, 2001), pp. 235-366. In my field research, I noticed that the young generations of Pentecostals in Ethiopia are showing an unusual interest in social and political activism.

36. Informant: Solomon Lulu.

37. R. Ronning Balsvik, *Haile Sellassie's Students,* .p. 240.

38. Informants: Mekonen Bishaw and Solomon Lulu.

39. Informant: Professor Legesse Watero, Astrophysicist, currently teaching in the AAU, Faculty of Science.

40. According to Shimelis Mazengia, members of the young generation of the 60's who took separate paths, one the religious, and the other the political, were essentially of the same ilk, both driven by idealism and a sense of mission. He makes the case that they both arose from the same conflictual encounters that obtained in Ethiopia in the 60's. Informant: Shimeles Mazengia.

41. Girma Amare pointed out that the church was a strong base and source of strength for many Ethiopians in the past, but has increasingly failed to be so for the emerging youth. On the contrary, unable to move with the time and adjust its teachings to changing conditions, it has become an object of bitter attack by its "enlightened" children. Amare Girma, "Need for Strong Convictions in the Student Body," *News and Views,* April 30, 1966, p. 16.

42. For further, see, Messay Kebede, *Radicalism and Cultural Dislocation in Ethiopia, 1960-1974.*

43. Brian Fargher, "The Charismatic Movement in Ethiopia, 1960-1980," *Evangelical Review Theology* 12(1988), p. 345. This is also a view shared by Bedru, a prominent church leader and one of the pioneers of the Pentecostal movement. See his, *Ye Ityopia Mule Wengel Amagnoch Bete Krestiyan.* February, 1985, p. 5.

44. Informants, who played a strategic role in leading the church during the revolution, maintain that their generation was supernaturally prepared for the task ahead. The evangelical church, with its rural background and limited resources, could have had tremendous difficulties to overcome the challenges of the military government. Organizing underground churches and maintaining their operations required combining spiritual and intellectual abilities. Informants: Dr. Solomon Mulugeta, Melesachew .Alem Bazezew, Tekeste , Abera Tilahun, and others.

45. Informants: Solomon Kebede, Solomon Mulugeta, and Bedru.

46. Following the fall of Haile Sellassie, Ethiopia's political culture has changed twice-to communism and to ethnic pluralism. The encounter between religion and politics during these changed periods, in the broader sense, including Islam and primal belief systems is a subject that needs critical inquiry.

47. Peter Berger, *A Rumor of Angels* (New York: Anchor Books, 1990), p. 16.

48. The White and Red Terror are terms used in reference to the slaughtering of the student radical among themselves either by standing on the government side or in opposition to it.

49. According to informants, the students actively taking part in the Crocodiles group were: Abay Abrha, Dawit, Tilahun, Gebru Mersha, Admasu, etc. Informants: Wubshet Dessalegn Ayalew, Solomon, Derese, and Amare.

50. Randi R. Balsvik, "Haile Sellassie's Students," Ph. D. dissertation, Michigan State University, 1983, p.222.

51. Sandra Richard, p. 19.

52. Informants: Wubshet, Solomon, Shiferaw, and Ayalew. In his book, *The Development of Higher Education and Social Change,* Teshome Wagaw, only make a passing reference by way of footnote, "Since 1972, there had been a student underground political party known as 'the Crocodiles.' Whether there was a direct link between this and EPRP cannot be ascertained." Teshome Wagaw, *The Development of Higher Education and Social Change: An Ethiopian Experience, (East Lansing, Michigan State University, 1990)* p.245.

53. Gerd Decke, "The Role of Gudina Tumsa in a Critical Dialogue between Marxism/ Socialism and Christianity," *The Life and Ministry of Rev. Gudina Tumsa* (Addis Ababa: MYC, 2001), p.110.

54. Informants: Tirunesh Yemar, Zewde Jimma, Ahenafi, and others.

55. Some of the leaders who chose that approach were derided by the Pentecostals themselves and were blamed of conflating *Marcos with Marcs* (mixing up Marx with the Biblical Apostle Mark).

56. Informants: Million Belete, Solomon, and Bekele.

57. Ethiopian Herald, 08-12-74.

58. Informants: Eshetu, Tekeste, Tiruwork, and others.

59. Informant: Miss Mildred Young, Tekeste Tiruwork and Alem. Overall informants maintain that except a few cases, most of the Christian students who participated in the *Zemecha* returned after finishing their assignment with their faith intact because of the strong backstopping of the works of Mrs. Young and the graduate fellowship; See also, EEMYC, Annual Report May 16, 1975(Mekane Yesus Seminary).

60. Informant: Alem.

61. Tesfaye Gabisso put it very succinctly: In the past the battle or the fight was between one forms of faith with another. Under the new regime the fight was between faith and its denial/ unbelief. The latter had to be fought more aggressively. Informant: Tesfaye Gabisso.

62. Hege, p. 167; Tilahun Beyene, *Ye-Meserete Kristos Bete Krsitiyan Tarik (Addis Ababa, Mega Publisher, 2001/2) p.* 110; The documents were prepared by Bedru Hussien, Solomon Kebede and others, who were graduates of HSIU and who were also key actors in the Pentecostal movement of the 1960's. Informants: Solomon Kebede, Bedru Hussien, and Balcha Deneged.

63. Informants: Alem Bazezew, Melesachew, Tekeste, Berhanu, and others.

64. Informant: Alem.

65. Informants: Betta, Girma Tessema, Zeleqe, and others. A word of caution is needed here. It might be possible that the term *Pente* by this time may have been used in reference to all evangelicals.

66. Taken from recorded cassette songs and personal interviews.

67. Lila W. Balisky, "Theology in Song: Ethiopia's Tesfaye Gabbiso," *Missiology: An International Review,* vol., 4, October, 1997, pp. 452-453.

68. This song was originally composed by Derge's brother who later joined the EPRP and lost his life.

69. Collected from various gospel songs composed and sung during the military regime.

70. Informant: Shiferaw.
71. Quoted in Reuben Makayiko Chriambo, "Mzimu wa Soldier" : Contemporary Popular Music and Politics in Malawi," *A Demography of Chameleons* (ed.) Harri Englund, (Blantyre : Christian Literature Association, 2002), p. 118.

6. FROM THE FRINGES TO THE CENTRE: PENTECOSTAL CHRISTIANITY IN THE PUBLIC SPHERE IN KENYA (1970-2009)

1. Philip Jenkins, *The Next Christendom: The Coming of Global Christianity*, New York: Oxford University Press, 2002, 75.
2. Harvey G. Cox, *Fire From Heaven: The Rise of Pentecostal Spirituality and the Reshaping of Religion in the Twenty-First Century*(Reading, MA: Addison-Wesley, 1996).
3. Innocent, Aguwuom, Indigenous Religiosity and the Reconceptualization of Catholicism in the Family of Jesus Crucified Movement, unpublished PhD Theses, 2005.
4. David, Barret and T. Johnson, 1998 '*Annual Statistical Table on Global Mission 1998*', in International Bulletin of Missionary Research, January, 26-27, as cited by David Maxwell, 2006.Also see World Christian Encyclopedia, (2001) and World Christian Database (2001).
5. World Christian Encyclopedia, (2001) and World Christian Database (2001).
6. The Pew Forum on Religion and Public Life; Pentecostalism in Kenya, http://pewforum.org/survey/pentecostal/countries/print.php?country.
7. Joel, Robbins, *The Globalization of Pentecostal and Charismatic Christianity*, Annual Reviews of Anthropology, 2004. 33: 117-43.
8. Ibid.
9. http://pewforum.org/survey/pentecostals/africa; see also Adogame (2005b) and Jones and Lauterbach (2005).
10. David, Maxwell, *African Gifts of the Spirit:* p. 6.
11. David, Maxwell, African Gifts of the Spirit. See also Damaris Parsitau, *Sounds of Change and Reform: The Appropriation of Gospel Music in Political Process in Kenya*, Studies in World Christianity Series 14.1 Edinburgh University Press 2008.
12. Ibid.

13. Damaris, Parsitau 'Then Sings My Soul': Gospel Music in the Spiritual Lives of Kenyan Pentecostal/Charismatic Christian', *Journal of Religion and Popular Culture*, Vol. XIV, the Fall 2006.http://www.usask.ca/relst/jrpc/art14-singsmysoul.html.

14. Simeon, O. Ilesanmi. *From Periphery to Centre: Pentecostalism is Transforming the State in Africa,* Harvard Divinity Bulletin, Vol. 35.No.4, 2007. See also Brigit Meyer, and Annelies, Moor, Religion, Media, and the Public Sphere, Indiana University Press, 2006, p.4. Marlene De Witte, *Alter Media's Living World: Televised Charismatic Christianity in Ghana* in Journal of Religion in Africa, 33,2 Leiden, Brill, p.178. Damaris, Parsitau, *Sounds of Change and Reform: the Appropriation of Gospel Music in Socio-political Processes in Kenya* in Studies in World Christianity Series 14.1, Edinburgh University Press 2008.p.55ff.

15. Harri Englund, *From Spiritual Warfare to Civic Virtues: Islamophopia and Evangelical Radio in Malawi,* a paper read at the 2008 International Conference on Religion and Public Culture at the University of Cambridge, on the 28th Feb-1st of March 2008.

16. Harri Englund, 2008. Also see Damaris Parsitau, *God Vs Allah: Islam, Pentecostal Christianity and the Contest for Public Space in Kenya,* a paper submitted to ISA International Sociological Association, in 2008.

17. Ibid.

18. Peter, Berger, The Desecularization of the World': A Global Overview. In The Desecularization of the World: *Resurgence Religion and their Politics.* Peter Berger. Eerdmans, 1999.

19. See interview here http://www.youtube.com/watch?v=7_niCKgH3LE&feature=related.

20. Mathew Ojo 'Pentecostalism, Public Accountability and Governance in Nigeria.' Paper presented at Discussion on Pentecostal- Civil Society Dialogue on Public Accountability and Governance available at http://www.boellnigeria.org/documents/PENTICOSTALISM.pdf.

7. THE CATHOLIC CHURCH AND CIVIC EDUCATION IN THE SLUMS OF NAIROBI

1. Larry Diamond, Juan Linz, and Seymour Lipset, *Democracy in Developing Countries*, Boulder, CO: L. Reinner Publishers, 1988, 26.

2. Peter Von Doepp, 'Liberal Visions and Actual Power in Grassroots Civil Society: Local Churches and Women's Empowerment in Rural Malawi,' *Journal of Modern African Studies*, 40 (2), 2002, 276.

3. See, e.g., Paul Gifford, 'Africa's Churches and the 'Second Liberation Struggle,' of 1989-93,' in Klaus Koschorke (ed.), *The Years 1989-90: Turning Point in European and Non-European Christian History*, Wiesbaden: Harrassowitz Verlag, 2008, 136-155; Agnes C. Aboum, 'The Churches' Involvement in the Democratisation Process in Kenya,' in Hizkias Assefa, and George Wachira (eds.), *Peacemaking and Democratisation in Africa*, Nairobi: East African Educational Publishers, 1996, 95-114; De Gruchy, *Christianity and Democracy*, 165-192 and Samuel P. Huntington, *The Third Wave: Democratization in the Late Twentieth Century*, Norman, OK: University of Oklahoma Press, 1991, 72-85.

4. By 2002, there were over 150 slums housing more than 2 million people; approximately 60% of the city's population occupied less than 5% of the city's total land area.

5. Burgeap, Seueca and Runji & Partners, 'Kibera Urban Environmental Sanitation Project,' Report prepared for the Ministry of Local Government, and Nairobi City Council, Nairobi, 2002, 12.

6. Daniel Biau, 'Three Things We Should Know about Slums,' *Habitat Debate*, March 2007, 6.

7. See Outreach Development Services, 'Participatory Urban Appraisal Study of Mashimoni, Kambi Muru, Lindi and Silanga Villages – Kibera Informal Settlement,' Report prepared for Oxfam GB, Nairobi, 2001, 22.

8. Mugo P. Kirii, *The Nairobi Basic Needs Basket: Cost of Basic Needs Basket in Twelve Informal Settlements, Nairobi-Kenya, 2004*, Nairobi: Paulines Publications Africa, 2004, 24.

9. There are 42 ethnic groups in Kenya; the largest groups are the Kikuyu (22%), Luhya (14%), Luo (13%), Kalenjin (12%), Kamba (11%), Kisii (6%) and the Meru (6%).

10. See Johan de Smedt, 'No Raila, No Peace!' Big Man Politics and Election Violence at the Kibera Grassroots,' *African Affairs*, 108 (433), 2009, 586.

11. For a detailed history of the Nubian claim, see Timothy Parsons, 'Kibra is our Blood: The Sudanese Military Legacy in Nairobi's Kibera, Location, 1902-1968,' *The International Journal of African Historical Studies*, 30 (1), 1997, 90.

12. Kenya Colony and Protectorate, *Report of the Kenyan Lands Commission*, Nairobi: Kenya Colony and Protectorate, 1933, 171.

13. Because the structure owners possessed the buildings and not the land, they were not landlords in the legal sense of the word and had no responsibility to maintain the premises or provide basic services.

14. de Smedt, 'No Raila,' 585.

15. Law Society of Kenya, 'Report: A Mission to Kibera', Nairobi: Law Society of Kenya Land Reform Program, 2002, 11-12.

16. Acacia Consultants, 'Investigation of Actors Operating in Kibera', Report prepared for Government of Kenya, and UN-Habitat, Nairobi, January 2004, 14.

17. For details on Pentecostal and AIC churches in Kenya, see Paul Gifford, *Christianity, Politics and Public Life in Kenya*, London: Hurst & Co., 2008, 86-108 and 109-172.

18. The Protestant churches were the Anglican, Presbyterian, Lutheran, Friends Church, Seventh-Day Adventist and Baptist.

19. St. Jerome's was established in Gatwikera village in the 1980s as a daughter church and became a parish in 2003. See Colin Smith, 'A Missiological Study of Pentecostal Churches in an Informal Settlement in Nairobi, Kenya', PhD diss., University of South Africa, February 2007, 207-208.

20. Kivutha Kibwana, George Kanyi Kimondo, and James Thuo Gathii, *The Citizen and the Constitution*, Nairobi: Claripress, 1996, 5 and Jennifer A. Widner, *The Rise of a Party State in Kenya: From "Harambee!" to "Nyayo!"* Berkley: University of California Press, 1993, 162-163.

21. The OHR coordinator solicited funds from her missionary organization and family and friends to cover the costs for teaching materials.

22. All quoted statements are taken from OHR minutes and evaluations or interviews conducted by the author.

23. In 2004 the number of SCCs increased from 16 to 21. The growth was attributed to revived interest by the parish priest who started saying nightly masses in the SCCs and assigned at least two catechists to each SCC.

24. The referendum campaign symbolized the power struggle between President Kibaki and Raila Odinga and by extension the ethnic communities. Amidst the political grandstanding on both sides, politicians failed to explain the complex document to the public and instead used the rallies (many became violent) to politick and jockey for power in anticipation of the 2007 election. For details, see Cottrell, and Ghai, 'Constitution Making', and Alicia Bannon, 'Designing a Constitution-Drafting Process: Lessons from Kenya', *Yale Law Journal*.

8. REFLECTING ON CHURCH-STATE RELATIONSHIP IN KENYA

1. John Lonsdale, 'Religion and Politics in Kenya', Trinity College, Cambridge, Lecture: Monday 7th February 2005. http://www.scribd.com/doc/5471228/Lonsdale-Religion-and-Politics-in-Kenya-I-Foundations.

2. Spirit and Power: a ten country survey of Pentecostals by the Pew Forum on Religion and Public Life, 5 October 2006. http://pewforum.org/Christian/Evangelical-Protestant-Churches/Spirit-and-Power.aspx.

3. http://www.telegraph.co.uk/comment/3558090/The-Church-isnt-dying-...-but-it-needs-to-evolve.html.

4. Mildred A.J. Ndeda, *The Struggle for Space: minority religious identities in post-independent Kenya*, CODESRIA, 12th General Assembly, http://www.codesria.org/IMG/pdf/Mildred_Ndeda.pdf.

5. Steve Lichty, The Church in Kenya: A cheerleader for Democracy or its competitors? Final Paper, 4 December 2007.

6. Ibid.

7. John Lonsdale, 'Religion and Politics in Kenya', Trinity College, Cambridge, Lecture: Monday 7th February 2005. http://www.scribd.com/doc/5471228/Lonsdale-Religion-and-Politics-in-Kenya-I-Foundations.

8. Ibid.

9. John Lonsdale, 'Religion and Politics in Kenya', Lecture, OCMS, 31 August 2004, Trinity College, Cambridge.

10. Oluoch, Jemimah, *The Christian Political Theology of Dr. John Henry Okullu*, Nairobi: Uzima, 2006, p.33.

11. P.L.O. Lumumba, interview with a Kenyan radio station, January 2008.

12. National Council of Churches of Kenya, Message by religious leaders during the national prayer day, 19 February 2009, http://www.ncck.org/index.php?option=com_content&view=article&id=104:irfmessage&catid=43:news&Itemid=29.

13. John L. Allen, Jr. Church leaders faulted in Kenya: African Christianity must come to terms with 'the contagion of tribalism', *National Catholic Reporter*, Jan 25 2008.

14. John Lonsdale, 'Religion and Politics in Kenya', Trinity College, Cambridge, Lecture: Monday 7th February 2005. http://www.scribd.com/doc/5471228/Lonsdale-Religion-and-Politics-in-Kenya-I-Foundations.

15. John L. Allen, Jr. Church leaders faulted in Kenya: African Christianity must come to terms with 'the contagion of tribalism', *National Catholic Reporter*, Jan 25 2008.

16. James Davison Hunter, To Change the World: The Irony, Tragedy, and Possibility of Christianity in the Late Modern World, Oxford University Press, 2010.

17. http://www.nation.co.ke/News/politics/-/1064/595414/-/view/printVersion/-/7a8xtc/-/index.html.

18. Rev. Timothy Njoya, Prophetic responses to political challenges in the context of existing Christianity, Reformed World, Vol. 52 No. 4 (December 2002).

19. Kwame Bediako, Africa and Christianity on the Threshold of the Third Millennium: The Religious Dimension, African Affairs (2000), 99, 322.

20. Michael Mundia Kamau, Kenya – A Nation in Despair, African Economic Analysis, http://www.africaeconomicanalysis.org/articles/gen/kenya1204.html.

21. See video here http://www.youtube.com/watch?v=DtFhwgyeVyI.

22. Bishop David Gitari, *In Season and out of Season: Sermons to a Nation*, Kenyatta University, 1978, p.31.

9. LITERACY TEACHING AND LEARNING IN SIERRA LEONE

1. I acknowledge the long time support and teachings of my colleague, Senior Lecturer Aske Gbla from Milton Margai College of Education (MMCET). I also thank Mr. James Tamba Koroma, the headmaster of Kabala Christian School who has played a large role in my learning.

2. "Illiteracy, Colonial Legacy and Education: The Case of Modern Sierra Leone." Kingsley Banya in *Comparative Education*, Vol. 29, No. 2 (1993), pp. 159-170.

3. United Nations Human Development Index is an annual ranking that lists countries in the order of quality of life indicators. These include such items as access to health, clean water, and schools; mortality rates and average daily incomes. See: http://hdr.undp.org/en/countries/.

4. Mehra, Rekha, 1997; McLoyd, Vonnie, 1998; Goonesekere Savitri & de Silva-de Alwis, Rangita, 2005.

5. Suso, Emmanuelle. Deutsche Volkshochshul Verbands – Internationale. Retrieved November 14, 2009. http://www.iiz-dvv.de/index.php?article_id=213&clang=1.

6. Daun 2000; Fuhriman et al. 2006; MacClure 1994; Williams 2007; Especially read Hough 1989. Inefficiency in Education- The Case of Mali which offers a thorough analysis of the gap between outcomes and the investment of resources and hope. *Comparative Education,* 25(1), 77-85.

7. http://www.eurodad.org/uploadedFiles/Whats_New/Reports/Old%20habits%20die%20hard.%20Aid%20and%20accountability%20in%20Sierra%20Leone.pdf (downloaded 15 March 2010).

8. World Bank. *Education in Sierra Leone: Present Challenges, Future Opportunities.* 2007: 96-116. Although a freeze was imposed on the hiring of tertiary level educators, significant funding has been assigned to emergency teacher training, distance training and certification as well as hiring of uncertified teachers.

9. Ibid: 78-81.

10. Ibid: 81-83. BECE Basic Education Certificate Examination, given at the end of 9 years of education.

11. Ibid: 83-84. West African Senior School Certificate Examination, at completion of secondary school.

12. Aske B. Gbla, West African Examination Council (WAEC) examiner in conversation. August 2009.

13. Freire, 1976, 2004; Heath 1999; Lee, 2007; Purcell-Gates 1995.

14. Aronowitz, Stanley & Giroux, Henry A. (1993).

15. Hornberger, Nancy. 2003: 449.

16. Brian Street in *Literacy and Development: Ethnographic Perspectives* presents 10 case studies, drawn from locations identified as "developing nations" where people's own needs and practices guide literacy program design.

17. See work on literacy as social praxis: Heath, 1983, Purcell Gates, 1999, 2004; Street, Brian.

18. Gee, James Paul (1990, 1992, 2010); Purcell-Gates, Victoria (1997, 2004) Heath, Shirley Brice (1983).

19. World Bank 2007.

20. Bledsoe, 1992; Daun 2000; Hough, 1989; Walter 1999.

21. Islamic teacher; sheik.

22. World Bank 2007.

23. Evans. Primary School Reader.

References

Aboum, Agnes. 1996. "The Churches' Involvement in the Democratisation Process in Kenya." In *Peacemaking and Democratisation in Africa: Theoretical Perspectives and Church Initiatives*, Ed. Hizkias Assefa, and George Wachira, Pp. 3-17 Nairobi: East African Educational Publishers.

Acacia Consultants, 2004. "Investigation of Actors Operating in Kibera." Report prepared for Government of Kenya, and UN-Habitat, Nairobi.

ACK Communications Department. 2009. "Anglican Church of Kenya: History." Available at http://www.ackenya.org/ack/history.html

Adogame, A. 2005a. "African Communities in Diaspora." In *African Christianity: An African Story*. Ed. O. U. Kalu, pp. 494-514. Pretoria: University of Pretoria.

_____. 2005b. "Politicization of Religion and the Religionization of Politics in Nigeria." In *Religion, History, and Politics in Nigeria: Essays in Honor of Ogbu U. Kalu*, Ed. C. Korieh and U. Nwokeji, pp. 125-139. Lanham, MD: University Press of America.

_____. 2004. *An Introduction to Pentecostalism: Global Charismatic Christianity*. Cambridge: Cambridge University Press.

_____. 2000. "The Quest for Space in the Global Spiritual Marketplace: African Religions in Europe." *International Review of Mission*, 89(354), 400 - 409.

Aluanga, Lillian. 2007. "Religion and Politics now get Intertwined." *Sunday Standard*, December, 3, p. 14.

Appadurai, A. 1990. "Disjuncture and Difference in the Global Cultural Economy." *Theory, Culture & Society*. Vol. 7:295-310.

Aronowitz, Stanley, and Henry A. Giroux. 1993. *Education still under siege*. Westport, Conn.: Bergin & Garvey.

Asamoah-Gyadu, J. Kwabena. 2005a. "Born of Water and Spirit: Pentecostal/ Charismatic Christianity in Africa." In *African Christianity: An African Story*. Ed. O. U. Kalu, pp. 376-398. Pretoria: University of Pretoria Press.

_____. 2005b. "'Christ is the Answer": What is the Question?' A Ghana Airways Prayer Vigil and its Implications for Religion, Evil and Public Space." *Journal of Religion in Africa*. Vol. 35(1):93-117.

Ashforth, A. 2005. *Witchcraft, Violence, and Democracy in South Africa*. Chicago: University of Chicago Press

Auslander, M. 1993. "'Open the Wombs!': The Symbolic Politics of Modern Ngoni Witchfinding." In *Modernity and Its Malcontents: Ritual and Power in Postcolonial Africa*. J. Comaroff and J. Comaroff, Ed. Pp. 167-192. Chicago: University of Chicago Press.

Banya, Kingsly. 1993. "Illiteracy, Colonial Legacy and Education: The Case of Modern Sierra Leone." *Comparative Education*. Vol. 29 (2):159-170.

Bardi, Mirela "Common Evaluation Frameworks for Language Teachers." Available at http://www.semlang.eu/Telechargement/Textes/SemLang%20-%20Bardi.pdf

Barrett, David B. 2001. *World Christian Encyclopedia: a Comparative Study of Churches and Religions in the Modern World*. 2nd ed. Oxford: Oxford University Press.

Bediako, Kwame. 1995. *Christianity in Africa: The Renewal of a Non-Western Religion*. Edinburgh: Edinburgh University Press.

Biau, Daniel. 2007. "Three Things We Should Know about Slums," *Habitat Debate*. General Council Session 21, March, 2007, pp. 6.

Bledsoe, Caroline. 1992. "The Cultural Transformation of Western Education in Sierra Leone." *Africa: Journal of the International African Institute*. Vol. 62(2):182-202.

Bornstein, E. 2001. "Child Sponsorship, Evangelism, and Belonging in the World of World Vision Zimbabwe." *American Ethnologist*. Vol. 28(3): 595-622.

Bujo, Benezet, 1992, *African Theology in Its Social Context*. Orbis Books.

Burgeap, Seueca and Runji & Partners. 2002. "Kibera Urban Environmental Sanitation Project," Report prepared for the Ministry of Local Government and Nairobi City Council, Nairobi.

Centre for Development and Enterprise (CDE). 2008. "Dormant Capital: Pentecostalism in South Africa and its Potential Social Economic Role," available at www.cde.org.za/attachment_view.php?aa_id=221

Chabal, Patrick, and Jean-Pascal Daloz. 1999. *Africa Works: Disorder as Political Instrument*. Oxford: James Currey.

Chazan, Naomi. 1992. "Africa's Democratic Challenge." *World Policy Journal.* Vol. 9 (2): 279-307.

CIA: The World Fact Book. 2009. Central Intelligence Agency. 26 Apr. 2009. Available at https://www.cia.gov/library/publications/the-world-fact-book/

Cobbert, Steve and Brian Fikkert. 2009. *When Helping Hurts: How to Alleviate Poverty Without Hurting the Poor.* Chicago: Moody Publishers.

Comaroff, Jean and John Comaroff 1993. "Introduction." In *Modernity and Its Malcontents: Ritual and Power in Postcolonial Africa.* Ed. J. Comaroff and J. Comaroff. Pp. xi-xxxvii. Chicago: University of Chicago Press.

_____. 1999. "Occult Economies and the Violence of Abstraction: noted from the South African Postcolony." *American Ethnologist.* Vol. 26(2):279-303.

Cooper, Fredrick. 1997. "Modernizing Bureaucrats, Backward Africans, and the Development Concept." In *International Development and the Social Sciences.* Ed. F. Cooper and R. Packard. Pp. 64-92. Berkeley: University of California Press.

_____. 2005. *Colonialism in Question: Theory, Knowledge, History.* Berkeley: University of California Press.

Cooper F. and R. Packard. 1997. "Introduction." In *International Development and the Social Sciences: Essays on the History of Knowledge.* Ed. F. Cooper and R. Packard. Pp. 1-30. Berkeley: University of California Press.

Cottrell, Jill, and Yash Ghai. 2007. "Constitution Making and Democratization in Kenya, (2000-2005)." *Democratization.* Vol. 14 (1):1-25.

Daun, Holgen. 2000. "Primary Education in Sub-Saharan Africa--a moral issue, and economic matter, or both?" *Comparative Education.* Vol. 36(1): 37-53.

de Gruchy, John W. 1995. *Christianity and Democracy: A Theology for a Just World Order.* Cambridge: Cambridge University Press.

De Smedt, Johan. 2009. "'No Raila, No Peace!' Big Man Politics and Election Violence at the Kibera Grassroots." African Affairs. Vol. 108 (433): 581-98.

Diamond, Larry. 1994. "Toward Democratic Consolidation." *Journal of Democracy.* Vol. 5 (3);4-17.

Diamond, Larry, Juan Linz, and Seymour Lipset. 1988. *Democracy in Developing Countries.* Boulder, CO: Lynne Reinner Publishers.

Dicklitch, Susan. 1998. *The Elusive Problem of NGOs in Africa: Lessons from Uganda.* New York: St. Martin's Press.

Easterly, William. 2006. *The White Man's Burden: Why the West's Efforts to Aid the Rest Have Done So Much Ill and So Little Good*. Penguin Press HC.

_____. 2001. *The Elusive Quest for Growth : Economists' Adventures and Misadventures in the Tropics*. The MIT Press.

Ela, Jean-Marc. 1986. *African Cry*. (R. R. Barr, Trans.) Maryknoll, NY: Orbis Books.

Elder, Glen. 2003. *Hostels, Sexuality, and the Apartheid Legacy: Malevolent Geographies*. Athens: Ohio University Press.

Ellis, Stephen and Haar, Gerrie Ter. 2004. *Worlds of Power: Religious Thought and Political Practice in Africa*. New York: Oxford University Press.

_____. 1998. "Religion and Politics in Sub-Saharan Africa." *The Journal of Modern African Studies*. Vol. 36(2): 175-201.

Englund, Harri. 2003. "Christian Independency and Global Membership: Pentecostal Extraversions in Malawi." *Journal of Religion in Africa*. Vol. 33(1): 83 - 111.

_____. (2001). "The Quest for Missionaries: Transnationalism and Township Pentecostalism in Malawi." In *Between Babel and Pentecostalism*. Ed. A. Corten and R. Marshall-Fratani. Pp. 235-255. Indiana: Indiana University Press.

_____. 1996. "Witchcraft, Modernity, and the Person: The morality of accumulation in Central Malawi." *Critique of Anthropology*. Vol. 16(3): 257-279.

Eshete, Tibebe. 2009. *The Evangelical Movement in Ethiopia: Resistance and Resilience*. Waco: Baylor University Press.

Evans-Pritchard, E. 1937. *Witchcraft, Oracles and Magic Among the Azande*. Oxford University Press.

Farber, A. 2003. Corridors or Peace: Adult Commitments to Doing Good For Children in Post-Apartheid South Africa. PhD Dissertation. Harvard University.

Fatton, Robert. 1992. *Predatory Rule, State and Civil Society in Africa*. Boulder, CO: Lynne Reinner.

_____. 1995. "Africa in the Age of Democratization: The Civic Limitations of Civil Society." *African Studies Review*. Vol. 38 (2):67-99.

Ferguson, James. 2006. *Global Shadows: Africa in the Neoliberal World Order*. Durham and London: Duke University Press.

_____. 1999. *Expectations of Modernity: Myths and Meanings of Urban Life on the Zambian Copperbelt*. Berkeley: University of California Press.

Foley, Michael, and Bob Edwards. 1996. "The Paradox of Civil Society." *Journal of Democracy*. Vol. 7 (3): 38-50.

Freidus, Andrea. 2010. "Raising Malawi's Children: Unanticipated Outcomes Associated with Institutionalized Care." *Children and Society*. Vol. 24 (24): 293-303.

Freire, Paulo. 1985. *The Politics of Education: Culture, Power and Liberation*. Translated by Donaldo Macedo. Massachusetts: Bergin & Garvey Publishers, Inc.

_____. 1970. *Pedagogy of the oppressed*. Continuum International Publishing House.

Freston, Paul. 2001. *Evangelicals and Politics in Asia, Africa and Latin America*.Cambridge: Cambridge University Press.

Fuhriman, A., Ballif-Spanvill, B., Ward, C., Solomon, Y. and Kacey, W.-J. 2006. Meaningful literacy? Gendered experiences with an NGO-sponsored literacy program in rural Mali. *Ethnography and Education*. Vol. 1 (1):103–124.

Gee, James Paul. 2009. "Language and Literacy: Reading Paulo Freire Empirically." Available at http://www.jamespaulgee.com/sites/default/files/pub/ReadingFreire.pdf

_____. 1990. *Social linguistics and Literacies: Ideology in discourses. Critical perspectives on literacy and education*. London: Falmer Press.

_____. 1992. *The social mind: Language, ideology, and social practice*. New York: Bergin & Garvey

Gekara, Mayaka. 2010. "Why churches pose the last hurdle to new constitution." *Daily Nation*. March 6, 2010.

Gifford, Paul. 2009. *Christianity, Politics and Public Life in Kenya*. New York: Columbia University Press.

_____. 2008. "Africa's Churches and the 'Second Liberation Struggle' of 1989-93." In *The Years 1989-90: Turning Point in European and Non-European Christian History*. Ed. Klaus Koschorke. Pp. 137-176. Wiesbaden: Harrassowitz Verlag.

_____. 2004. *Ghana's New Christianity: Pentecostalism in a Globalizing African Economy*. London: Hurst & Co.

_____. 1999. *African Christianity: Its Public Role in Uganda and other African Countries*. Kampala: Fountain Publishers.

_____. 1998. *African Christianity: Its Public Role*. London: Hurst & Co.

_____. Ed. 1995. *The Christian churches and the Democratization of Africa*. Leiden: E. J. Brill.

Goonesekere, Savitri & de Silva-de Alwis, Rangita. 2005. "Women's and Children's Rights in a Human Rights Based Approach to Development." Division of Policy and Planning Working Paper. UNICEF. NY: New York

Gulyani, Sumikla, and Debabrata Talukdar. 2008. "Slum Real Estate: The Low-Quality High-Price Puzzle in Nairobi's Slum Rental Market and its Implications for Theory and Practice." *World Development*. Vol. 36 (10):1916-1937.

Gupta, Akhil. 1997. "Agrarian Populism in the Development of a Modern Nation." In *International Development and the Social Sciences*. F. Cooper and R. Packard, eds. Pp. 320-344. Berkeley: University of California Press.

Hall, Stuart. 1992. "The West and the Rest: Discourse and Power." In *Formations of Modernity*. Ed. S. Hall and B. Gieben. Pp. 275-320. Oxford: Polity Press.

Harbeson, John W. "Civil Society and Political Renaissance in Africa." In *Civil Society and the State in Africa*. Ed. John W. Harbeson, Donald S. Rothchild, and Naomi Chazan. Pp. 1-30. Boulder, CO: L. Reinner Publishers, 1994.

Heath, Shirley Brice. 1999. *Ways with words*. Cambridge, U.K.: Cambridge University Press.

Hearn, Julie. 2002. "The 'Invisible' NGO: US Evangelical Missions in Kenya." *Journal of Religions in Africa*. Vol. 32 (1): 32-60.

Herr, Harvey, and Karl Guenter. 2003. "Estimating Global Slum Dwellers: Monitoring the Millennium Development Goal 7, Target 11." UN-Habitat working paper, Nairobi.

Hoekema, David. 2010. "Religious Rights: Christians and Muslims in Kenya." *The Christian Century*. June 15, 2010, pp. 10-11.

Hornberger, Nancy. 2003) "Literacy and Language Planning." In *Social Linguistics: Essential Readings*. Ed. Christiana Bratt Paulston & Richard Tucker, Pp. 449-459. Cornwell, UK: Blackwell Publishers.

Hough, J. R. 1989. "Inefficiency in Education: The Case of Mali." *Comparative Education*. Vol. 25(1):77-85.

Huchzermeyer, Marie. 2006. "Slum Upgrading Initiatives in Kenya within the Basic Services and Wider Housing Market." COHRE Discussion Paper No. 1/2006, COHRE, Geneva.

Hulme, David, and Michael Edwards. Eds. 1997. *NGOs, States and Donors: Too Close for Comfort?* New York: St. Martin's Press.

Huntington, Samuel. 1991. *The Third Wave: Democratization in the Late Twentieth Century*. Norman, OK: University of Oklahoma Press.

Jeffrey, Paul. 2001. "Short Term Missions Trips." *The Christian Century*. December 12, 2001: 5-7.

Joof, Amy E. "The UNESCO Teacher Training Initiative for Sub-Saharan Africa." First Meeting of National Coordinators. March, 7-9, 2006. Available at http://unesdoc.unesco.org/images/0014/001446/144680E.pdf

Kalu, Ogbu. 2008. *African Pentecostalism: An Introduction*. New York: Oxford University Press.

_____. 2007. "Pentecostalism and Mission in Africa." *Mission Studies*. Vol. 24 (1): 9-45.

_____. 2006. *Power, Poverty, Prayer: The Challenges of Poverty and Pluralism in African Christianity, 1960-1996*. Asmara, Eritrea: Africa World Press.

_____. 2005. *African Christianity: An African Story*. Pretoria: University of Pretoria Press.

_____. 2003a. "Pentecostal and Charismatic Reshaping of the Africa Religions Landscape." *The Mission Studies*. Vol. 20: 1 – 39.

_____. 2003b. "Faith and Politics in Africa: Emergent Political Theology of Engagement in Nigeria, 1970 - 2002." Paul B. Henry Lecture, Calvin College, Grand Rapids, Michigan. Available at www.calvin.edu/henry/archives/lectures/kalu.pdf

Kasfir, Nelson. 1998. "Civil Society, the State and Democracy in Africa." In *Civil Society and Democracy in Africa: Critical Perspectives*. Ed. Nelson Kasfir, Pp. 123-140. London: Frank Cass, 1998.

Kenya Colony and Protectorate. 1933. *Report of the Kenyan Lands Commission*. Nairobi: Kenya Colony and Protectorate.

Kirii, Mugo. 2004. *The Nairobi Basic Needs Basket: Cost of Basic Needs Basket in Twelve Informal Settlements, Nairobi-Kenya*. Nairobi: Paulines Publications Africa.

Law Society of Kenya.2002. "Report: A Mission to Kibera." Nairobi: Law Society of Kenya Land Reform Programme.

Lee, Carol and Peter Smagorinsky. 2000. *Vygotskian Perspectives on Literacy Research*. Cambridge University Press.

Lee, Carol. 2007. *Culture, Literacy, and Learning: Taking Bloom in the Midst of the Whirlwind*. New York: Teachers College Press.

Livermore, David A. 2006. *Serving with Eyes Wide Open: Doing Short Term Missions with Cultural Intelligence*. Grand Rapids: Baker Books.

Lytle Susan. and Wolf, Michael. 1989. "Adult Literacy Education: Program Evaluation and Assessment" *Eric Digest, No. 103*:5-17. Available at http://www.ericdigests.org/pre-9217/adult.htm

Maxwell, David. 2006. *African Gift of the Spirit: Pentecostalism and the Rise of a Zimbabwean Transnational Religious Movement.* Oxford: James Currey.

Martin, David. 1990. *Tongues of Fire: The Explosion of Pentecostalism in Latin America.* Oxford: Blackwell.

Mazrui, Ali. 1999. *UNESCO General History of Africa, Vol. VIII: Africa since 1935.* Berkeley, CA: University of California Press.

McCall, John. 1995. "Rethinking Ancestors in Africa." *Africa: Journal of the International African Institute.* Vol. 65 (2): 256-70.

McLoyd, Vonnie. 1998. "Socioeconomic Disadvantage and Child Development." *American Psychologist.* Vol. 53 (2):185-204.

Mehmet, Ozay. 1995. *Westernizing the Third World: The Eurocentricity of Economic Development Theories.* Routledge, London.

Mehra, Rekha. 1997. "The Role of NGOs: Charity and Empowerment." *Women, Empowerment, and Economic Development: Annals of the American Academy of Political and Social Science.* Vol. 554: 136-149.

Meredith, Martin. 2006. *The Fate of Africa: A History of Fifty Years.* New York: Public Affairs Books.

Meyer, Birgit. & Moors, Annelies. 2006. *Religion, Media, and the Public Sphere.* Indiana: Indiana University Press.

Miller, Donald & Yamamori, Tetsunao. 2007a. *Global Pentecostalism: The New Face of Christian Social Engagement.* University of California Press, Berkeley & Los Angeles, California.

_____. 2007b. *Global Pentecostalism: the new face of Christian social engagement.* Berkeley: University of California Press.

Moore, Henrietta and Todd Sanders. 2001. "Magical Interpretations and Material Realities: An Introduction." In *Magical Interpretations, material Realities: Modernity, Witchcraft and the Occult in Postcolonial Africa.* Ed. H. Moore and T. Sanders. Pp. 1-27. London and New York: Routledge.

Moreau, Scott, Gary R. Corwin, and Gary B. McGee. 2004. *Introducing World Missions: A Biblical, Historical, and Practical Survey.* Grand Rapids: Baker Academic.

Mudimbe, Valentine. 1994. *The Idea of Africa: Gnosis, Philosophy, and the Order of knowledge.* Bloomington: Indiana University Press.

Mwaura, Philomena. 2005. "Nigerian Pentecostal Missionary Enterprise in Kenya." In *Religion, History, and Politics in Nigeria: Essays in honor of Ogbu U. Kalu.* Ed. Chimah Korieh, Pp. 246-262. Lanham: University Press.

Ndegwa, Stephen. 1992. *The Two Faces of Civil Society: NGOs and Politics in Africa*. West Hartford, CT: Kumarian Press.

Nkrumah, Kwame. 1967. "African Socialism Revisited." Retrieved from http://www.marxists.org/subject/africa/nkrumah/index.htm

Nyerere, J. 1998 [1966]. "Leaders Must Not be Masters," In *African Philosophy: An Anthology*. Ed. E. C. Eze, pp. 77-80. Malden, MA: Blackwell.

Office of Human Rights. 2008. "Kibera East Baseline Survey." Unpublished report, Nairobi.

Ojo, Matthew. 2004. "Pentecostalism, Public Accountability and Governance in Nigeria." Paper presented at the Conference on Pentecostal-Civil Society Dialogue on Public Accountability and Governance, Lagos, October 18th

Omenyo, Cephas. 2002. *Pentecost outside Pentecostalism: A Study of the Development of Charismatic Renewal in the Mainline Churches in Ghana*. Zoetermeer, The Netherlands: Boekencentrum.

Onsrud, Line. 1999. "East Africa Pentecostal Churches: A Study of 'Self-Historisation' as Contextualisation." *Svensk missionstidskrift*. Vol. 87(3): 419-46.

Outreach Development Services. 2001. "Participatory Urban Appraisal Study of Mashimoni, Kambi Muru, Lindi and Silanga Villages – Kibera Informal Settlement." Report prepared for Oxfam GB, Nairobi.

Parsitau, Damaris. 2009. "'Keep Holy Distance and Abstain till He Comes': Interrogating a Pentecostal Church Discourses and Engagements with HIV/AIDS and the Youth in Kenya." *Africa Today*. Vol. 56 (1):44-64

_____. 2008. "Sounds of Change and Reform: The Appropriation of Gospel Music in Political Process in Kenya." *Studies in World Christianity*. Vol. 14(1):55-72

_____. 2007. "From the Periphery to the Centre: The Pentecostalization of Mainline Christianity in Kenya, Missionalia, Southern Africa". *Journal of Missiology*, Acad SA Publishing (35) 3.83-111

_____. (2006). "'Then sings my Soul': Gospel Music as Popular Culture in the Spiritual Lives of Kenyan Pentecostals." *Journal of Religion and Popular Culture*, XIV, http://www.usask.ca/relst/jrpc/articles14.html

Parsons, Timothy. 1997. "Kibra is our Blood: The Sudanese Military Legacy in Nairobi's Kibera, Location, 1902-1968." *The International Journal of African Historical Studies*. Vol. 30 (1):87-122.

p'Bitek, Okot. 1964. "The Self in African Imagery." *Transition*. Vol. 1 (15): 32-35.

Pew Forum. 2010. "The Historical Overview of Pentecostalism in Kenya." Available at http://pewforum.org/Christian/Evangelical-Protestant-Churches/Historical-Overview-of-Pentecostalism-in-Kenya.aspx

Pikkert, P. n.d. "African Primal Religion: Themes and Substance," available at http://www.pikkert.com/downloads.php?group=10&PHPSESSID=787 8a3a0f0be3b19d574f562b7f1d1f2 accessed August 9, 2009.

Purcell-Gates, Victoria. 2007. *Cultural practices of literacy: Case studies of language, literacy, social practice, and power.* Mahwah, NJ: Lawrence Erlbaum Associates.

_____. 1995. *Other People's Words: The Cycle of Low Literacy*: Harvard University Press.

Putman, Robert. 2000. *Bowling Alone: The Collapse and Revival of American Community.* New York: Simon and Schuster.

Ramphele, Mamphela. 2001. "Citizenship Challenges in South Africa's Youth Democracy." *Daedalus.* Vol. 130 (1):1-18.

Ranger, Terrence. 1999. *Voices from the Rocks: Nature, Culture, and History in the Matopos Hills of Zimbabwe.* Bloomington: Indiana University Press.

Research International. 2005. "Kibera Social and Economic Mapping: Household Survey Report." Report prepared for Government of Kenya and UN-Habitat, Nairobi.

Rist, Gilbert. 1997. *The History of Development: From Western Origins to Global Faith.* London: Zed Books.

Samita, Z. 2003. Involvement in Development within African Evangelical and Pentecostal Churches. In *Quests for Integrity in Africa.* Ed. G. Wamue & M. Theuri, pp. 23-45. Nairobi: Acton Publishers.

Sanneh, Lamin. 2008. *Disciples of All Nations.* Oxford: Oxford University Press.

Schwartz, Glenn. 2004. "Two Awesome Problems: How Short-term Missions can Go Wrong." *International Journal of Frontier Missions.* Vol. 20(4):27-34.

Scott, Lindy. 2007. "Letter from the Editor." *Journal of Latin American Theology: Christian Reflections from the Latino South.* Vol. 2(2): p. 5

Senghor, Leopold. 1998. "Negritude and African Socialism." In *The African Philosophy Reader.* Ed. J. M. Coetzee, pp. 442-447. New York: Routledge.

Sheppard, Kylie. 2006. Pentecostalism and Sustainability: Conflicts or Convergence. PhD Thesis, Murdoch University, Australia.

Skurnik, W. A. 1965. "Leopold Sedar Senghor and African Socialism." *Journal of Modern African Studies.* Vol. 3(0303): 349-369.

Smith, C. 2007a. "Informal Pentecostal: The Emergence and Growth of Pentecostal Churches within Kibera Informal Settlement, Nairobi." *Missionalia*. Vol. (35) 3.67-82

_____. 2007b. A Missiological Study of Pentecostal Churches in an Informal Settlement in Nairobi, Kenya. PhD diss., University of South Africa.

Street, Brian, ed. 2001. *Literacy and Development: Ethnographic Perspectives.* London: Routledge.

Syagga, Paul, Winnie Mitullah, and Sarah K. Gitau. 2001. *Nairobi Situation Analysis: Consultative Report*. Nairobi: Government of Kenya, and UN-Habitat.

_____. 2002. *Nairobi Situation Analysis Supplementary Study: A Rapid Appraisal of Rents in Slums and Informal Settlements*. Nairobi: Government of Kenya, and UN-Habitat.

Taylor, John. 1963. *The Primal Vision, Christian Presence Amid African Religion*. London: Student Christian Movement Press, Ltd.

The Puritans Board. n.d. "Perceptions of Missionaries by Nationals- a Romania Case Study," available at http://www.puritanboard.com/f71/perceptions-missionaries-nationals-romanian-case-study-60949/ accessed July 7, 2010

Tutu, Desmond. 1999. *No Future Without Forgiveness*. New York: Doubleday.

Ubah, C N. 1982. "The Supreme Being, Divinities and Ancestors in Igbo Traditional Religion: Evidence from Otanchara and Otanzu." *Africa: Journal of the International African Institute*. Vol. 52(2): 90-105.

Van Dijk, R. 2001a. "Time and Transcultural Technologies of the Self in the Ghanaian Pentecostal Diaspora." In *Between Babel and Pentecost: Transnational Pentecostalism in Africa and Latin America*. Ed. A. Corten and R. Marshall Fratani. Pp. 216-255. Bloomington: Indiana University Press.

_____. 2001b. "Witchcraft and Skepticism by Proxy: Pentecostalism and laughter in urban Malawi." In *Magical Interpretations, material Realities: Modernity, Witchcraft and the Occult in Postcolonial Africa*. Ed. H. Moore and T. Sanders. Pp. 97-117. London and New York: Routledge.

Van Engen, JoAnn. 2000. "The Cost of Short Term Missions." *The Other Side*. January & February: 20-23.

Verbeek, Kurt Alan. n.d."International Service Learning: A Call to Caution." *Commitment and Connection: Service-Learning and Christian Higher Education*. Ed. Gunst Heffner, Gail and Claudia DeVries Beversluis. Chapter 5. New York: University Press of America.

_____. 2008. "Lessons from the Sapling: Review of Quantitative Research on Short Term Missions." *Effective Engagement in Short Term Missions;*

Doing it Right! Ed. Robert Priest Pp: 475-497. Pasadena: William Carey Library.

_____. 2005. "The impact of Short Term Missions: A Case of House Construction in Honduras After Hurricane Mitch." *Missiology*. Vol. 34 (4): 445-477.

Walls, Andrew. 1982. "The Gospel as the Prisoner and Liberator of Culture." *Missionalia*. Vol. 10(3):98-99.

Walter, Pierre. 1999. "Defining literacy and its consequences in the developing world." *International Journal of Lifelong Education*. Vol. 18(1), 31-48.

Werlin, Herbert. 1974. *Governing an African City: A Study of Nairobi*. New York: Africana Publishing Co.

Widner, Jennifer. 1993. *The Rise of a Party-State in Kenya: From "Harambee!" To "Nyayo!"* Berkeley: University of California Press.

World Bank. 2007. *Education in Sierra Leone: Present Challenges, Future Opportunities*. Washington DC.

Wuthnow, Robert. 2009. *Boundless Faith: The Global Outreach of American Churches*. Berkeley, CA: University of California Press.

Contributors

Ross Acheson, grew up in Ann Arbor and graduated with honors from Calvin College in May 2009, with a major in International Development Studies and minors in Religion and Greek. Acheson has a strong interest in Christianity in Africa. During his time at Calvin College as a student, he participated in an interim course in Kenya that focused on Christian leadership and development, and also spent a semester in Ghana studying politics and culture and researching about the Charismatic Renewal movement in the Catholic Church there. He currently lives an intentional community in Grand Rapids, Michigan. He can be reached at ross.acheson@gmail.com.

Christine Bodewes received a PhD from the University of London's School of Oriental and African studies, a B.A. from Saint Mary's College, Notre Dame, and a J.D. degree from the University of Illinois, Urbana-Champaign. From 1997 to 2006 Bodewes volunteered with the Maryknoll Lay Missioners in Nairobi, Kenya where she founded the Office of Human Rights in Kibera, and co-founded the land rights program at the Kituo Cha Sheria (Legal Aid Clinic). Her publications include: *Parish Transformation in Urban Slums, Voices of Kibera, Kenya,* Paulines Publications Africa, 2005; 'Chang'aa Drinking in Kibera, Kenya,' *African Journal of Drug and Alcohol Studie*s, 9, 2010 and 'Civil society and the consolidation of democracy in Kenya: an analysis of a Catholic parish's efforts in Kibera slum,' *Journal of Modern African Studies*, 48 (4), 2010. She can be reached at bodeweschristine@yahoo.com.

Tibebe Eshete holds a PhD in African history from Michigan State University, where he also serves as adjunct professor in the Religious Studies Program. He has taught at Missouri State University, Calvin College, Asmara University, and Addis Ababa University. Eshete has published extensively on the Horn of Africa as it pertains to Ethiopo-Somali relations and on issues related to new religious movements in Ethiopia. His recent research interests have focused on social and cultural changes, youth movements, and the like. His publications include the following: *The Silent Revolution* (World Vision, 2001) and *The Evangelical Movement in Ethiopia* (2009), which has been considered as one of the most outstanding books of the year in the field of mission studies for 2009. He can be reached at tibebees@msu.edu.

David A. Hoekema received his Ph.D. from Princeton University and served on the faculty of St. Olaf College and as Executive Director of the American Philosophical Association at the University of Delaware, before he moved to Calvin to serve as Academic Dean from 1992-98. Hoekema is currently professor of philosophy regularly teaching a course on African philosophy. His publications include *Rights and Wrongs: Coercion, Punishment and the State* (Susquehanna University Press, 1986), *Campus Rules and Moral Community* (Rowman and Littlefield, 1994), and a book in progress on *Finding the Hidden Path: Contexts of Conflict and Possibilities for Peace*, based in part on sabbatical research in South Africa. He can be reached at dhoekema@calvin.edu.

Josh Kuipers graduated with an interdisciplinary major from Calvin College and is currently a graduate student at Emory University's Chandler School of Theology. A year after graduating high school he spent 8 months in Kibera, Kenya serving with Adventures in Missions. During that time he worked closely with a local pastor of a Pentecostal church. It is in that church that a passion for African Christianity was planted in him. Following that year Kuipers began studying Biblical Studies at Columbia Bible College and eventually transferred to Calvin College. He can be reached at Joshua.s.kuipers@emory.edu.

Johanna Kuyvenhoven holds a PhD from British Columbia, Canada and is currently associate professor of education at Calvin College.

She has worked on matters related to teacher training and curriculum development in Sierra Leone since 1994 and has been international consultant for UNICEF. Her research interests are centered by the relationships between orality and literacy education, especially in school classrooms. She can be reached at jck8@calvin.edu.

Caitlin McGill is a graduate student at the Bush School of Government and Public Service, Texas A&M University where she is getting an MA in International Affairs focusing on national security and American diplomacy. Caitlin received her BA in political science from Calvin College and has traveled to Kenya and Uganda for study and service abroad. She can be contacted at Caitlin.mcgill@gmail.com.

Njonjo Mue is a Human Rights Lawyer and advocate of the High Court of Kenya. He is the Head of the International Centre for Transitional Justice's Kenya Office in Nairobi. Prior to that Mue served as the Head of Advocacy at the Kenya National Commission on Human Rights. He was educated at the University of Nairobi where he obtained an LL.B degree in 1990; Widener University School of Law, Delaware, USA; Kenya School of Law; Oxford University, UK, where he was a Rhodes Scholar and read for a Masters in International Law and Comparative Human Rights; Helsinki University where he obtained a diploma in Problems in Contemporary International Law; and the Nairobi International School of Theology where he obtained an MA in Christian Ministry and Leadership. Mue has vast experience in leading successful human rights organizations both in Kenya and abroad. He can be reached at njonjomue@gmail.com.

Mwenda Ntarangwi is a cultural anthropologist and currently executive director Office of Global Initiatives, Indiana Wesleyan University. He earned his PhD in cultural anthropology from the University of Illinois Urbana-Champaign. He has taught for St. Lawrence University, Augustana College, and Calvin College. Mwenda's research is on popular cultural expressions, the practice and history of anthropology, and inter-cultural engagement. He is the author of, among other works, *Reversed Gaze: an African Ethnography of American Anthropology* (Illinois, 2010), *East African Hip Hop: Youth Culture and Globalization* (Illinois, 2009), *Gender Identity and Performance: Understanding*

Swahili Cultural Realities Through Song (Africa World Press, 2003), and co-editor of African Anthropologies: History, Critique and Practice (Zed, 2006). He can be reached at mwendantarangwi@gmail.com.

Damaris Parsitau holds a PhD in religion from Kenyatta University, Kenya and is currently lecturer of African Christianities at Egerton University, Kenya. Her research interests focuses on Pentecostal Christianity and its interface with various themes such as mass media, music, health, politics, democracy, gender, and trans-nationalism, and Faith Based Humanitarianism, Christian-Muslim relations, Religion and Sports and the impact of Kenya's Post Election Violence on women and children. Damaris has published numerous articles and book chapters on these and other themes in peer reviewed journals such as *Africa Today*, Edinburgh University Press, Brill, Missionalia (Southern African Journal of Missiology) and is co-editor of *Weaving the Feature Together: Doing Collaborative Post Colonial Feminist Theologies* (an edited volume resulting from the Global Feminist Theologies Kenya Project, 2009). She can be reached at dparsitau@yahoo.com.

Index

Adogame, Afe 124, 125

Africa Inland Church (AIC) 69, 79, 153

Africa Inland Mission (AIM) 87, 88

African Independent Churches (AICs) 181

AIDS 3, 5, 50, 58, 133, 149, 153, 156, 161, 166, 200

Alliance of Protestant Missions 179

ANC (African National Congress) 26, 35, 45

Ancestor 14, 49, 53-56

Apartheid 2, 9, 32, 44

Asamoah-Gyadu , J. Kwabena 13, 124, 125

Barrett, David 84, 87, 124

Bediako, Kwame 18, 51, 84, 94, 186

Berger, Peter 114, 132, 198

Blackness 39, 40

Bonk, Jonathan 6

Calvin College 64, 191, 200

Capitalism 10, 11, 16, 28, 32, 36

Catholic Charismatic Renewal (CCR) 70-78

Catholic Relief Services (CRS) 200

Charismatic Renewal 20, 21, 67-75, 77-79, 81, 83, 85-87, 89, 91, 93, 95, 97, 99

Christendom 179

Church Mission Society (CMS) 84

CIDA 191

Citizenship 163

Civic Education 22, 147, 149, 151, 153-155, 157-169, 171, 173, 174, 181, 182

Civil Society 9, 22, 124, 126, 127, 138-140, 147, 148, 152, 154, 167, 169, 173, 187, 188

Classical Pentecostalism 85

Cold War 36, 37, 105, 114, 148

Collectivism 49, 51, 52, 54

Colonialism 27, 30, 31, 34, 151, 179, 180, 215

Communism 28, 105, 115

Corruption 5, 22, 34, 132, 133, 139, 140, 143-145, 147, 148, 151, 154, 163, 165, 170, 171, 173, 182, 187, 215

Dependence 3, 5, 26, 27, 30, 33-39, 41, 49, 53, 54, 69, 85, 86, 141, 172, 180, 181, 194, 202

Derg 39, 65, 90, 113, 119, 120, 208

Development 2, 3, 9-19, 22, 27, 28, 34, 36, 43, 44, 48, 59, 61, 63, 64, 71, 82, 87, 94, 102, 104-107, 109, 110, 113, 116, 123, 127, 129, 130, 133, 138, 141, 142, 150, 152, 153, 191-199, 201, 203-205, 209-211, 213, 214

Dutch Reformed Church 9

Ela, Jean-Marc 39-41, 45, 46

Englund, Harri 14, 126, 131, 136

Ethiopia 9, 21, 22, 37, 87, 98, 101-117, 119-121

Ethiopian Christian Business Men's Association 111

Ethiopian Revolution 104, 110, 113-115, 119, 121

Faith 2-4, 6, 8, 9, 12, 15-17, 19, 20, 23, 25, 27, 29, 31, 33, 35, 37, 39-41, 43, 45, 49-51, 56, 57, 59, 61, 67-69, 74, 77, 79, 83-85, 88, 96, 97, 99, 102,

104-109, 111-120, 124, 130, 134-136, 138, 143, 144, 147, 161, 163, 176, 181, 185-187, 192

Finland Pentecostal Missionaries (FPM) 106

Freire, Paul 198, 199

Ghana 12-15, 20, 21, 27, 30, 45, 67-79, 86, 125, 127, 128, 131

Gifford, Paul 2, 7, 85, 93, 124, 127

Gitari, David 7, 181, 184

Governance 20, 133, 139, 145, 148, 151, 154, 156, 159, 161, 163-165, 170, 195, 197, 200-202

Haile Sellassie I University 21, 103, 104

Hastings, Adrian 6

Human Rights 1, 12, 22, 28, 132, 136, 139, 147, 148, 153, 154, 159, 161, 163, 167-173, 176, 181, 186, 188

Individualism 10, 15, 49, 51, 53, 56, 60

Intercultural Communication 65

Islam 25, 37, 42, 44, 50, 105, 132-137, 143, 182

Jenkins, Philip 5

Johnston, Todd 124

Kadhi Courts 42, 133-136, 189

Kalu, Ogbu 85, 86, 95, 124-127, 139, 141, 143

Kasali, David 7, 94

Kenya 1, 7-9, 21-23, 26, 42, 43, 58, 62, 67, 81-91, 93-97, 99, 107, 123, 127-129, 131-145, 147-154, 158, 163, 168, 172-181, 183-185, 187-189

Kenyatta, Jomo 150, 152, 153, 158, 180

Kibaki, Mwai 140, 158, 176, 181-183

Kibera 21, 22, 83, 87-92, 94, 95, 98, 147-153, 155, 157, 159, 160, 163, 165-171, 173, 174

Knowledge CQ 65

Krapf, Johann Ludwig 84

Literacy 23, 94, 149, 191-207, 209, 211-215

Livermore, David 60, 63, 65

Livingstone, David 10, 48

Longman, Timothy 8

Lonsdale, John 7, 181, 184

Lutheran World Federation (LWF) 104, 105

Mainline Church 67-71, 79, 126, 127, 131, 132, 138, 141, 142, 180

Malawi 7, 9, 14, 18, 126, 127

Marshall, Katherine 2

Marxism 21, 22, 37, 101, 102, 105, 109, 110, 112, 113, 115-117, 119, 120

Maryknoll 153

Mau Mau 85, 86, 180

Maxwell, David 127, 130, 143

Mbiti, John 14, 84, 121, 143

McCall, John C. 52, 53, 55

Mekane Yesus Youth Hostel 102, 104

Millennium Development Goals (MDG) 195

Missionaries 10, 11, 14, 18, 19, 21, 38, 48, 49, 53, 59, 61, 70, 81-84, 87, 91, 93, 94, 96, 98, 99, 106-108, 126, 153, 179, 192, 201

Modernity 9-13, 15, 18, 86

Moi, Daniel Arap 151, 153, 156, 178, 180-182, 185, 189

Mudimbe, V. Y. 4

Muge, Kipsang 181

Muslim 2, 22, 42, 45, 50, 67, 98, 131-133, 135, 136

Musyimi, Mutava 138, 184, 185

Nairobi Chapel 90

National Council of Churches in Kenya (NCCK) 8, 9, 138, 181, 183-185

National Prayer Breakfast 138-140

National Prayer Day 139, 141

Naude, Beyers 9

Négritude 31, 39, 40

Neo-Pentecostal 68, 82, 85, 86, 88-95, 98, 127, 128

Non Governmental Organization (NGO) 7, 9, 13, 15-17, 38, 44, 91, 127, 148, 152, 153, 157, 168, 186, 200

Njoya, Timothy 134, 181, 184, 185

Nkrumah, Kwame 29-33, 37

Nyerere, Julius 29, 30, 32, 33, 37, 38

Occult 11, 13, 14, 16

Office of Human Rights (OHR) 153-157, 159-162, 164-170, 173

Ojo, Mathew 125-127, 142

Okullu, Henry 181, 184

Omenyo, Cephas 71

Orthodox Church 106, 107, 109, 112

Otabil, Mensa 12

P'Bitek, Okot 52

Pentecostalism 11, 20-22, 67, 71, 77, 82, 85, 86, 90, 92, 93, 95, 101, 102, 107, 109, 110, 113, 114, 119, 121, 123-129, 132, 138, 142, 143

Presbyterian Church 181

Protestant 5, 12, 13, 16, 17, 78, 84, 98, 106, 124, 128, 153, 179, 180

Qale Heywet Church 103

Radio Voice of the Gospel (RVOG) 102, 105, 106

Ranger, Terrence 11, 14, 40

Redeemed Christian Church of God 90, 96

Romero, Oscar 175

Rwanda 7, 8, 85, 87, 140

Salvation 12, 13, 17, 49, 51, 79, 85, 92, 93, 96, 103, 108, 136, 180, 181, 189

Sanneh, Lamin 6, 84-86, 94, 97

Sarpong, Peter Kwesi 70, 71

Senghor, Léopold 31-33, 37

Short-Term Missions 20, 47, 48, 57, 59-61, 63-65

Sierra Leone 23, 191-193, 195, 197, 199, 201-209, 211, 213-215

Skurnik, Walter 31, 32

Small Christian Community (SCC) 153-156, 158-167, 171-174

Socialism 28-34, 36-38, 43, 115, 117

South Africa 2, 7, 9, 26, 30, 32, 33, 35, 38, 41, 44, 45, 87, 90, 127

Sudan Inland Mission (SIM) 102, 103

Supreme Council of Kenyan Muslims (SUPKEM) 135

Swahili 29, 30, 89, 92

Swedish Philadelphia Mission (SPM) 107

Taylor, John 50-52, 54-56

Traditional Religion 25, 58, 70, 79, 112

Tutu, Desmond 9, 32, 33, 38

Ubuntu 4, 32, 38

Ufungamano House 1, 176, 177

Uganda 18, 26, 30, 41-43, 50, 52, 59, 64, 85, 127, 150

Ujamaa 29, 30, 38

UNESCO 196

UNHDP 194, 195

UNICEF 191, 200, 212

United Nations (UN)

University Student Union of Addis Ababa (USUAA) 111

USAID 191, 213

Van Hoyweghen, Saskia 7

VerBeek, Kurt 57, 60-64, 66

Victoria Faith Assembly 96

Walls, Andrew 18, 50, 51, 97, 166

Weber, Max 16

Winners Chapel International 96

Witchcraft 11, 14-17, 75, 78, 126, 136, 162

World Impact Center 85, 89, 92, 93, 95, 97

Worldview 11, 13, 15, 20, 49-51, 53-59, 65, 68, 79, 85, 95, 116, 141

Wuthnow, Robert 5, 6, 12, 57, 58, 63

Zimbabwe 10, 11, 14-16, 41, 57, 127